KINGS OF THE RING

THE HISTORY OF HEAVYWEIGHT BOXING

KINGS OF THE RING

THE HISTORY OF HEAVYWEIGHT BOXING

GAVIN EVANS

WEIDENFELD & NICOLSON

Contents

Introduction

The 'Brown Bomber' got me started. Nine years old and left behind with the babysitter, I turned on the radio and heard a quiz programme where the expert topic was the life of Joe Louis. Within minutes I was utterly transfixed, within days had cancelled my subscription to *Tiger* magazine, replacing it with *Boxing News*, and within weeks I had launched my low-achieving amateur career. I milked my long-suffering father for memories of Louis and persuaded him to take me to see rare films of the great champions in action – obsessed with the old masters, until the modernists won the fight for my attention.

Inevitably, Muhammad Ali took over, and when he fought George Foreman in Zaire in 1974 I felt immensely proud of the fact that my letter to our local paper, predicting a victory for 'The Greatest', was published. I watched a delayed transmission of his unlikely triumph at Cape Town's Alhambra cinema, after which I devoured every book, film and article on the man that I could find. Four years later, living in Texas, I watched Ali lose and then regain his world heavyweight title from Leon Spinks, the same year that Larry Holmes so effortlessly outclassed Ernie Shavers and then, one armed, outboxed and outlasted Ken Norton – so he took over; not quite a hero because the pear-shaped, abrasive Larry never won that kind of devotion, but still, a fighter deserving of immense respect. And from there to Tyson, Lewis and onwards.

The story of the heavyweight title-holders is seldom short of compelling. The title – 'the supreme prize in world sport' – and the status it brings – 'strongest unarmed man in the world' – is the essence of the attraction, but often the more interesting story comes in how these men got there and what happened next. They were all inspiring characters in their different ways and many were tragic too. Researching this book I was reminded, as if I needed it, that the qualities necessary for becoming the best fighter in the world did not always make for nice human beings. In retrospect their flaws probably seem more remarkable than in their own airbrushed times: the extreme racism of most of the early white gloved champions, the violence against women and other men, the greed, the stupidity, the links with organised crime, the alcohol and the drugs. It would be dishonest to downplay all this, but with every one of these men the dark side co-existed with noble and even heroic qualities: that ability to drive their bodies to extremes of pain and discomfort. Some of them did it so many times that in the end it threatened to destroy them. And for a few the heroism was taken beyond the ring and into the rest of their lives.

The story starts in London in the early 1700s with a hardy swordsman and cudgeller, James Figg, who introduced what was known as boxing to England, and ends in Los Angeles with a giant American-based, German-trained Ukrainian PhD, Dr Vitali Klitschko, who is attempting to assert his will on the division and the sport.

The intervening 300 years saw the sport break out of its English confines, acquire the veneer of legality (if not full respectability), move close to the centre stage of the American sporting universe and then drift away again, back to the fringes and peripheries where, against all odds, it continues to flourish. When 'Dr Ironfist' fights it may not excite mainstream America but in Germany, the Ukraine and Russia he stops the traffic.

Throughout this long spell boxing, and particularly its premier division, has always shown the capacity to astonish. Jack Johnson, the first black heavyweight champion, cleansed the ranks of its pale pretenders and, in the process, brought out the worst in white America, inspiring a wave of hatred and fear so intense that it took another 22 years before a black man was again allowed to fight for the title. That man, Joe Louis, rose during one of the division's periodic slumps to become a symbol of hope for his own people and ultimately for America as a whole. Twenty years later Muhammad Ali transcended his sport and then all sport by converting to a black-exclusivist version of Islam and then refusing to serve in a military engaged in a war he did not support. He paid a high price but when he was finally allowed to return it was, after a while, as a figure of universal delight rather than hatred.

Each of these great champions soared high above his calling. But others who flew closer to the ground also had moments of grace – like the Nazi-backed Max Schmeling, who helped to smuggle two Jewish boys out of Germany, or Jack Dempsey and Gene Tunney, whose post-boxing success was complemented by their heroism in the Second World War, or the quiet charitable generosity of champions like Floyd Patterson and Lennox Lewis.

But ultimately these kings are judged according to their assets as fighting men. That is why we know of them and read their stories. Inevitably there is an element of choice here. The history of the world heavyweight title is fraught with periodic dispute. For this book we have confined ourselves to those champions who won universal recognition – or at least something close to it – with six exceptions.

In the gloved era we have included three 'coloured' world heavyweight title holders who, because of their skin colour, were never given the chance to fight for the world title – Peter Jackson, Sam Langford and Harry Wills. The reason is that each of these men had a spell when he was clearly the best heavyweight in the world. We have also included a few champions who won partial recognition – Marvin Hart in the 1900s (because he ushered in the next universally recognised champion), Ken Norton in the 1970s (because he was one of the big four in the division's best decade and for a brief spell was the best in the world) and Klitschko today (because he is, by far, the best qualified of the current claimants). So that's it then – after 54 kings of the ring and 300 years I'm back to where I started 36 years ago: suitably obsessed.

Following pages: An engraving of a bare knuckle fight between Daniel Mendoza and Richard Humphries on 9 January 1788 at Odiham, Hampshire, England. Humphries won this fight when Mendoza injured his leg after 29 minutes of fighting, but in two subsequent fights Mendoza – the first jewish champion – used his superior skill to prevail against his bigger opponent.

The Bare Knuckle Era

Roots

In one sense boxing is as old as humanity. For as long as people have lived together in organised groups, boys and men, and sometimes women too, have fought to settle disputes, achieve status or earn their keep.

A mosaic in Tunisia and a bas-relief in Iraq, both carbon dated at around 5,000 years, show men fighting with thong coverings on their hands. The first clear references to organised fist fighting go back even further – to the Hindu poem *Mahabharata* and early Egyptian hieroglyphics and archaeological digs which suggest even earlier antecedents. But it was ancient Greece where boxing was introduced as a sport. It was widely practised in the villages, prompting its introduction to the Olympics in 688 BC. Greek boxers fought under the sun in outdoor arenas wearing nothing more than 10 foot strips of soft leather wrapped around their hands. Layers of harder leather were added to the knuckle to increase the impact of the blows while the inner portions were lined with wool to protect the palms of the hands. In the *Iliad* Homer describes a fight between Epeius and Euryalus, with both men wearing on their hands 'well cut thongs of the hide of an ox of the field'.

Later, under Roman influence, the caesteus was introduced – a glove studded with iron and lead (and some Roman variants used iron spikes). This transformed the sport into a gladiatorial fight to the death (or submission), without time limit. To prevent bouts dragging on too long the fighters were offered the option of 'klimax', which meant one man would remain still while the other hit him and vice versa until one of them collapsed or surrendered. The most celebrated of the Greek boxers was Theagenes of Thaos, who won the Olympic tournament in 450 BC. He was said to have won 1,406 fights, mainly using the caesteus – and, apparently, most of his opponents died. The Greek Olympics were abolished in 394 AD but boxing continued in Greece and the Roman Empire as a village sport for several centuries. Variants can also be found in China, Japan, Korea, Thailand, Burma and India – in some cases matching the Romans for brutality. In parts of Southeast Asia boxers covered their wrapped hands in resin and then dipped them in ground glass – all the better to carve up the opposition.

Boxing arrived in Britain with the Roman invasion but it died out after they departed. The sport's contemporary Western origins lie in 17th-century England, where it began to emerge as a village sport, although boxing, or 'milling' as it was sometimes called, was a loose term in these early fights, which also involved 'purring' (kicking) and wrestling. Samuel Pepys wrote of a boxing match in a 1662 entry in his diary while the early British newspaper, *The Protestant Mercury*, described a fight in 1681 between the Duke of Albermarle's footman and a local butcher. Right from the start this practice of servants and other commoners fighting on behalf of aristocratic backers, usually for wagers, became a key factor in the bare knuckle scene, and there was a symbiotic relationship between the fighting men and their wealthy patrons.

The calling card of pugilist James Figg who declared himself to be England's first heavyweight champion. Figg was an expert swordsman and cudgeller and was respected with his fists. He developed his reputation through teaching gentlemen the art of self defence while periodically engaging in prize fights.

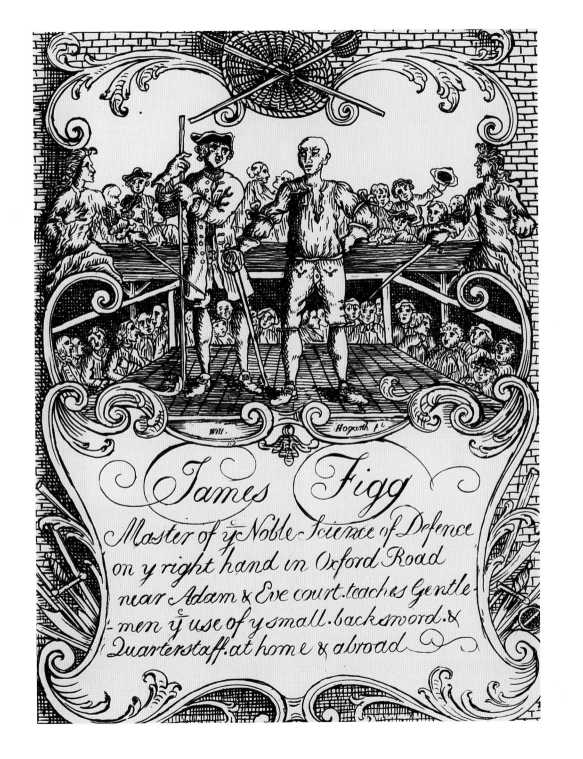

James Figg

The style of early British boxing owed a great deal to fencing. Pictures of the bare knuckle fighters show them leaning back, head up, with a wide stance – which prevailed until well into the gloved era of the early 20th century. The first English champion was James Figg, a master cudgeller and fencer, who issued a calling card, designed and engraved by his great friend Hogarth and distributed to patrons at his London 'School of Arms and Self Defence'. Calling himself a 'Master of the Noble Science of Defence' his card stated: 'He teaches gentlemen the use of the small backsword and quarterstaff at home and abroad'. Figg declared himself champion at the age of 24 in 1719 and attracted the backing of aristocratic 'bloods', some wanting to learn a thing or two about fighting while others, such as the Prince of Wales and Figg's patron, the Earl of Peterborough, sponsored him and backed him in fights against other men.

Figg conducted regular exhibitions at his Amphitheatre in Oxford Street and engaged in several listed fights – fought either in a roped circle on the turf or in elevated rings, with wooden rails instead of ropes and a referee standing outside the ring. Some involved cudgels (a short stick); others fists. For example, he fought Ned Sutton three times, first with cudgels, then swords, then bare fists, winning all three. He would also take on all-comers at the Southwark Fair, helping spread the appeal of the sport among working men. Figg, a huge man for his time (6ft, 185 lb.) 'resigned' as champion in 1734, appointing his pupil George Taylor as his successor. He died at the age of 45 in 1740, leaving a tidy sum to his wife and children.

Jack Broughton

By then several rival boxing academies had sprung up around London, including one set up by the next great champion, Jack Broughton. He was backed by the Duke of Cumberland, who secured him the position of Yeoman of the Guard for King George II. The powerfully built, 5'10½, 196 lb. Broughton, known as the 'Father of the English School of Boxing', was a clever man who knew how to make money out of his calling and how to develop the sport. Building on his knowledge as a swordsman he worked on parrying, blocking, retreating and different techniques of punching and wrestling, which gave him an advantage over the fairground brawlers of his day. Teaching well-healed students at 'Broughton's Amphitheatre' in Tottenham Court Road, he also introduced soft, feather-filled boxing gloves – known as mufflers – for sparring sessions and exhibitions. He became recognised as English champion in 1738, when, at the age of 34, he beat the one-eyed Taylor.

Three years later one of Broughton's opponents, George Stevenson, died as a result of a 45-minute beating, prompting the distraught champion to introduce the first Rules of Boxing in 1743. They allowed wrestling and grappling but declared: 'That no person is to hit his adversary when he is down, or seize him by the ham, the breeches, or any part below the waist: a man on his knees to be reckoned down.' The rules prohibited all but the fighters and their seconds from the ring (meaning that in most fights six people were in the ring – each boxer having two seconds). Rounds were of

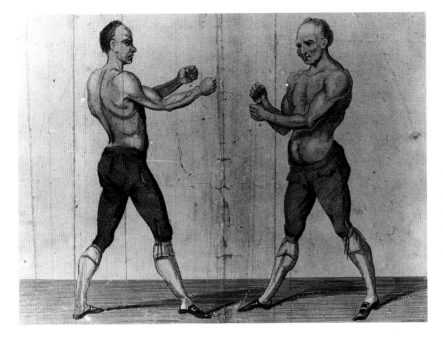

Jack Broughton (*left*) and Jack Slack square up in their bare knuckle bout on 10 April 1750. Slack won and reigned as champion until 1760. Broughton is credited with bringing a element of defensive skill to prize fighting. He also introduced the first boxing gloves – known as mufflers – for sparring and, after killing an opponent in the ring, the first rules of boxing, known as the 'Broughton Rules'. Slack was very different – a dirty fighter known for throwing fights in return for bribes.

indeterminate length, ending whenever one of the boxers touched down or when they had to be 'parted from the rails' (the wooden barriers or ropes defining the 'ring'). The 'Broughton Rules' gave a downed man half a minute to get up. Fights could end by knockout, capitulation or police intervention, with the winner receiving two-thirds of the prize money. These rules soon became universally accepted and governed boxing for nearly a century.

Broughton finally lost his title claim to Figg's grandson, the 202 lb. Norwich butcher Jack Slack, who called himself 'Knight of the Cleaver', on 10 April 1750. The bout lasted only fourteen minutes because Broughton could not recover from a punch that temporarily blinded him after his other eye was already closed. Boxing's first historian, Pierce Egan, wrote in his 1812 book *Sketches of Pugilism* that Cumberland had thousands of pounds riding on the outcome and implored Broughton to fight on. He yelled at his 46-year-old charge 'What are you about, Broughton? You can't fight! You're beat!' to which Broughton replied 'I can't see my man, your Highness; I am blind, but not beat; only let me be placed before my antagonist, and he shall not gain the day yet.' Cumberland withdrew his patronage and Broughton never fought again, transforming his academy into an antique shop. He died at the age of 85, and was buried in Westminster Abbey.

Boxing was sustained by betting and Slack, a dirty fighter who specialised in rabbit punching (behind the neck), was accused of 'throwing' fights in exchange for extra money and of fixing other boxers' bouts. After Cumberland's setback with Broughton he transferred his allegiances to Slack until 1760 when his charge lost to the Duke of York's fighter, William 'The Nailer' Stevens. An enraged Cumberland accused Slack of a double-cross and began to campaign against the sport.

Daniel Mendoza

The next great English champion was Daniel Mendoza, a comparatively small Spanish-Jewish Londoner who was credited with introducing 'science' into boxing by concentrating on footwork – particularly sidestepping as well as blocking, parrying and jabbing – as much as on power and strength. At 5'7 and 160 lb. 'Mendoza the Jew', as he was often called, was invariably the smaller man in an era before weight divisions were introduced, but used his advantages in speed, agility and technique to get results. Egan called him 'a complete artist' and 'a star of the first brilliancy' and there was great enthusiasm among some aristocrats and amateur boxers for his grace and defensive brilliance, although there was also much criticism, some of it taking on an anti-Semitic hue. His approach was sometimes called 'the Jewish School', criticised as cowardly, although it proved highly effective.

Mendoza, a descendent of Spanish Marranos Jews (who had been coerced into Christianity and had lived in London since the mid-1600s), was raised in a poor family in London's East End. His father was an artisan and Daniel worked as a glass cutter, labourer, greengrocer's lad and actor before having his first recorded fight when he beat Harry the Coalheaver in 40 minutes. After several more victories he beat Sam 'The Bath Butcher' Martin in 1787, which secured him the patronage of the Prince of Wales (later King George IV). This was apparently the first time the future king ever spoke to a Jew, and Mendoza's position was credited with easing the tide of anti-Semitism in late 18th-century England.

His first loss was to his great rival Richard 'The Gentleman' Humphries on 9 January 1788 when his seconds threw in the towel at the 29-minute mark after he suffered a leg injury. But they fought twice more over the next two years with Mendoza winning easily in 52 minutes and then in 15 minutes. In 1791, when the reigning English champion, Ben Brain, retired, Mendoza claimed the title. This was contested, however, by another leading fighter, Bill Warr, and they settled it in 1792, with Mendoza winning in 23 rounds. They fought again at Bexley Common in 1794 and this time Mendoza stopped him in 15 minutes. Another who contested Mendoza's supremacy was the Irish champion Squire Fitzgerald, who spiced his invective with anti-Semitic insults. Daniel, who was touring England, Scotland and Ireland with the Aston Circus, paused to thrash Fitzgerald in 26 minutes. He later helped to establish a school in Ireland where he taught art as well as self-defence – helping to spread the popularity of the sport there. His victories over bigger men and his willingness to travel made him a renowned figure throughout Britain and Ireland.

The 30-year-old Mendoza lost his title at Hornchurch, Essex, on 15 April 1795 to another highly skilled London

An engraving of Mendoza (*left*) and Humphries during their third public contest for superiority on 29 September 1790. Mendoza won in 15 minutes.

boxer, the 25-year-old 5'11, 202 lb. 'Gentleman' John Jackson, who dominated the early action before grabbing Daniel's long hair with his left hand and battering him with the right. This was not a foul according to the Broughton Rules, and it helped to secure a knockout victory for Jackson after 11 minutes. Mendoza retired after this but blew his money and returned to action at the age of 41 with a 53 round victory over Harry Lee in 1806. Fourteen years later, aged 56, he had a final fight, losing to Tom Owen in 12 rounds. In the interim he owned a tavern and became a celebrated boxing teacher, running a 'school-at-arms' that was patronised by the nobility. He died at the age of 72 in 1836.

John Jackson

Jackson was even more popular and helped to improve the image of the sport. He cultivated a polished demeanour and made a point of carrying out charitable deeds. Unlike most of the boxers of his and subsequent eras, he was one step removed from poverty. The son of a builder, John had the time and space to pursue sports at school and became an outstanding sprinter and long jumper as well as a highly accomplished amateur boxer with an educated jab and a sound defence. At the age of 18 he shocked his parents when he told them of his plans to become a prizefighter.

His first recorded bare-fisted fight was against the previously unbeaten, 230 lb. William Fewterall in Croydon on 9 June 1788, attended by several aristocrats including the Prince of Wales. Weighing 195 lb. he had no trouble evading Fewterall's swings, stopping him after 67 minutes (by grabbing Fewterall's left hand and pounding him). In his next bout, 11 months later, Jackson easily won the first two rounds against George 'The Brewer' Ingleston but a rainstorm made the turf slippery and he was variously reported as having sprained his ankle or broken it. In any event he was forced to quit and was so mortified by this embarrassment that he declined to box professionally for the next six years. But the offer to fight Mendoza in 1795 drew him back. Despite his questionable tactics in ending the fight, he made a big impression with his skill, strength and power. Gentleman John retired on this note and never fought again, instead devoting his efforts to running his London boxing academy where he used mufflers to teach the nobility, including his friend Lord Byron (who praised him in several of his literary works, calling him 'The Emperor of Pugilism'). He died at the age of 76 and was buried in Brompton where the marble monument at his grave carries a statue of a crouching lion to symbolize his great skill and strength.

Jem Belcher

The next champion, the 5'11½, 182 lb. Bristol-born Jem Belcher, was also praised for his skill, speed and agility but came from very different stock to the relatively refined Jackson. The grandson of former champion Jack Slack, and the brother of another prizefighter, Jem took to boxing as a family business, turning professional at the age of 18. After a series of wins in and around London, including two over rival title claimant John Bartholomew, he was recognised as English champion and became known as the

'Napoleon of the Ring.' He took to drinking and cultivating an image as something of a dandy – his speciality being a dotted Ascot tie. In 1803 he was blinded in one eye after being hit by the ball in a game of racquets and for the next two years fought only exhibitions.

Henry Pearce & John Gully

The man who emerged as his premier challenger was a fellow Bristolian, Henry 'The Game Chicken' Pearce. Standing 5'9 and weighing 175 lb. Pearce was more slugger than boxer – tough, resilient and determined. After a series of wins in the London area he was a champion-in-waiting. One of his friends was a young butcher's son, John Gully, known as an extremely talented amateur boxer in the Bristol area. But Gully failed in a business venture, racking up big debts. He ended up in the King's Bench debtors prison and the only way out was to find someone to pay his debt. Pearce visited him and their get-out-of-jail strategy involved an exhibition bout with mufflers within prison grounds. To the astonishment of those in attendance, the 6'0, 190 lb. Gully held the edge. The news spread to London where a wealthy sportsman, Fletcher Reid, paid off Gully's debts on condition that he fight Pearce without the protection of gloves, and the contest was set for 8 October 1805 in Hailsham. In the early rounds the 28-year-old Pearce dominated, dropping his 22-year-old friend seven times. But Gully worked his way into the fight and took over. By round 20 Pearce's face was a bloody mess and one of his eyes was closed. And yet he kept on firing and Gully gradually began to weaken. Finally, after 1 hour 17 minutes of brutal fighting, the Game Chicken landed a vicious punch to the throat and with Gully no longer able to breathe properly, the fight was stopped. The reputation of both men grew as a result of this battle.

John Gully, after becoming a bare knuckle prize fighter went on to be a wealthy man owning a colliery, several prize race horses and representing Pontefract as Member of Parliament.

By the time Belcher defended his title against Pearce, near Doncaster on 6 December 1805, the 24-year-old champion was a shadow of the fighter of earlier years, and was stopped in 18 rounds. Pearce then retired, declaring that Gully was the only man worthy of the title. This former debtor won universal recognition through dishing out a bloody beating to Bob 'The Lancashire Giant' Gregson in 28 bloody rounds, lasting 1 hour 15 minutes, at Six Mile Bottom on 14 October 1807. Seven months later they met again in Woburn and this time Gully won in eight rounds, after which he announced his retirement, refusing all offers to fight again, including a plea from the Duke of York. Pearce became an alcoholic, dying of tuberculosis in 1809, but Gully prospered, partly because of his connection with the renowned sportsman and nobleman Captain Robert Barclay, who walked one mile every hour for 1,000 hours to win a wager of 1,000 guineas (over £40,000 in today's values, although when side bets were taken into account around £40 million was at stake). He felt obliged to take measures to guarantee his safety, including employing 'Big' John Gully to accompany him at night. Using these ties and the money and fame he earned from fighting, Gully became a highly successful businessman and stable owner. His horses twice won the English Derby and in 1832, as the result of a bet he won, he became a candidate for parliament and was duly elected. He served two terms before retiring and died in 1863, at the age of 80, leaving his large family well cared for.

Bill Richmond, Tom Cribb & Tom Molineaux

The Belcher-Pearce-Gully era was followed by an even more intense rivalry between an outstanding English fighter, Tom Cribb, and two black Americans, the small and extremely lithe Bill Richmond and the powerful Tom Molineaux.

Richmond, the son of a Georgia plantation slave, was born on Staten Island, New York on 5 August 1763. His fortune was set as a young teenager when one of the commanders of British forces General Earl Percy (later the Duke of Northumberland) watched him fend off a trio of Redcoats who attacked him. Percy took the lad under his wing, using him to entertain guests by fighting British soldiers. Although he was a mere 5'6, his speed and reflexes invariably secured him victory. In 1779 Percy sent the 16-year-old Richmond to England. After a few years of schooling he was apprenticed to a cabinet-maker in York, while living and occasionally fighting under Percy's auspices. Still weighing 152 lb. he periodically beat far bigger men by dodging their blows, moving around and throwing quick counters. The first fight that brought him to public notice was against a 196 lb. soldier and York fighting terror George 'Docky' Moore, who insulted him on the racecourse. Richmond's friends tried to persuade him against the fight but he refused to back down and, as Egan wrote, 'in the course of twenty-five minutes, our hero punished Docky so completely that he gave in, and was taken out of the ring totally blind.' He followed this with at least five victories in York and London before getting on with life as a carpenter.

He came back at the age of 40 to take on another old professional, George Maddox, at Wimbledon Common and was knocked out in three rounds. But after two notable wins he was picked as an opponent for the rising 24-year-old heavyweight Tom Cribb, an immensely powerful, 5'10, 195 pounder. One of seven children of a poor family, Cribb grew up in Hanham on the outskirts of Bristol. At the age of 13 he left for London, eventually finding work as a stevedore on the Thames wharves then went to work as a coal heaver before joining the navy as a seaman. After surviving two serious work place accidents he developed a fearsome reputation as a fighter and began boxing for pay in 1805, beating George Maddox in a fight that lasted 2 hours 12 minutes.

Bare knuckle boxing allowed wrestling and throwing, and most fights included long spells of grappling, with the boxers attempting to throw their opponent down and then fall on them. Cribb excelled in these tactics. Although he was essentially a slugger and wrestler he was not devoid of defensive technique – particularly 'milling in retreat' (boxing on the back foot) before mounting his next attack. After two more wins and a 52 round defeat to the more experienced George Nichols, he met Richmond in Hailsham on 8 October 1805 in another marathon battle. In the end Cribb's advantages in size and youth were decisive and he wore down and then, at the 90 minute mark, knocked out the 42-year-old.

When the one-eyed, faded, 26-year-old Jem Belcher fought Cribb at Moulsey Hurst 18 months later he was so sure he would prevail that he bet his fortune on the result and easily outboxed the bigger, cruder man in the early rounds. He dropped his rival and looked set for victory, but Cribb's notorious seconds started a debate about wagers on the fight, which persisted long enough to allow their man to recover. Cribb was able to

Following pages: An artist's depiction of the first epic bout between Tom Cribb (*left*) and Tom Molineaux. Behind Molineaux is his chief second Bill Richmond. Cribb won, but only after his supporters invaded the ring and broke one of Molineaux's fingers. They fought in a rain storm in near-freezing conditions which favoured Cribb, who prevailed after 55 minutes.

close Belcher's good eye to gain the victory after 35 minutes. After three more wins Cribb fought Belcher again – at Epsom Downs on 1 February 1809 – and this time won without much trouble, stopping Belcher after 40 minutes. When John Gully formally retired Cribb won widespread recognition as English champion.

A week after Cribb's second victory over Belcher, Bill Richmond made his return to the ring, stopping Isaac Wood in 23 rounds. Five days later he took on one of England's top heavyweights, Jack Carter. He was knocked down early but rose to batter the big man to submission in 25 minutes. Another couple of wins set him up for a return with the first man to have beaten him, George Maddox, whom he stopped in the 52nd round. But after one more victory, he drifted out of boxing for four years – then came back for a couple more wins, and retired again. In 1818, when Richmond was 55 years old, Jack Carter challenged him to a return fight. As always, the boxer known as 'The Black Terror' accepted, stopping Carter in three rounds. In the meantime he married a wealthy woman who helped him to buy a public house, the Horse and Dolphin, near Leicester Square, and he also ran a boxing academy where one of his pupils was the writer William Hazlitt. He died at the age of 66.

Richmond's success helped persuade another black American boxer, Tom Molineaux, to try his luck in England. The 5'8½, 198 lb. Molineaux was born a slave in Virginia in 1784. Plantation owners entertained each other by ordering their strongest slaves to fight and the young Tom soon proved the toughest of the lot. Tutored by his father, he excelled in these bare knuckle battles, earning betting money for his owner, and this proved to be his route to freedom. His owner bet what was then the massive sum of $100,000 on Tom to beat another plantation owner's champion slave. To ensure Tom fought as ferociously as possible he offered the slave his freedom plus $500 if he won – which he duly did in fine style. The freed Molineaux then travelled to New York where he continued fighting for pay. It was then that he heard of Richmond's English exploits and in 1809 he took a job as a deckhand on a boat bound for Liverpool. He immediately went to find Richmond, who became his trainer, mentor and agent. His first English fight was against one of Tom Cribb's Bristol protégés, Jack Burrows. Molineaux delivered a severe, 65 minute beating. Cribb was so incensed by the idea of this American 'Moor' beating his friend that he ensured Molineaux's next opponent was the more formidable veteran 'Tough' Tom Blake. Molineaux knocked him out in eight rounds. The American then began to question inactive Cribb's right to call himself champion of England – declaring himself the rightful king of the ring. The Englishman was not amused and at this point agreed to accept the impostor's challenge, at Copthall Common a week before the Christmas of 1810.

The fight took place in a rainstorm in near-freezing weather, with a chilling wind further reducing the temperature – conditions that suited the Englishman better. But in the early rounds the 26-year-old American dominated, drawing first blood. He seemed the harder puncher and the more skilled boxer and in the 19th round drove the 199 lb., 29-year-old Cribb into the ropes, held him and began to pound him. Cribb's vociferous band of supporters leapt into the ring, grabbed Molineaux and broke one of his fingers. Despite this injury Molineaux fought on and in the 28th round knocked Cribb down heavily. It seemed clear he'd scored a legitimate knockout because Cribb failed to recover within the allotted 30 seconds, but at this point the Englishman's supporters invaded the ring again, making the bizarre accusation that Molineaux was carrying lead bullets in his hands. By the time they had accepted he was lead-free, Cribb had recovered. By this stage the driving, icy rain had made the ring's wooden floor into a precarious surface. Molineux slipped and cracked his head on one of the ring posts. It was the edge Cribb needed and he took over, dropping his injured opponent several times and closing both his eyes. Finally in round 33, after 55 minutes, Molineaux, who could barely see and was shivering from the cold, collapsed, raising his hand and telling his chief second, Bill Richmond: 'Me can fight no more.' He then 'fell into a stupor' and was carried from the ring.

The American was widely praised for his performance, with many sharing his view that he would have won had it not been for the two ring raids by the champion's supporters. Meanwhile Cribb announced his retirement and turned down Molineaux's plea for a return. He returned to his hard drinking ways and his weight rose to 225 lb. At this point the American issued a public challenge to any man willing to try his luck. A leading English fighter, Joe Rimmer, answered the call and Molineaux stopped him in 21 rounds – and once again claimed the English championship. The idea of 'The Moor' as champion was too much for Cribb's legion of followers to take, so they persuaded their man to come back to fight the foreigner at Thistleton Gap on 28 September 1811. At this point Captain Robert Barclay, having recovered from his 1,000 hour walk, took Cribb in hand – a product of his close relations with John Gully who, in turn, was one of Cribb's backers. Barclay took him off to Scotland for two months of intense training – the first training camp in boxing history. Long walks and, more unusual for the time, long runs, combined with hard physical labour and abstinence from alcohol brought the English fighter to the best condition of his career. Weighing 189 lb. he looked sleek and muscular and as soon as Molineaux saw him he knew he was in trouble. The American, meanwhile, had fallen out with Richmond and had taken to alcohol, and was not nearly as fit as he had been for the first fight.

The result was a shorter, but no less intense, encounter watched by 25,000 spectators. Once again Molineaux dominated at first, closing one of Cribb's eyes with his punches, forcing Gully, the Englishman's second, to lance it. He also broke Cribb's nose and bloodied his mouth. But the superbly conditioned Englishman absorbed the beating and began attacking the body, throwing heavy hooks to the ribs and one to the groin in round six. In round nine Cribb landed a huge left swing that broke the American's jaw, knocking him down and out. But the Bristol man was determined to prove his point and allowed his rival to continue. Finally, in the 11th round, after 19 minutes 10 seconds of action, the exhausted American was knocked out after a sustained assault. Pierce Egan, calling the loser, 'the Tremendous Man of Colour', wrote 'Molineaux proved himself as courageous a man as ever an adversary contended with … He astonished everyone, not only by his extraordinary power of hitting and his gigantic strength, but also by his acquaintance with the science, which was far greater than any had given him credit for.'

Molineaux continued fighting but he also continued drinking. Such was his strength and talent that for a while these two co-existed but gradually the alcohol brought him down. He kept borrowing money from friends, and particularly from Richmond, but was not good at paying them back and his relationships deteriorated. He was arrested and held for a few days in 1813 for a failure to pay a debt to Richmond. His last notable win came against a leading fighter, William Fuller, whom he beat on a disqualification after 68 minutes of intense fighting. Pierce Egan was so impressed that he wrote that the fight was 'without parallel'. Nine months later Molineaux was stopped in 20 minutes by George Cooper – his last official fight, although he continued to box exhibitions. While touring Ireland with a circus in 1818 he contracted tuberculosis, exacerbated by his alcoholism. He died in Dublin at the age of 34.

The immensely popular Cribb continued to fight periodically, including 'private' fights, exhibitions and sparring sessions (one for the benefit of the Russian Tsar). In 1820 he beat Jack Carter in a one-hour fight – his last recorded win. He formally retired on 18 May 1822, at the age of 40 and was presented with the first-ever title belt, made from a lion skin. He died in London in 1848, shortly before his 68th birthday. This period – the first quarter of the 19th century – was known as a golden era of bare knuckle boxing, with the sport gaining immense popularity and producing several extremely popular champions.

Tom Spring

Cribb's successor was Tom 'The Light Tapper' Spring, who was born Thomas Winter in Townhope, Hertfordshire. He began boxing as an amateur and at the age of 17 was spotted by a highly impressed Cribb. Spring had his first bare knuckle fight at the age of 19, using his speed and evasive skills to beat a bigger slugger, John 'Hammer' Hollands. After this Cribb began coaching Spring, teaching him the tricks he'd learned over the years. But unlike his mentor the youngster relied on quickness and defence rather than power and was called 'a lady's maid fighter' because of his lack of a knockout punch. However, his style was extremely effective. One of his moves became known as 'Spring's Harlequin Step' – he would feint while in range, dodge the incoming punch and then counter.

Spring went undefeated for four years until fighting a return with a tough and experienced opponent called Ned Painter, whom he had beaten four months earlier. Spring had to forfeit after 42 rounds because he was bleeding profusely from a badly cut right eye. In 1819 he went on a public sparring tour with Cribb and over the next two years he beat five of Britain's top prizefighters. When Cribb retired he declared Spring the new champion but this was disputed by the extremely tough and hard-hitting Bill Neat (who gained widespread recognition through his place in William Hazlitt's novel, *The Fight*). They fought at Hinckley Downs on 17 May 1823 and the more skilful Spring beat him in 37 minutes – Neat retiring after suffering a broken arm. The 5'11½ , 190 lb. Spring had two more title fights, twice beating the 176 lb. Irish champion Jack Langan in lengthy and bloody bouts. He retired because of broken hands, which were a common hazard with bare knuckle fighters, and went on to become a wealthy innkeeper, famed for his kindness. He died at the age of 56.

Several popular champions followed Spring, including James 'The Deaf 'Un' Burke, who won 18 of his 20 bare knuckle fights, gaining recognition as champion by beating

Simon Byrne (who died after their 3 hour 16 minutes fight). Two others were the tough, little William 'Bendigo' Thompson and his great rival, the huge Ben Caunt, although none of these men achieved the fame of Gully, Cribb, Molineaux and Spring.

Tom Sayers

A significant change was the introduction in 1838 of a new set of regulations governing the sport, the London Prize Ring Rules. There was now a 30 second break between rounds after which the umpire would call 'Time' and boxers were required to walk to the 'scratch' line (in the centre of the ring) unaided in no more than eight seconds. A boxer who went down deliberately, without being hit, was declared the loser. Long spikes on boots were banned, as were butting, biting, gouging, kicking, 'squeezing' on the ropes and using stones inside the hands.

The first great English champion to emerge under these rules was the small, hard-hitting and skilful bricklayer, Tom Sayers. Born and raised in Brighton he began fighting as a 112 lb. 16-year-old although his prizefighting career only really took off in 1849, when he was nearly 23. By then he had reached his full height of 5'8½ and weighed 140 lb., which meant he did most of his fighting at middleweight (a new weight division introduced in this period). Some of his victories were marathons (his win over Jack Grant in 1852, for example, lasted two and a half hours and a later fight, against Harry Poulson, lasted 3 hours 8 minutes). In his 10th recorded bare knuckle fight, in Suffolk on 18 October 1853, he challenged a great fighter, Jack Langham, for the English middleweight title. He won the early rounds but as the fight progressed it became clear he was out of his depth against a bigger and far more experienced champion. Both eyes were closed when his seconds threw in the towel after 2 hours 2 minutes. He promptly called for a return but Langham retired.

After several more victories he moved up to heavyweight, even though he seldom weighed more than 150 lb. On 16 June 1857 he took on one of the claimants to the English title, William 'Tipton Slasher' Perry. Giving away 50 lb. he lost the early rounds but used his speed and skill to wear Perry down. Finally after 1 hour 45 minutes he dropped Perry and split his lip, and the big man's seconds threw in the sponge. Sayers's evasive tactics prompted accusations of cowardice but over the next few years he gained respect with a series of wins over far bigger men, including a 1 hour 20 minute win over Tom Paddock, which won Sayers universal recognition as English champion in 1858. He consolidated his position with two more title victories before agreeing to take on the American champion John Heenan in Farnborough on 17 April 1860.

John Heenan

The big-hitting and well-skilled Irish-American 'Benicia Boy', as Heenan was called, began boxing professionally in San Francisco at the age of 20 in 1855, and came to prominence when facing his premier rival, John Morrissey, for the US title at Long Point in Canada on 20 October 1858. The 6'2, 190 lb. Heenan had a festering leg ulcer going into the fight and soon broke his right hand when it struck a stake in a neutral corner. He fought on, dropping Morrissey in the fifth round, but hampered by his ulcer and fighting one-handed he took a beating and collapsed in the 11th round, to be carried to his corner. Morrissey refused to give him a return and instead retired, after which Heenan was recognised as American champion. Boxing was still in its infancy in America and there were no suitable challengers, so Heenan's friends talked him into issuing a challenge to Tom Sayers in what would effectively be a world title fight. Sayers agreed and Heenan sailed to England for a fight that generated huge excitement on both sides of the Atlantic, with several American publications sending reporters to cover it.

By then British and American boxing had entered a long period of twilight legality – permitted in some locations and banned by the police in others – yet it still enjoyed significant support from gamblers and other wealthy patrons, which meant it continued to prosper, although sometimes police had to be bribed to stay away. Still, the threat of police action meant that the run-up to the Sayers-Heenan contest had a clandestine dimension, which only added to its appeal. Heenan had to change training camps regularly, after warnings that the police were on their way to arrest him. Guarded by a bull terrier, he completed his preparations in a Wiltshire barn, where his trainer, Jack Macdonald, introduced an innovation to English boxing: they hung a 30 lb. bag of sand from one of the beams and the American used it to practise his punches. On the morning of the fight, 17 April 1860, Sayers and Heenan met in disguise at London Bridge before heading off to Farnborough for the fight. The event was the talk of London and two long steam trains were used to transport Sayers's supporters to the fight. The police could easily have prevented it but instead they sent their constables to another area, to allow it to proceed. The crowd included Charles Dickens, William Thackeray, senior army and navy officers, clergymen, MPs and members of the aristocracy.

The Englishman, who was almost 34 years old, was quicker and more skilful but at 152 lb. he was at a huge disadvantage against the powerful 195 lb. American, who was also nine years younger. A pattern emerged of Sayers landing quick jabs and rights to the face before getting tossed to the ground or knocked down with body blows. In the 37th round Sayers began to wilt and Heenan charged at him, forcing him against the ropes, pressing his neck against the top strand and digging his fist into the throat. The partisan English crowd went wild, storming the ring and cutting the ropes. The referee disappeared and Heenan and his seconds had to ward off angry spectators. A hard-core group of betters then linked arms to make their own ring and the boxers fought for five more rounds, until the referee forced his way back into the makeshift ring declaring the bout a draw.

The two men became friends and went on an exhibition tour together, re-enacting their famous fight, although neither fully recovered from it. Sayers retired and as a result Heenan gained universal recognition as the first world heavyweight champion. He returned to England to avoid the Civil War and in December 1863 agreed to face the new English champion, Tom King, with his friend Sayers as his chief second. But by then he was a faded fighter and he was beaten in 35 minutes, after which he joined Tom in retirement. Sayers died of diabetes and tuberculosis on 8 November 1865, at the age of 39. Heenan became a Tammany Hall politician for a few years, before losing all his money and returning to boxing as a sparring partner. He died on 28 October 1873, aged 38.

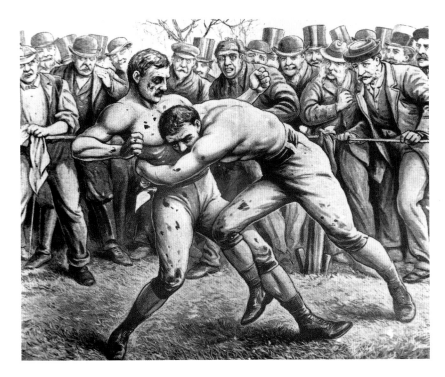

English boxing champion Tom King endures a rib cracking courtesy of American John Heenan in the sixth round of their international fight on 8 December 1863. King eventually won after 24 rounds. Heenan's first trip to Britain saw him fighting a 42 round draw with then English champion Tom Sayers. When Sayers retired Heenan was recognised as world champion. He returned to England to avoid fighting in the Civil War and was backed by his new friend, Sayers, who was his chief second against King.

Jem Mace & Tom King

The Sayers-Heenan fight prompted the police to become ever more vigilant in stopping fights, partly because of outcries from sections of the clergy and from evangelical preachers, who ranted against the 'ruffians of the ring'. It was still hugely popular among the common people but the upper classes, whose money sustained the sport, began to shy away. As a result, the standard of the professional game began to decline. At the same time, boxing was experiencing its most sustained period of international expansion, and the man who deserved most credit for this was the last great English bare knuckle champion, Jem Mace, who, aside from being a brilliant boxer, took on the role of missionary for the sport. In a boxing career that spanned an astonishing 55 years, he imparted his skills and enthusiasm to hundreds of good boxers all across the world.

Known as the 'Swaffham Gypsy', but in fact born into a non-Romany, Norfolk-based travelling family, he always stood out as exceptional. His three brothers became blacksmiths but Jem became a cabinet maker while also travelling the country as a talented fiddler. He started boxing as a way of earning extra money in circus booths, where he was noted for his agility and quick reflexes. His first recorded fight took place in Cambridge in 1849 when he was 18 years old and he won after a two-hour marathon battle. Standing 5'9½ and weighing 144 lb., he fought for the British welterweight title in 1858 but was knocked out by Bob Brettle after three minutes. Seventeen months later he took the welterweight title by stopping Bob Travers in a 91 minute battle and later in 1860 he avenged his defeat against Brettle, stopping him in seven minutes.

After this he decided his fortune lay in fighting heavyweights. He beefed up to 158 lb. and challenged the 6'2½, 200 lb. champion, Sam Hurst, effortlessly evading his charges before knocking him out after forty minutes. This fight, at Medway Island on 18 June 1861, made Mace the new English heavyweight champion. He toured the country with a circus before making his first defence, at Godstone on 28 January 1861 against the 6'2, 176 lb. Tom King, who had learnt his craft in the Royal Navy. Despite giving away 21 lb. the quicker, more elusive Mace gradually gained the ascendancy but he was fighting with his left eye closed and his right swollen. In the 30th round he backheeled King, who fell on his head and after that it became one-sided. In the 43rd round, after 68 minutes, Mace landed a hard left to the throat and then threw King to the ground to end the fight. The public demanded a return, which took place on the banks of the Thames on 26 November of the same year. This time King, at 180 lb., was ground down to a state of exhaustion by the 19th round, but as Mace moved in his rival landed a huge left swing, catching him on the temple. Two rounds later, after 38 minutes of fighting, Mace collapsed and lost his title. The 26-year-old King immediately announced his retirement, refusing Mace's plea for a third bout. Mace then took him on in a street fight. But with John Heenan in Britain, the press and public urged King to reconsider, and he finally agreed to return for the sole purpose of fighting Heenan. His victory secured him recognition as world champion but he retired for good to earn a fortune on the racetracks. When he died in 1888, aged 53, his estate was valued at £150,000 – a massive amount for the time.

In Mace's next recorded fight, on 1 September 1863, he came in at 149½ lb. to beat Joe Goss in 1 hour 55 minutes for the English middleweight title. He also won British recognition as world heavyweight champion – a claim disputed by the Irish-born American champion, Joe Coburn. Jem accepted his challenge and they were set on 4 October in Pierstown, near Dublin, but Coburn made the outrageous demand that his personal friend James Bowler should be the referee. This demand was declined and Coburn refused to fight. Mace returned to England for a draw and a win over Joe Goss, the second bout securing him the English heavyweight title again.

By then several of his bouts had been cancelled at the last minute because of police intervention and he decided to seek his fortune in America, starting with an exhibition tour with John Heenan in 1869. His next major fight was against the leading US-based Englishman, Tom Allen, at Kennerville, Louisiana on 10 May 1870. Mace had no trouble stopping the 173 lb. Allen after 44 minutes – a bout that secured him American recognition as world champion. This was followed by three scheduled bouts with the volatile Joe Coburn. The first – a strange bout in which both men were so adept at ducking, dodging and blocking that neither landed a decent blow – was declared a draw when police stopped it after 1 hour 17 minutes. For the second Coburn simply did not turn up and the third, lasting 3 hours 48 minutes, with Mace breaking his hand in the fifth round, was again declared a draw. Jem Mace then announced his retirement at the age of 40 but he could not keep away from the ring, and over the next five years he travelled around America, fighting and winning.

After a brief return to England he toured Australia with another outstanding professional, Larry Foley, whom he taught the fine points of self-defence. Along the way Mace set up tournaments in several towns, and one of the boxers to emerge was Bob Fitzsimmons, who went on to become boxing's first three weight world champion. Mace fought his last bout in Cape Town on 18 January 1904, when he was 73. He died in 1910 at the age of 79, having done more to spread the appeal of his sport than any other man.

A Cambridge oarsman and amateur athletics organizer, John Graham Chambers, devised a fresh set of rules for amateur boxing contests and exhibitions in 1867. He got his old college friend, John Sholto Douglas, the Eighth Marquess of Queensberry, to sponsor these changes, which became known as the Queensberry Rules. Douglas, a notorious wife beater and aristocratic thug, later achieved notoriety for his obsessive campaign to charge Oscar Wilde with sodomy because of his relationship with the Marquess's son – a campaign that led to Wilde's imprisonment. It was perhaps appropriate that he should sponsor a set of rules for fighting, but not that he should be associated with the 'civilising' of the sport. Still, from then on his name was associated with the rules that continue to govern boxing. They mandated the use of boxing gloves for all contests, created the first three-minute rounds with a minute's break between them, banned wrestling and 'hugging', banned seconds from being in the ring and introduced the 10 second unassisted knockout count rather than the old 30 second limit. They also created the possibility of a limited number of timed rounds with a result decided when the fight reached this limit – a verdict reached by the referee in the British ring.

But these changes were not quite so sudden and dramatic as is sometimes suggested. For one thing, they were designed for the rising sport of amateur boxing and it was nearly 15 years before they made an impact on prizefighting, after which the two forms co-existed for another 15 years. Many early gloved professional fighters also fought bare knuckle fights while almost all of the bare knuckle fighters in the late 19th century did their share of gloved fighting. The limit on the length of bouts under the Queensberry rules was not always applied. In fact, some of the gloved bouts were longer than the protracted bare knuckle wars – the record being a 110 round bout in New Orleans in 1893 that lasted 7 hours 19 minutes. Also, the fighting style of the early gloved boxers drew a great deal from the bare knuckle tradition – plenty of holding, mauling, upper-body wrestling and punching from the clinches.

By the last quarter of the 19th century, with British boxing experiencing a slump, the sport's centre of gravity shifted firmly to the United States. Most of the top heavyweights to emerge in this period were either immigrants or first generation Americans, and in particular Irish-Americans (including Joe Coburn, Sullivan and Jim Corbett). They ferociously battled among themselves while doing their best to freeze out another group of hyphenated Americans – the descendants of slaves. This was the backbeat to the story of the next half century of heavyweight boxing, spanning the end of the bare knuckle era and the early decades of the 20th century, starting with the rise of the last bare knuckle world champion and the first gloved world champion, John L Sullivan.

Following pages: Mike Tyson hits British and Commonwealth champion Julius Francis with a vicious left hook during his two round victory in Manchester in 2000. Francis's astute manager, Frank Maloney, sold advertising space on the soles of his boxer's boots which was bought by the *Daily Mirror* newspaper.

The Heavyweights

John L Sullivan – 'The Boston Strong Boy'

American heavyweight champion 1882–89; world heavyweight champion 1889–92. Last bare knuckle champion and first gloved champion.

'When Sullivan hit me, I thought a telegraph pole had been shoved against me endways.'
Paddy Ryan, the man Sullivan stopped to win the world title.

Height: 5'10¼
Peak weight: 190–200 lb.
39 wins (33 stoppages),
1 loss, 4 draws
Born: Boston, Massachusetts
15 October 1858
Died: 2 February 1918

John L Sullivan, the world champion who bridged the bare knuckle and gloved eras, was the first all-American sporting celebrity – an heroic figure, famed for his brawling, boozing and braggadocio. A quick temper, a bullying streak and a virulent strain of racism were all part of the package, but he was adored for his big right, hard chin and his refrain, 'I can lick any sonofabitch in the house.'

His most severe test came in the fight that secured him general recognition as world champion – the last ever bare knuckle battle, against his fellow Irish-American, Jake Kilrain on 8 July 1889 in Richburg, Mississippi, at a time when the champion was doing far more boozing than boxing. Sullivan's friend, the wrestler, physical trainer and future New York boxing commissioner, William Muldoon, drove him to give up alcohol for the duration of his preparations and hone his body into prime fighting shape for one of the most brutal encounters ever seen in a boxing ring.

The two men fought for a side bet of $10,000 within a 24 foot square ring, pitched on turf, with a 'scratch' line drawn in the centre, where the fighters would meet at the start of each round (after one man went down). It was an extraordinarily draining encounter with both men taking horrendous punishment to the delight of the 3,000-strong crowd. After 2 hours 16 minutes of wrestling, clinching and bare-fisted slugging, Kilrain was finished and his trainer, 'Professor' Mike Donovan, refused to allow him to come up to scratch for the 76th round because he feared for his man's life. Kilrain's nose was broken, his lips split, one eye was shut, his body covered in bruises and welts and he'd been reduced to sipping whiskey between rounds to dull the pain. Sullivan had a black eye, bleeding ear and grotesquely swollen hands but was in better shape overall. As the *New York Times* put it on their front page, 'The Bigger Brute Won'.

John Lawrence Sullivan inherited his short fuse – and love of a good malt – from his father, Mike Sullivan, a brawling builder's labourer from County Kerry, and his powerful physique from his Irish immigrant mother, Catherine, and although it is hard to separate myth and fact, the boy seems to have been a born fighter, being bigger and more robust than anyone else. His first recorded fight took place when he was 19 when another local thug, Jack Scannell, challenged him. John removed his coat, laced up a pair of woolly muffler gloves, took a punch on the head from Scannell and duly lost his rag, belting Scannell over the on-stage piano. The legend of the 'Boston Strong Boy' was born.

His advantages in size and strength were invariably decisive and took him to a fight in Mississippi City on 7 February 1882 against fellow Irish-American, Paddy Ryan, who held the American heavyweight title. Sullivan overcame Ryan using his power to out-wrestle the champion and his heavy right to batter him to a one-sided defeat in the ninth round.

The 'Boston Strong Boy', John L Sullivan, became the first fighter to win universal recognition as world heavyweight champion. He was the last man to win a world title fight with bare knuckles and the first to defend the world heavyweight title with gloves.

John embarked on a non-stop spending, drinking and brawling splurge. He married chorus girl Annie Bates a year after beating Ryan and they had a son, John Junior. When the toddler died of diphtheria he drowned his sorrows, abandoned his wife and moved in with a burlesque queen. But he was seldom home. He took his world title show on the road, travelling to Ireland, England and France as well as all over the USA, meeting with the future King Edward VII and building his reputation as a wild, rather odd and often generous character. His many eccentricities included a passion for chasing fire engines.

Sullivan is credited with 31 official fights in the seven years after winning the title. However, in common with several of his successors he 'drew the colour line', refusing to fight black men. 'Any fighter who'd get into the same ring with a nigger loses my respect', he said. Which was also a rather convenient way of sidestepping several good boxers, and one brilliant one, the black Australian Peter Jackson, who arrived in America in 1888. While Sullivan's stance attracted mild criticism, he could get away with it because of the shift in the social climate in the late 1880s. A permissive abolitionist ethos prevailed for a few years after the Civil War, but the end of Reconstruction was accompanied by an extremist white backlash, and Sullivan's attitude fitted this changing milieu.

What we can say is that he beat the best white heavyweights of his day. At one stage, while touring America, he offered what was then the huge sum of $1,000 to any man who could stand up to him for four rounds (using gloves and fighting under the relatively new Queensberry Rules). Needless to say, few survived.

The physical condition of the flamboyant John – who liked to wear brightly coloured outfits, the look completed by a long black cigar – deteriorated as his fame grew, prompting doubt that he could still call himself the hardest man around. The man to beat

John L Sullivan shown at Muldoon's Farm, Belfast, New York, getting in shape to meet with Jake Kilrain. The fight lasted 76 rounds and was fought under the old bare knuckle London Rules. Sullivan was temporarily off alcohol for this fight and arrived in peak condition – needed for an intense, brutal battle that lasted two hours 16 minutes.

MR. MULDOON'S HOME

RUBBING DOWN AFTER THE BATH.

SULLIVAN'S TRAINING QUARTERS

RUNNING TO REDUCE WEIGHT

WEIGHING

A SWEATER.

PRACTICING FOOTBALL

A SHOWER-BATH

"FEEL MY ARM."

was Kilrain and when John achieved that feat he won universal recognition as world champion. He had always preferred fighting with gloves but now he vowed never again to fight without them – a decision effectively ending the bare knuckle era.

Sullivan froze his world title over the next three years, preferring to eat and drink out on his growing celebrity – appearing on stage as the hero of a melodrama called *Honest Hearts and William Hands,* while boxing in the occasional gloved exhibition bout. His most deserving challenger was Jackson, but by appealing to the racist sentiments of his followers he managed to sidestep the black man without much condemnation. Instead he signed to meet Corbett at the Olympic Club, New Orleans, on 7 September 1892 in a title contest under the Queensberry Rules. Sullivan, who was nearly 34 years old, didn't bother to train properly, even by his own shoddy standards, and came in at a soft 212 lb.

The quick-moving 26-year-old Corbett was in superb condition at 178 lb. and had little trouble side-stepping the old man's wild swings, spearing him with single jabs and rights. After ten rounds Corbett was landing without much resistance because the exhausted Sullivan had little to offer in return. Now and then the old champion would rush him but Corbett invariably managed to evade his efforts. In round 21, with the thoroughly depleted Sullivan falling over his own feet, Corbett felt it time to end the one-sided fight, releasing a series of stiff punches. Sullivan, pouring blood from his nose, backed off, holding the top rope for support. He no longer had the energy to raise his arms. Corbett teed off with a right hand that sent the old warrior to his knees. John bravely hauled himself up but a left and right sent him down again. He landed on his face and chest and was counted out after 1 hour 20 minutes of fighting. Once he recovered his balance and breath the former world champion told the ringside crowd: 'Gentlemen, gentlemen, I have nothing at all to say. All I have to say is that I came into the ring once too often – and if I had to get licked I'm glad I was licked by an American.' He ended his impromptu speech with the words: 'I remain your warm and personal friend, John L Sullivan'.

The long Sullivan era was finally over but for many years his legion of fans continued to regard him as the true champion of the world. Whatever his limitations as a man and a fighter there is no doubt he made an immense contribution to the future of boxing.

John returned to the stage and for a while drinking, fighting and acting co-existed but eventually the booze got the upper hand and Sullivan became a pathetic figure – a sad, boastful, penniless drunk. He had one final fight at the age of 46, defeating Jim McCormick in Grand Rapids, Michigan on 1 March 1905, and while recovering from this effort he decided to turn around his life. Four days later, with typical 'Boston Strong Boy' bravado, he announced he'd had his last drink and was as good as his word. He took to the road, preaching on the 'Evils of John Barleycorn', while making money through celebrity appearances where his catchphrase was: 'shake the hand that shook the world.'

Sober and cured of his temper he divorced his estranged wife, Annie, and married his childhood sweetheart Kate Harkins, and they lived in apparent bliss on a small farm near Boston. He died of a heart attack on 2 February 1918, at the age of 59, and was sent off with a huge Boston funeral, after which the frozen earth had to be blasted to make his grave. For many years those who had known or seen or heard of him would make the offer: 'Shake the hand that shook the hand of John L Sullivan.'

Peter Jackson – 'The Black Prince'

World 'Coloured' heavyweight champion, 1888–99;
British Empire heavyweight champion 1892–99.

*'I thought Peter Jackson was a great fighter then and today, after thirty-three years,
I still maintain he was the greatest fighter I have ever seen.'*
Jim Corbett, 1925

Height: 6'1¼
Peak weight: 192–198 lb.
47 wins (32 stoppages),
3 losses, 3 draws,
41 no decisions
Born: Frederiksted, St Croix,
Virgin Islands
3 July 1861
Died: 13 July 1901

Peter Jackson may well have been the finest heavyweight of the 19th century – a boxer whose blend of skill, power and natural athleticism was considered astonishing in his time. At his peak, in the late 1880s, he dominated most of the world's best big men during his travels through America, Canada, England, Ireland and Australia and the only reason he never won the world title is that John L Sullivan refused to fight him. Jim Corbett also made his excuses and in the end Jackson's early demise from despair, alcohol, pneumonia and TB was as sad as it gets in this game. Contemporary accounts suggest an extraordinary level of adoration for this unusual man. White Americans, Australians and Englishmen, whose views were coloured by the prejudices of their day, fell over themselves extolling his gentlemanly virtues of intelligence, grace, forbearance and dignity, as well as his brilliance in the ring.

He started life on what was then the Danish Caribbean colony of St Croix as one of five children of what he described as a loving family. His father was a carpenter on the orange grove plantation where they lived, and Peter attended school in nearby Frederiksted, where he made an impression as an athlete and swimmer. He became an apprentice on a merchant ship, sailing between Europe and the Caribbean, before visiting New York at the age of 16 to try to find one of his brothers. A year later he made it to Sydney, Australia and took work on a plantation during the day and in a hotel at night, before taking a job as a deckhand on a tugboat. On one occasion it was reported that the propeller was entangled in a thick rope and the captain asked for a volunteer to dive into the shark-infested waters to free it. Jackson didn't hesitate, and years later the captain told a reporter 'I always knew Peter would make a name for himself in the world. The material was there, the man was there, no more is ever necessary.'

Some accounts say his introduction to boxing came through using his fists to put down a mutiny, but the more likely story is that he followed a friend to a local boxing hall. Fascinated, he bought a boxing manual by ex-fighter Ned Donnelly and found an outstanding trainer in the bare knuckle warrior Laurence Foley. 'It came as natural to me as if I had been to the manner born,' Peter explained. He won his first fight as an 18-year-old in January 1882 and after eight more took on the experienced Melbourne foundryman Bill Farnan for the Australian title but was knocked out in three rounds. Two years and much learning later he won the Australian title by knocking out Tom Lees (who had beaten Farnan) in the 30th round. By then he was in a different class from the crude sluggers he faced, but when a local rival, Jack 'The Irish Lad' Burke, refused to fight him on racial grounds, he decided it was time to leave and set sail for

Peter Jackson was the world's best heavyweight during the later years of Sullivan's reign. However, he was denied a shot at the title due to the champion's refusal to fight black challengers. When he died in 1901 the London *Sporting Times* wrote: 'Peter had a soul above all the miserable hicks that so frequently degrade the professional pugilist. In short he was at heart a gentleman and boxing would be all the better today for a few more like him.'

San Francisco, arriving in April 1888 with a record of just that one loss in 44 fights and a reputation as a master pugilist.

In his second American fight he took on George Godfrey for what was billed as the 'Coloured World Heavyweight Title'. Jackson had no trouble outboxing him, winning on a tenth-round knockout. Next came the white Californian champion, Joe McAuliffe who announced: 'I'll fight the nigger for a purse of $1,000, winner take all, and no gloves.' Jackson took his time, ending it in round 14 with a left to the stomach and a right between the eyes. Californian reporters wrote of a broad-shouldered, wasp-waisted boxer of remarkable defensive skill, speed, poise, timing and power. His reputation grew as he toured America, packing in 12 more effortless performances. But Sullivan refused to budge, despite receiving two unprecedented offers of $30,000. Years later Sullivan's manager and trainer, William Muldoon, admitted he persuaded John L to refuse the match because he wanted to 'save him the humiliation of being defeated by a Negro'. The disillusioned Jackson decided to try his luck in England, Ireland and Australia before returning to America to take on the rising star, James J Corbett on 21 May 1891.

Corbett and Jackson battle it out in their one and only fight. Despite lasting 61 rounds, the fight was declared a draw. Some reports suggest Jackson – who came into the fight with a viral infection and sprained ankle – may have held the slight advantage.

In his autobiography Corbett describes watching an exhibition match where Jackson dished out a one-sided boxing lesson to future world heavyweight champion Bob Fitzsimmons, but he also knew of Jackson's indiscipline between fights. With 86 fights to his name, Jackson had plenty of wear and tear on his body and he had taken to drinking, gambling and hiring prostitutes – a lifestyle that affected his condition. The unbeaten Corbett was a quick-stepping, superbly conditioned 182 lb. 25-year-old who had reached his peak. He was prepared to forgo his racial prejudices because he knew that a good showing would secure him a shot at the world title. His chances were improved by two pre-fight setbacks for Jackson. Giving himself only four weeks to train he lost a week when he was thrown from a buggy and severely sprained his ankle – an injury that restricted his movement in the ring. On top of that he came down with a bad cold a few days before the event. The fight was a disappointment with Corbett moving exclusively in retreat and both men struggling to land. After 30 rounds spectators began leaving while others 'stretched themselves out on the vacated benches and went to sleep'. After 61 rounds, lasting 4 hours 5 minutes, both men were in a state of severe exhaustion and the referee, Hiriam Cook, waved it off without declaring a winner.

Peter, disgusted with his showing, remained in San Francisco to do some serious drinking, briefly opening his own saloon to pay his bills, but when he heard Corbett was about to secure a shot at Sullivan's title he decided to return to England. Corbett sneered that his rival 'sneaked out of the country like a cur'. Part of Jackson's motivation was a fight for the Commonwealth title against Frank Slavin, an Irish-Australian he hated from his Sydney days. Slavin had taunted Jackson that he would never let a black man beat him but on three occasions they brawled out of passion for a local girl – who ended up rejecting both men. The 185 lb. 30-year-old was a formidable boxer, unbeaten in 57 fights, including a recent stoppage win over Jake Kilrain. 1,300 members of the British ruling class packed into the National Sporting Club to watch a vicious, entertaining fight with Jackson's skills gradually giving him the edge until, in round ten, he battered the bleeding Slavin, pausing to ask the referee, 'Must I do any more?' before knocking him out. Jackson was fêted by British society. Even Peggy Bettinson, the curmudgeonly boss of the National Sporting Club, fell over himself with his praise for this 'gentlemanly' black visitor.

Jackson still held out hope of being accommodated by the new world champion, Corbett, and published a long letter, pleading: 'Before age has impaired my powers I hope to have the pleasure of again meeting James J Corbett in the ring. Not that I have a feeling of animosity for him. On the contrary, I like him very much … Age is now coming on me. I am 32 and I hope to get a match on with him.' Corbett took two years to enter talks for a Jackson fight, by which stage Peter was in serious decline. With Corbett insisting they fight in the former Confederate South they failed to agree to terms and after a fiery meeting in August 1894, went their own ways.

Disillusioned, Jackson sailed back to England, from where he mounted periodic exhibition tours of Europe, using a giant Irish boxer as his foil, before returning to London to offer boxing lessons. But his main activity was drinking and his physical condition deteriorated remarkably. When he finally returned to San Francisco in late 1897 he found the racial climate had hardened and there were no openings other than the ring. Desperate for money he agreed to a contest against the strong but crude James Jeffries. In the previous five years he'd fought only six rounds and was in no condition to face such a powerful young man. Jeffries later said Jackson hit him harder than anyone else, but he overwhelmed the flabby 37-year-old, dropping him three times and stopping him at the end of round three. Peter then made his way to Vancouver where a local heavyweight, Jim Jeffords, knocked him out in four rounds.

He followed this with a gold-fossicking expedition in the Klondike and returned suffering from viral pneumonia. Doctors told him his only hope lay in a warmer climate and so his still-adoring friends agreed to pay his berth back to Australia. Rather oddly, considering that country's treatment of its aboriginal population, they too loved Peter and he was given a hero's welcome when he made it to Sydney. He staged a brief recovery, allowing him to travel with a circus and put on a 25 round boxing exhibition. But within a year he declined again – first with crippling sciatica and then tuberculosis. Another group of friends paid for his admission to a sanatorium in the town of Roma, where his carer described him as 'one of the finest characters I have ever met'.

Peter Jackson died, aged 40, on 13 July 1901. The news spread fast and tributes poured in from America, England, Ireland and Europe. Australian supporters chipped in for an impressive funeral and burial in Brisbane. Seven years later Jack Johnson visited Australia where he became the first-ever black man to win the world heavyweight title. He took time out from his post-fight tour to visit Jackson's grave, hanging his head to pay his respects to his greatest predecessor before looking up to read the simple Shakespearian words etched into the two metre high sandstone tombstone: 'This was a man.'

James J Corbett – 'Gentleman Jim'

World heavyweight champion 1892–97.

'I honestly think Corbett is a better boxer than Benny Leonard. It was the greatest thing I've ever seen in the ring. I learned plenty.'
Gene Tunney, after boxing an exhibition with the 59-year-old Corbett in 1925.

Height: 6'1
Peak weight: 178–188 lb.
13 wins (six stoppages),
4 losses, 4 draws, 3 no contests
Born: San Francisco
1 September 1866
Died: 18 February 1933

Old-timers talked of 'Gentleman Jim' as the man who revolutionised boxing – a beautifully poised dancing master, near impossible to tag, possessing astonishing speed of hand and foot and a repertoire of skills long since forgotten. 'He was the cleverest man I ever fought,' said one of his successors, Jim Jeffries. 'There isn't a fighter of any weight, living or dead, who could measure up to him as a boxer.' Asked to compare Corbett and Jeffries, William Brady, who managed both, replied, 'I have a leaning toward Corbett. He combined the most desired qualities of brain and brawn to a degree I have never seen in any other fighter, past or present.' This was the picture of Corbett portrayed in the 1942 Errol Flynn vehicle *Gentleman Jim* and if we embrace it at face value we might be tempted to accept Tunney was being frank in his gushing assessment rather than simply gracious.

It has to be said, however, that this misty-eyed image of Gentleman Jim as the meeting point between science and art is dented by the two surprisingly clear films of the man at his peak. The first was a staged match with middleweight Peter Courtney, filmed by Thomas Edison in 1894. Jim plays with Courtney in the early one-minute rounds and then, on cue, knocks him over in the sixth. The second is his world title defeat against Bob Fitzsimmons three years later. These reveal Jim's assets – sharp reflexes and far more movement than usual for his era – but also his limitations. He boxed with his head high and hands low, clinching frequently, lunging and swatting, with no combinations, no in-fighting and not much weight behind those single blows. At times he seems crude and certainly by the standards of Benny Leonard – the brilliant 1920s' lightweight champion Tunney referred to – Corbett's skills are rudimentary. In other words, he was a creature of his time, which is what we should expect.

Also not quite appropriate is the gentleman bit. It came, in part, from the white-collar contrast he presented to the raw Sullivan, but it never really fitted until later in life. Aside from being a high-school graduate and a bank teller who spoke of the 'value of a good tailor' and usually remembered how to behave in public, he was a bully capable of thuggish behaviour. One of 10 children of Irish immigrants who became livery stable owners, he was a big lad who loved throwing punches. He dropped the idea of becoming a priest and began boxing in his late teens at the San Francisco Olympic Club under the tutelage of an old pro, Walter Watson, and later worked as an instructor while also playing professional baseball. He won the club middleweight championship after a year and progressed to gloved professional fights as 'Joe Dillon' while retaining his amateur status under his original name. He fought for pay in Utah and Wyoming before returning to California in 1889 for three fights against the outstanding Jewish-American

'Gentleman Jim' Corbett punches a heavy bag whilst in training for an unsuccessful attempt to regain the world heavyweight title from his former sparring partner Jim Jeffries.

middleweight Joe Choynski, winning two, while the third fight was stopped by the police after four rounds. Their best bout was their second, fought with two-ounce gloves on a San Francisco barge on 30 May 1889. After wobbling several times, Jim came back to knock Joe out in round 27, and then collapsed. 'That was the toughest battle I ever fought,' he said after retiring, 'one in which I was to receive more punishment than I ever had in all my battles put together.'

Corbett came into contention by beating Jake Kilrain over six rounds, in New Orleans in 1890, six months after the bare knuckle hero's defeat at the hands of Sullivan. A year later Corbett and Peter Jackson fought their 61 round marathon, with the *Los Angeles Times* noting that both were 'boxer-types with a lot of quickness' but that after 30 rounds 'the bout became tame with a lot of walking around taking place and with very few, if any, blows landing.' After this he focussed on Sullivan, irritating him by bowing to the crowd after arriving late for John L's San Francisco theatrical debut. Sullivan then agreed to box Jim in an exhibition at the Grand Opera House in San Francisco in June 1891, although to hide his ample belly, he insisted they spar in formal evening dress. At the end of four rounds Corbett concluded Sullivan was a sucker for a counter-punch and had nothing but a wild right to offer. The next step was to entice Sullivan into defending his title – a task eventually managed by Brady, who raised the required $10,000. Corbett's one-sided, 21 round victory in New Orleans on 7 September 1892 was testament not just to skill over brawn, but to sobriety over alcoholism, dedication over neglect and youth over age.

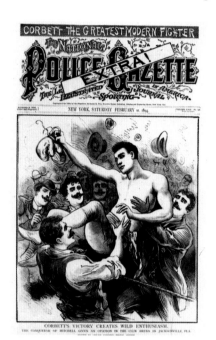

The conqueror of Charlie Mitchell is given an ovation in Jacksonville, Florida, 1894. His fans lift the boxer above their heads as Corbett holds out his boxing gloves. Cover of the *Police Gazette*, 10 February 1894.

Faced with persistent calls for a return with his premier rival, Corbett responded by saying he had 'no objection to fighting Peter Jackson because he is coloured. I think he is a credit to his profession.' But first he wanted to accommodate Charlie Mitchell because of a personal grudge – and it took him 14 months as champion to get around to it. Charlie had insulted his Irish ancestry, home life and ability to fight, prompting an enraged Jim to charge at him, receiving a cut to the lower lip in the process. He vowed to punish this English rogue in the ring, for a $20,000 winner's purse. The 32-year-old Mitchell, a petty criminal as well as an excellent boxer, was at the end of a 17-year career and at 158 lb. was giving away 26 lb. He was knocked out in three rounds. The pressure increased on Corbett to fight Jackson. After rejecting a $15,000 offer from the National Sporting Club in London (with Jackson adding he was prepared to have an American referee), Jim set out his stall: a fight to the finish (reasoning this would give him an edge over an out-of-shape 33-year-old) held in the Confederate town of Jacksonville, Florida. Jackson said no to fighting in the South, after which Corbett refused to pursue the matter, prompting criticism in American and Australian newspapers for his unreasonable negotiating tactics, with some suggesting he was simply biding his time until Jackson was too old to be a threat.

Corbett transferred his focus from the ring to the stage, although unlike most boxers he was rather good at it, earning well by acting in lowbrow productions, including one called 'Gentleman Jack' in which he played a boxer much like himself. Over the next three years he had just one fight – a four round draw with a tough Irish-American, Tom Sharkey – with most of his time spent travelling America, Canada and Europe as an actor. He announced his retirement, naming former Jackson victim, Peter Maher, as his successor. But Maher was twice knocked out by the reigning world middleweight champion, Bob Fitzsimmons. Cornish-born, New Zealand-raised, Australian-tutored, American-based Fitz was almost 34 years old and usually weighed under 165 lb. and although he hit extremely hard Jim figured on an easy night's work. The fight, on St Patrick's Day, 17 March 1897, was held in Carson City, Nevada, which legalised boxing specifically to accommodate the event, with Bat Masterson as time-keeper and Wyatt Earp patrolling the ring with his six-gun to ensure 'fair play'. It was the first-ever fight to be filmed from beginning to end, with Edison's people designing a special camera for this occasion, resulting in a film of surprising detail and clarity.

The main controversy came in round six when Corbett landed a series of stiff punches. Subsequent reports talked of a 'long count' with Bob resting on his right knee while clinging to Corbett's leg and only letting go when referee George Siler politely insisted, after which the count finally began – a 16 second process that denied Jim a knockout. The film gives a different perspective – Fitz clinching when hurt and then going down on one knee, ready to leap up at the count of eight, after which he resumed his attack. In round 14 he landed a right in the face, then feinted with another. Jim raised his hands and Bob shifted to the left and dug in with his left fist, landing hard below the heart. Corbett fell, winded, and was counted out. He was out of action for 20 months, returning in November 1898 to take on his old rival Tom Sharkey. Three months earlier he'd learnt that his father had killed his mother before committing suicide, and this might have affected his performance. Whatever the cause, the 5'8, 177¼ lb. Irish-born sailor proved too much for him and Corbett was disqualified when one of his cornermen jumped into the ring.

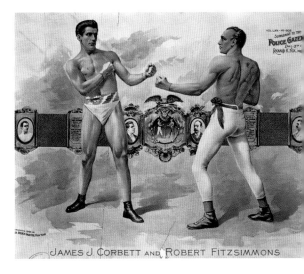

JAMES J CORBETT AND ROBERT FITZSIMMONS

An illustration depicting heavyweight boxers James Corbett and Bob Fitzsimmons facing off. Fitzsimmons rose from a sixth round knockdown and went on to knock Corbett out with a left to the solar plexus in the fourteenth round. This was the first title fight to be filmed.

Jim returned to his theatrical, restaurant-owning life and took to binge drinking, but when his former sparring partner, Jim Jeffries, won the world title it was too much to bear and he begged William Brady (who now managed Jeffries) for a fight. Brady accepted, thinking Corbett was out of shape, but the 33-year-old had been in secret training, on the wagon and working hard. By the time they met in Brooklyn on 11 May 1900, Jim weighed a sleek 188 lb. – 30 lb. less than Jeffries. Corbett used his footwork to get out of trouble while spearing his former sparring partner with jabs and quick rights until Jeffries flattened him in round 23. One of Corbett's cornermen made a bid to pour water over his stricken man in the hope of reviving him before the count reached 10, but Jeffries booted him in the face and out of the ring and the count continued. 'The finishing blow came suddenly and was a startling surprise,' the *Durango Democrat* reported. 'Corbett had been making a wonderful battle. His defence was absolutely perfect and while he was lacking in strength, he had more than held his own and stood an excellent chance of winning had it gone the limit. He had not been badly punished and had managed to mark his man severely. The winning punch was a short left to the jaw. Corbett dropped like a weight and was clearly out. Jeffries showed his ability to take hard punishment at any distance. He was clearly outboxed and at times was made to look like a novice.' Years later Corbett could laugh about it. 'I knew I'd won back the championship and from the twentieth round I kept thinking the banners would read, "Corbett Re-wins the Championship of the World!" and kept wondering would I have letters three feet high or six feet high. That was the problem bothering me, not Jeffries. I was in a corner as I had often been. He rushed me, just as he had rushed time and again. All I had to do was to sidestep and slip out, as I'd done a hundred times. And then it happened.'

Three months later he knocked out the former world middleweight champion Kid McCoy in five rounds (although it was revealed that the loser bet on himself to get knocked out at that point) and retired again. But he could not resist the call to arms and agreed to a return with Jeffries two weeks before his 37th birthday. Trained by the great little fighter Tommy Ryan he once again got himself into mint shape at 190 lb. but his reflexes had dulled while the 220 lb. Jeffries had improved. The *Elbert County Banner* reported: 'Jeffries played with Corbett for nine rounds and a half. The end came shortly after the beginning of the tenth when Jeffries planted one of his terrific left swings on Corbett's stomach. The man who conquered Sullivan dropped to the floor in agony, and the memorable scene at Carson, when Bob Fitzsimmons landed his solar plexus blow, was almost duplicated. This time however, Corbett struggled to his feet and again faced his gigantic adversary. With hardly a moment's hesitation, Jeffries swung his right and again landed on Corbett's stomach. Jim dropped to the floor, and then it was that. Tommy Ryan, seeing it was all over, motioned to Referee Graney to stop the punishment.'

Corbett was an enthusiast for the 'White Hope' campaign to unseat Jack Johnson – one of his roles, as an aide to Jeffries, was to dish out racist insults to the first black champion. But most of his attention focussed on acting. He became a popular Broadway vaudeville headliner and also appeared in silent movies. He'd married his childhood sweetheart, Olivia Lake, at the age of 19, but they divorced nine years later to allow him to marry Jessie Taylor (known by her stage name of Vera Stanwood) and this union lasted 38 years until his death. When the pickings from vaudeville grew sparse he had success as a Manhattan salon owner. He wrote his autobiography, *The Roar of the Crowd*, which was serialised by the *Saturday Evening Post* in 1924 and then published as a bestselling book. Over his last decade he was treated as a celebrity of both the stage and the ring. Five years before his death he wrote, 'Mrs. Corbett and I sort of like a little ostentation. We like a fast car, we like to move around and see folks and places, we like the hustle and bustle of life. I like to read a little poetry myself – Edgar Allen Poe and James Whitcomb Riley are my favourites. Sometimes I'll even go half an hour of Shakespeare. But that is not the feature of my existence. I also like to get money and I like to spend it. Not that Jim Corbett is a spendthrift. I don't think they'll ever have to hold a benefit for me or mine. But retirement is not in my blood.' He died of cancer at his home in Bayside, Long Island, in 1933, aged 66.

'Gentleman Jim' Corbett posing with Jim McVey. Corbett was world champion for four and a half years but made only one successful title defence in that time.

Corbett   Mckey
a left hand and

Bob Fitzsimmons – 'Ruby Robert'

World heavyweight champion 1897–99; world middleweight champion 1891–7; world light heavyweight champion 1903–4.

'He was the trickiest man who ever fought in the heavyweight division and he could hit like hell. A guy could make just one mistake against old Fitz.'
Jim Jeffries

Height: 5'11¾
Peak weight: 150–167 lb.
54 wins (47 stoppages),
8 losses, 7 draws,
17 no decisions
Born: Helston, Cornwall,
England, 26 May 1863
Died: 22 July 1917

Throughout his career Bob Fitzsimmons insisted that he could still make the 158 lb. middleweight limit, yet he beat many of the best heavyweights of his time, including Corbett for the world heavyweight title and George Gardner for the world light heavyweight title.

Fitzsimmons has many firsts to his name: first middleweight to win the heavyweight title, first to win world titles in three divisions, lightest-ever heavyweight champion, first English-born heavyweight champion. He was a remarkable boxer and also a remarkably strange-looking boxer. A freckled, prematurely balding redhead, he had skinny legs and broad shoulders, creating an odd appearance, complemented by a curious style. Fighting in the manner of his bare knuckle heroes, he leaned back, head high, left leg well forward. It hardly looked imposing but such was his accuracy, timing and power that he could knock out far bigger men with one punch.

Bob, the youngest of 12 children of a policeman, left Cornwall at the age of ten along with his parents and five of his 11 brothers and sisters and sailed to Timaru in New Zealand, never to return. He excelled at running and football at school but was soon sent to train as a blacksmith's apprentice in his brother Jarrett's shop, where he developed his strength. He took to boxing as a 17-year-old after the great British boxer Jem Mace organised an amateur tournament. He won at lightweight one year and middleweight the next. Tutored by another English professional, Dan Lea, he began fighting regularly, sometimes with bare knuckles – a tradition he greatly respected.

The money wasn't good so he relocated to Sydney, Australia in 1883, training under Larry Foley alongside Peter Jackson, and picked up another bare knuckle win and a clutch of gloved victories. Bob, an asthma sufferer, took three years off to work as a blacksmith and then, when he was cured, resumed boxing. At the age of 22 he married Louisa Johns but the relationship was soon under strain. Their daughter and first son both died as babies and they divorced when their third child, Robert Junior, was born – and then Louisa died. Shortly after her funeral, in February 1890, Bob took on Jim Hall, a boxer he'd previously stopped, and was knocked out in four rounds – a fight widely believed to have been fixed. He wanted a fresh start and sailed to San Francisco. After three wins he secured a shot at the world middleweight title, held by the Irishman John Kelly, better known as 'Nonpareil' Jack Dempsey, because he was considered without equal. Their bout in New Orleans on 14 January 1891 saw the 27-year-old Fitz, who weighed 150½ lb. dropping 'Nonpareil' 13 times. Bob pleaded with Jack to give up but it was only when the champion was wounded by a throat punch that his corner threw in the sponge.

He made two middleweight title defences – knocking out his old rival, Jim Hall, in two rounds in 1893 and doing the same to Dan Creadon a year later – but his priority was beating heavyweights. He once knocked out seven men in one night, the heaviest weighing 240 lb. His lean-back style was deceptive because he was hard to tag and with

his little feints and shifts of stance he would position himself to counter with knockout blows. Freckled Bob, as he was called, liked to joke, tease and play outside the ring, but when it came to his profession he was ruthless. In an 1894 exhibition bout he knocked out a boxer called Con Riordan, who fell into a coma and died soon afterwards, but if it affected Bob, it didn't show – he was back in the ring ten days later. Jim Corbett retired in 1895 and named the Irishman Peter Maher as champion. Fitzsimmons took on Maher in Coahuila, Mexico on 21 February 1896, under the authority of Judge Roy Bean, who bypassed the Texas Rangers by holding the bout on a Rio Grande sandbar. High rollers were transported on a special train and a footbridge was built for easy access. It took the 163 lb. New Zealander 90 seconds to knock out the 180 lb. Irishman. Nine months later he beat up the tough Tom Sawyer and in the eighth round felled him with a body punch. The referee, the famous ranger Wyatt Earp, who had a financial interest in Sawyer's success, promptly disqualified Fitz for a foul that no one saw. This moral victory set up his title bout with Corbett.

Bob was weighed privately on the morning of 17 March 1897 – a few hours before the fight – and came in at 156½ lb. (under the middleweight limit). It was said he went to the official weigh-in with weights in his pockets and this time weighed 167 lb. – still 16 lb. less than Corbett. And yet he was wonderfully confident. Making his way to the ring, he paused to kiss his second wife, Rose (a famous acrobat he had married four years earlier), and then proceeded to stalk the champion. The film of the fight shows both men fighting cautiously, throwing single punches and then clinching. The fast moving Corbett dropped his shuffling challenger in round six and yet, despite a bloody nose and mouth, Fitz looked the fresher fighter in the later rounds. Before round 14 Rose yelled from her box: 'Hit him in the slats, Bob! Hit him in the slats!' and finally her husband caught the tiring Corbett with a blow that later became known as his 'solar plexus punch' – in fact, just a good whack to the 'slats'. As Corbett crumpled Fitz landed another cuff to the ear and then looked down at the agonised champion. 'How do you like the view from there, you son-of-a-bitch?' he spat.

Fitzsimmons treated Corbett pretty much like Jim had treated Peter Jackson: despite the 'Gentleman' pleading Fitz had no interest in a return. In fact he had no intention of giving anyone a title shot for as long as he could help it. For over two years he had no official fights (only exhibitions) and instead toured America with a theatrical group. His first defence in San Francisco on 9 June 1899 came against a man he considered no more than a novice, James J Jeffries, for a record purse of $40,000. Fitz's weight dipped to 160 lb. the day before the fight, but again he managed to weigh in at 167 lb. – 39 lb. less than Jeffries. 'The bigger they come, the harder they fall,' he quipped. But, stale and out of form, he was worn down and then stopped in the 11th round. Soon back in the ring, he picked up a string of knockouts, including one over Tom Sharkey. After a failed try at wrestling he embarked on a tour of the western states with Jeffries and then, at 39, challenged for the title. This time he was in far better shape and Jeffries felt the impact of those accurate blows, landed with 5 oz. gloves. His eyes were cut and swollen, one ear was ripped, his nose broken and lips bleeding. But in round eight Jeffries, who had a 47 lb. advantage, hurt Fitz with a left to the ribs and then finished him with a hook to the chin. Afterwards it was said that Fitz, who broke both his hands, fought with 'loaded' gloves.

His life was again hit by sadness when Rose, the mother of three of his children, died in April 1903. Shortly afterwards, Bob killed another man, Con Coughlin, in the ring. But these tragedies had no obvious effect. Three months after Rose's death he married vaudeville singer Julia Giffard and 15 days after Coughlin's death he boxed again. He then won a 20 round points decision over George Gardner to win the world light heavyweight title (a new weight division). His next fight came against the skilful Philadelphia Jack O'Brien – a six round no decision bout. Fitz went 17 months without fighting before fighting a return with O'Brien in San Francisco five days before the Christmas of 1905. The bout was billed as a world heavyweight title eliminator but because both men weighed within the light heavyweight limit (Fitz was 165 lb.; O'Brien 164 lb.), Bob's new title was also at stake. At the age of 42 he no longer had the reflexes to cope with the 27-year-old's speed and was stopped in 13 rounds.

It was time to retire but, like so many, he was the last man to see it. 'I will meet any man in the world for the middleweight championship at 158 lb. or I will meet O'Brien and agree to stop him inside of ten rounds or forfeit all claim to any purse,' he declared in 1907. Instead, he took on Jack Johnson, who was then at the peak of his powers. Hampered by torn ligaments in his right elbow, he was stopped in two rounds. 'Fitzsimmons did not show a trace of his former prowess and it is probable Johnson could have stopped him in the opening round if he had cared to do so,' Associated Press reported. 'The blow that put Fitzsimmons out was a light right to the jaw. The old man fell to the floor and as he made no attempt to rise, the referee stopped the bout. The hissing which usually follows knockouts of this character was absent, the spectators evidently taking compassion on the former pugilistic star.' Fitz, who was notorious for demeaning his opponents, respected Johnson and was notably absent from the parade of champions who joined the anti-Johnson 'White Hope' campaign. He continued boxing, touring Australia and New Zealand. Julia would sing while Bob would box exhibitions and make well-rehearsed speeches in his surprisingly high voice. In December 1909 he suffered a 12th round knockout at the hands of the Australian heavyweight, Bill Lang. The film shows Fitz battered to the canvas, rising and then being knocked cold, after which his seconds haul his prostrate body to the corner to revive him. He fought twice more in 1914 and protested bitterly when the New York State Athletic Commission withdrew his boxing licence later that year. His final fling came at 53 when he boxed several exhibitions with his 28-year-old son Robert – also a professional boxer. Julia had left him by then, complaining that his whiskey drinking had ruined their marriage. In 1915 he married the 32-year-old Temo Ziller, and after a religious conversion they became travelling evangelists. Bob Fitzsimmons died of pneumonia in Chicago at the age of 54.

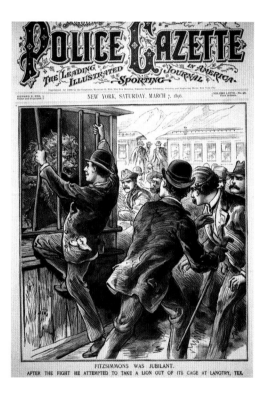

An engraving of Bob Fitzsimmons attempting to release a lion from its cage at Langtry, Texas, after he beat Peter Maher. Bystanders run away in fright.

James J. Jeffries – 'The Boilermaker'

World heavyweight champion, 1899–1905.

'There's no style to him, but he's the hardest hitter I ever saw and that includes Dempsey. Jeffries would have knocked out Dempsey. You never seen an athlete in all the world like Jeffries. Boy what I would have given to see the real Jeffries tackle Johnson.'
Tex Rickard, who promoted Jeffries, Johnson and Dempsey.

Height: 6'2½
Peak weight: 206–220 lb.
19 wins (15 stoppages),
1 loss, 2 draws
Born: Carol, Ohio, 15 April 1875
Died: 3 March 1953

Jeffries was regarded as a colossus in his time: an immensely powerful grizzly who became the first world heavyweight champion to retire unbeaten, and he achieved this after a long and relatively productive reign. In the first half of the 20th century there were several leading pundits who rated 'The Boilermaker' as the greatest of them all, preferring to judge him on this impressive record as champion rather than on his folly in returning six years later to tangle with Jack Johnson. Two films of his fights are still around: his 25 round brawl with Tom Sharkey in 1899 and his humiliation at the hands of Johnson 11 years later. What they show is that he was indeed a massive block of bone and muscle, which meant he was impervious to punishment; able to wear opponents down with strength. He fought out of a crouch – unusual in an era when most boxers leaned with their heads high – and so despite his rudimentary technique, he was hard to catch cleanly. As was common in his time he did plenty of clinching, with his strength giving him an advantage. He was an extremely heavy hitter and worked the body diligently. What the films also show is that he was crude, slow, unimaginative and vulnerable to the attentions of more agile and skillful operators.

Jim was one of eight children of Rebecca and Alexis Jeffries, his father doubling as farmer and preacher. In 1881 the family moved to a farm near Los Angeles, where Jim started school, excelling in wrestling and athletics – later running the 100 yards in 11 seconds, and clearing 5'10 in the high jump – but his main asset was his strength. He was once said to have shot a large deer and carried it on his shoulders nine miles to camp without resting. He further developed this muscle power when working as a boilermaker and for a meat packing company after leaving school. It was in this period that Jim began boxing at the East Side Athletic Club but his decision to fight for pay followed an impromptu rumble on the beach with his wrestler friend, Jim Barber. 'We wrestled all over that beach, tore up half an acre of sand and gravel and when we were finally finished we were skinned from head to foot,' he said. 'Barber, panting, said, "It's lucky they didn't get us to fight. You're a better man than I am." Until then I had thought him as the strongest man in California and to beat him at rough and tumble wrestling settled the matter. That night I made up my mind finally, to be a fighter. If I was strong enough to beat Jim Barber, I need fear no one.'

Jim won his first professional fight at the age of 20 but his parents disapproved and he promised them he would desist until he came of age. Eight months on he started again, picking up a few more knockouts, which encouraged Corbett to take him on as a sparring partner while preparing to fight Fitzsimmons. The world champion handled him with

Jeffries held the world heavyweight title for nearly six years, defending it six times. He announced his retirement on 13 May 1905, claiming to have 'defeated all logical challengers'.

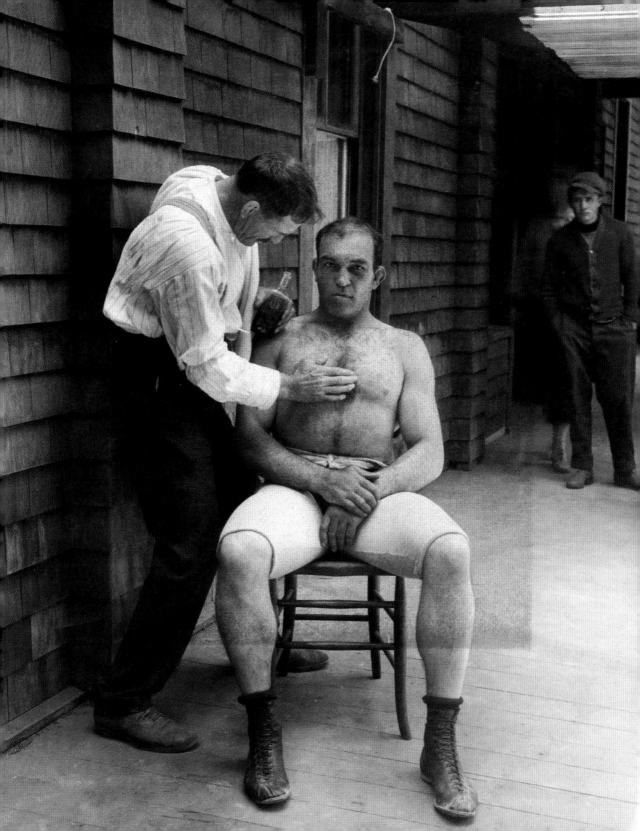

ease but the youngster emerged a better fighter. Soon after, he fought a pair of draws – the first, a hard 20 rounds with the powerful novice Gus Ruhlin; the second an even harder 20 rounds with the small but highly experienced Joe Choynski in San Francisco on 30 November 1897. After 15 give-and-take rounds Jeffries was advancing when the veteran Jewish boxer caught him with a perfectly timed right cross in the mouth and nose, which he said was the most painful punch he ever absorbed. It broke his nose and forced his top lip into the gap between his front two teeth. At the end of the round his trainer had to cut loose the flesh and he then had to spit out mouthfuls of blood, rather than swallowing it.

Four more wins, including a close 20 rounder against the tough Irishman Tom Sharkey, prompted his new manager, William A Brady, to pursue a title bout. But in his next outing – his New York debut, in which he was supposed to fight two men in one night – he broke his thumb and struggled to win a 10 round decision over a small journeyman, forcing the cancellation of the second bout. Disheartened by the boos, he talked of quitting but the world champion, Bob Fitzsimmons, decided this slow oaf was just the ticket needed after two years out of action, and so the fight was secured for Coney Island Athletic Club on 9 June 1899. The middleweight champion, Tommy Ryan, came in to assist Jim's usual trainer, Billy Delaney, teaching him to crouch with his left arm extended and his face covered by his right. He also helped develop Jeffries's hook and jab. But most of their work was on getting him into the shape needed for 25 rounds. He ran 14 miles each morning, alternating between jogging and sprinting, then played three games of handball, punched the bag for 20 minutes, and skipped rope 1,500 times, sparred at least 12 rounds and either put in some wrestling practice or tossed an 18-pound medicine ball. By fight time he was in magnificent shape, weighing in at his career lightest of 206 lb. When Bob went to his dressing room to discuss the rules Jim demonstrated how he planned to break the clinches. 'I mean like this,' he said, grabbing Bob and throwing him across the room. And he continued this treatment in the fight, dropping the New Zealander in the second round and gradually breaking him with body blows. 'The first time he hit me in the body, I thought his fist had gone right through me,' said Fitzsimmons. He dropped Fitz twice more in round ten and moved in for the kill in the 11th. After a few clinches, he landed two rights to the heart, a left to the neck and one to the ribs. Fitzsimmons crowded in, missing with a right, and Jeffries responded with a hard left to the head and a right to the point of the chin. As Bob fell with his shoulders quivering, Jim looked down, satisfied with a job well done. 'Jeffries was as firm and steady as the proverbial rock, fighting a carefully planned battle,' the *National Police Gazette* reported. 'He demonstrated his ability to hit the champion and likewise demonstrated he had nothing to fear from the latter's punches.'

The new champion travelled around America; then sailed to England and Ireland, putting on exhibitions, before returning for a 25 round return with Tom Sharkey on Coney Island, 3 November 1899. Fighting under the intense glow of 400 low-slung artificial lights (used for filming the evening event), it turned out to be one of the hardest title fights of all time. The 183 lb. Sharkey was six inches shorter than the 215 lb. Jeffries but he was a rough, dirty, hard-hitting handful. He worked the champion over in the early rounds, but Jeffries, who severely injured his left arm in the second round, absorbed everything, taking over in the later rounds with brutal body punches. The sailor was hospitalised after the bout with two cracked ribs, one poking through the skin, as well as a broken nose, several facial cuts and a grotesquely swollen ear. As the *New York Times* reported: 'For more than two hours they banged and battered each other in a fashion that was highly approved by the 19,000 spectators. It was a battle of giants, and two more magnificent specimens of physical manhood it would be difficult to find.' Jeffries won a disputed decision, prompting rumours that the referee, George Siler, was bribed, although the majority opinion was that Jeff deserved it. 'That fight was the hardest of my life, and perhaps the greatest combat ever waged in a ring between two human beings,' he later said.

Jeffries acted in a play called *The Man from the West*, put on exhibitions against all comers, and then returned to knock out the novice Jack Finnegan in one round. But his next challenger, Jim Corbett, was a far tougher proposition and it took 23 rounds of chasing before the bigger, younger, cruder Jeffries found his chin. He then beat Gus Ruhlin by tossing him into the ropes in the fifth round, after which the 200 lb. challenger quit in protest. This was followed by a return with Fitzsimmons, who cut him up for seven rounds, breaking both hands along the way. But, once again, Jim's giant left hook got him out of trouble, this time in round eight. When Fitz woke up he promptly tossed his gloves into the crowd, prompting rumours that he'd tampered with them. They shook hands afterwards and Jeffries made a point of feeling the tape around Fitz's broken fingers. 'Those things on your hands cut me up a lot,' he said. 'You didn't wear them the last time and your blows never cut me up the way they did tonight.' But he was magnanimous in victory and invited Bob along for an American exhibition tour before fighting Corbett again, dishing out a one-sided beating before stopping him in round 10. The *San Francisco Chronicle* reported: 'The body blows that stung Corbett's stomach and kidneys with such unerring accuracy hurt the ex-champion grievously.' Referee, Ed Graney, added: 'I was not prepared to see Jeffries outbox Corbett. I doubt the equal of his present self will ever exist.'

The black boxer, Jack Johnson, knocked out Jim's brother, Jack Jeffries, in five rounds 1902, after which he turned to the world champion who was sitting at ringside and said, 'I can whip you, too, Jim.' A year later Johnson won the 'coloured' world title and several US newspapers called on Jeffries to do the honourable thing. The *Los Angeles Times*, for instance, wrote: 'Jack Johnson is now the logical opponent for champion Jeffries. The color line gag does not go now. Johnson has met all comers in his class; has defeated each and every one. Now he stands ready to box for the world's championship. When they meet the world will see a battle before which the gladiatorial combats of ancient Rome pale into childish insignificance. And meet they some day will. It is up to Jeffries to say when.' Instead, Jim waited a year before defending against the novice Jack Monroe who had dropped him in an exhibition bout. Jeffries knocked him out in round two – hitting him again after he rose because he didn't realise the fight was over. Soon after, Johnson confronted him in a San Francisco saloon, but Jim refused to fight him in the ring. Instead he announced his retirement on 13 May 1905, claiming to have 'defeated all logical challengers'. He wanted to spend time on his farm with his new wife, Frieda, and nominated two white men, Marvin Hart and Jack Root, to fight for the vacant crown.

But Johnson's world title victory on Boxing Day 1908 set off a frantic clamour for a

'White Hope' to rescue the crown, beginning with Jack London's ringside report, calling on Jim to leave his farm to 'wipe the golden smile off Johnson's face'. London concluded his report: 'Jeff, it's up to you.' At first, Jim desisted, but when three other potential white hopes failed, the offers became more enticing. Shortly after his 34th birthday he announced he was acceding to 'that portion of the white race that has been looking for me to defend its racial superiority' and would begin training for the bout. He waited another six months before signing with Tex Rickard, a former horse wrangler, US marshal, saloon owner and gold panner, who made him an offer of $158,000 if he lost and $668,000 if he won. The fight was set for Reno, Nevada, on Independence Day,

James J Jeffries shadow boxing at the height of his career. He defended his title six times in nearly six years but refused to meet his most logical challenger, the world 'coloured' champion Jack Johnson, drawing the colour line just as Sullivan and Corbett had done before.

4 July 1910, in a 16,500 seater stadium built especially for the occasion. Jeffries's title reign had been relatively low key but now he was hailed as an heroic figure. Sullivan and Corbett rallied to his cause, Jack London called him 'the chosen representative of the white race' and Democratic presidential nominee William Jennings Bryan sent a telegraph, saying: 'God will forgive you everything you do to that nigger in this fight. Jeff, God is with you.'

Jeffries trained with the same frantic intensity he showed on winning the world title over a decade earlier. In 1909 he weighed around 300 lb. Eight months later he was a hard, muscular 227 lb. Among his sparring partners was Sam Langford, who must have discouraged him because he was reported to have handled Jeffries with ease. But Jeffries remained confident that Johnson could never match his strength and was too slow on his feet to keep away, and he also held to the idea that he'd bring out a latent 'yellow streak' intrinsic to black men. 'That nigger can never lick me,' he said.

But Jim took a terrible licking. The smiling Johnson taunted him throughout, while also enjoying the insults from an enraged Corbett. Despite being 19 lb. lighter, he seemed the stronger man; at one point bending Jim's hand behind his back to make a point, and he slowly sapped the resistance of the older man. It was a methodical beating, with Jeffries unable to land his big swings and finding himself raked with hurtful counters. Jim's only moment of success came in round four when he bloodied Jack's mouth but for the rest of the fight Johnson effortlessly avoided his best efforts and kept catching him with uppercuts, most thrown as they came out of their many clinches. Johnson wriggled loose from yet another clinch in round 15 and landed a short left to the jaw. Jim grabbed but was caught by three more lefts on the inside that sent him reeling. Jack moved in, landing a right to the jaw and then a left uppercut and Jeffries was down. He rose at the count of nine and Johnson pounced, knocking him halfway out of the ring. The referee – Rickard – gave him a slow count and Jim wobbled up again, clearly too dazed to respond. Johnson charged, landing a right and a left to the head before dumping him in the corner with a hook to the jaw, after which Jim's cornermen jumped in to save their man and Rickard raised Johnson's hand.

Bruised and bleeding, with two fewer teeth than before, Jim blamed his demise on age, inactivity and hubris (although he would later offer a more generous assessment of his conqueror). 'I did not have the snap of youth I used to have,' he said. 'I guess it's all my own fault. I was getting along nicely and peacefully on my alfalfa farm, but when they started calling for me and mentioning me as the white man's hope, I guess my pride got the better of my good judgement. I just didn't have it today. Six years ago it would have been different.' Johnson saw it differently: 'I won from Jeffries because I outclassed him in every department of the fighting game. He came back at me with the heart of a true fighter. No man can say he did not do his best.' Jeffries returned to the farm to spend more time with Frieda and their daughter, Mary. He bought a bar and bred prize cattle, but was forced to declare bankruptcy because of several bad investments. After that he performed a series of exhibitions with his brother Jack and with Tom Sharkey, continuing until his late 50s. He also acted in vaudeville and movies. He died in his sleep in 1953, shortly before his 78th birthday.

Marvin Hart – 'The Fightin' Kentuckian'

World heavyweight title claimant 1905–06.

'A friend to countless hundreds. A man among men, an ideal of children, a clean fighter whose example will continue to inspire the coming generations.'

Inscription on Marvin Hart's headstone.

Height: 5'11½
Peak weight: 185–190 lb.
31 wins (21 stoppages),
9 losses, 7 draws, 1 no decision
Born: Fern Creek, Kentucky,
16 September 1876
Died: 17 September 1931

Marvin Hart would be no more than a footnote in heavyweight history were it not for one curious result: his win over a peak Jack Johnson on 28 March 1905.

Hart, the 28-year-old underdog, gave his usual plucky show, pressing forward and working the body. Johnson, two days short of 27, fought with even more nonchalance than usual, throwing less but landing more. After 20 rounds Marvin was bruised and bleeding; Jack unmarked. 'Hart's face was battered to a pulp,' the *Washington Post* noted and their report hinted that Johnson was not punching his weight but that referee Alec Greggains's verdict was still questionable. Whatever the truth, Hart was appointed by Jim Jeffries as one of the two white men to fight for his old title three months later – a dramatic turnaround from a career that had been chugging aimlessly

Marvin seemed to have the appropriate genetic material for his calling – both parents had been noted for their size and strength. After high school he learned his trade as a plumber and it was in this period that he started boxing. In his first professional fight at the age of 23 the novice won on a seventh round knockout and remained unbeaten for two years, until running into 'Wild Bill' Hanrahan, who knocked him out in the first round, with Hart claiming he was drugged. He regrouped until 1902 when he fought one of the world's best light heavyweights, the Austrian-born Jack Root, who was too quick and skilful. He paused to marry his sweetheart, Florence Ziegler, and then went into a fight for the world light heavyweight title with another classy veteran, George Gardner, and had to retire in the 12th round after breaking his wrist.

But he improved after moving to heavyweight and in the return with Gardner seemed unlucky to get only a draw, after which he secured that disputed win over Johnson. This prompted Jeffries to nominate him for the vacant heavyweight title against his former conqueror, Root. By then Hart was significantly stronger and hit harder, but Root was quicker and in round seven he opened up, dropping Marvin just before the bell. But Hart recovered and worked his way back, wearing down the smaller man before knocking him out with a right to the chest in round 12. Jeffries held his hand up, anointing him the new world heavyweight champion.

The first defence of his crown was against 5'7 Canadian middleweight Tommy Burns at the Pacific Athletic Club in Los Angeles. Hart went in for the kill but found himself handily outboxed by the quicker, more skilful challenger and after 20 rounds the decision was a formality. Marvin pleaded for a return, but no one was listening. Hart fought on with mixed success but after losing three more fights he retired with Florence to Louisville, Kentucky, at the age of 34. He died from liver disease and high blood pressure in 1931 at the age of 55.

Hart's most controversial fight was against the up and coming African-American fighter, Jack Johnson, in 1905. Johnson claimed he was blackmailed to throw the fight and that the sight of a revolver in the lap of a ringsider persuaded him the threat was serious.

Tommy Burns – 'The Little Giant of Hanover'

World heavyweight champion 1906–08.

'Let me say of Mr Burns: that he has done what no one else ever done; he gave a black man a chance for the championship. He was beaten, but he was game.'

Jack Johnson, three months after beating Burns in 1908.

Height: 5'7
Peak weight: 168–181 lb.
48 wins (39 stoppages),
6 losses, 8 draws,
2 no decisions
Born: Hanover, Ontario, Canada
17 June 1881
Died: 10 May 1955

Tommy Burns is known for the distinction of being the shortest boxer to lift the world heavyweight title and the man who took a bad beating in the service of ushering in the first black champion, Jack Johnson. But he is worth far more: strong for his size, nimble on his feet with quick hands, sharp timing, sound defensive technique and a cracking left hook.

Born Noah Brusso, a French-Canadian of Italian descent, he grew up in a log cabin as one of 13 children of a poor Catholic family, left school at 10 and worked in the mining camps where he first came across boxing. He moved to Detroit where he started fighting and after winning the Michigan middleweight title he dished out a ferocious beating to a boxer called Ben O'Grady who nearly died. The 22-year-old Noah hurriedly left town, moved to Chicago and began fighting under the name Ed Burns and then Tommy Burns.

He boxed all over America in a bid to secure a title shot, usually winning on knockouts but suffered setbacks along the way to world light heavyweight champion Philadelphia Jack O'Brien and top middleweight Jack 'Twin' Sullivan. Six weeks after the Sullivan loss, world middleweight champion Tommy Ryan agreed to fight him for the 158 lb. title. But Burns, who was struggling to make the weight, then received a better offer to fight Marvin Hart for the heavyweight title. So instead of boiling down, he beefed his way up to 180 lb. and outboxed the larger, slower favourite. Later that year he met the other title claimant, his old rival Philadelphia Jack O'Brien. They delivered a battle of skill and speed, with Tommy holding a slight edge. However, referee Jim Jeffries, who had previously declared O'Brien as his preference, made the result a draw, so they fought again five months on and this time Burns won decisively to gain universal recognition as world champion.

He took his show on a world tour – racking up a record for heavyweight title bouts of eight knockouts in a row. A fellow traveller, Jack Johnson, made a point of calling him out from ringside after every defence but Burns had no desire to take on a man as dangerous as Johnson unless for a record fee. He finally said yes to an unprecedented $30,000 purse offer, agreeing to fight on Boxing Day in Sydney.

The author Jack London backed Burns when he defended his title against the African-American Jack Johnson. 'I am with Burns the whole way,' London wrote. 'He is a white man and so am I. Naturally I want to see the white man win.' Burns was knocked out in round 14. Many years later Burns publicly apologised for making racist comments to Johnson in the ring.

The 168 lb. Hart was installed as a 3–1 betting favourite, but the 192 lb. Johnson was too big, strong and elusive. Burns was down in the first and everything he tried after that was evaded or countered. Johnson replied with stiff single jabs and quick uppercuts, which cut Tommy's face, bruised his body and drained his resistance. In round 14 Johnson dropped Burns with a heavy right. When he rose Jack pounced, raining punches on his bleeding face. The referee promptly stopped the fight, declaring Johnson the winner.

Tommy fought intermittently over the next 12 years, finally ending his career aged 39. He owned a couple of bars before becoming an evangelist, denouncing the brutality of boxing. He was destitute when he died of a heart attack a month before his 74th birthday.

Jack Johnson – 'The Galveston Giant'

World heavyweight champion 1908–15; world 'Coloured' heavyweight champion 1903–8.

'I could never have whipped Johnson at my best. I couldn't have reached him in a thousand years.'
Jim Jeffries, a few months after losing to Johnson in 1910.

Height: 6'1¼
Peak weight: 185–208 lb.
82 wins (52 stoppages),
14 losses, 11 draws,
20 no decisions
Born: Galveston, Texas,
31 March 1878
Died: 10 June 1946

When Johnson entered the ring to fight Jeffries he was greeted by the crowd singing: 'All Coons Look Alike to Me' – lyrics inspired by an offhand remark made by the former champion six years earlier. And this was about as mild as it got for the man known first as 'Li'l Arthur' and later as 'Papa Jack'. After the fight a man armed with a shotgun tried to break into his Chicago home – aiming to kill him for the general offence of beating a white man and the specific offence of beating the beloved Jeff. And Jack wasn't alone in getting this kind of treatment. His victory prompted race rioting all over the United States, with at least 26 people killed, and hundreds injured, mainly black.

Arthur John Johnson was the second of six children – his father a janitor and freed slave, his mother a laundress. He left school after five years and avoided fighting until he was 12 when he discovered he was exceedingly good at it. As a young teenager he went to find work in Dallas where a shop owner introduced him to boxing and he took work as a sparring partner while taking part in fights against other black boxers for the entertainment of white patrons who would throw coins into the ring after the end of each match. He returned to Galveston and worked as a janitor, stable boy, hotel porter and longshoreman, before securing a job cleaning a gym and it was then that he decided on his profession. His first official fight was on the beach in 1894, shortly before his 16th birthday, against dockworker John Lee. Johnson won on a 15th round knockout to take the $1.50 purse.

He left home to seek his fortune in 1899. 'There was nothing more for me to do in Galveston,' he explained. 'The purses offered were truly minimal – 10, 15 or 20 dollars at most. If I stayed there, all I'd have is debts for I had to pay one or two seconds and their wages absorbed the whole purse and sometimes more. So I decided to travel the world, to try to box from one coast to the other, and to attach myself to the training camp of a famous boxer.' He paused in Chicago, then Springfield, Illinois, where a saloon owner employed him to fight in a 'battle royal' when several black boxers were blindfolded and placed in a ring, with the last man standing winning the coins tossed to them by white patrons. Johnson won another $1.50, but was left with nothing after having to pay a white agent. This secured him a fight in Chicago against a decent black heavyweight, known as Klondike. Jack lacked the experience to cope and quit in round five. After this he fought whenever he could and filled in the time by working as a sparring partner, until offered a return with Klondike, battling his way to a 20 round draw. They fought once more and this time Li'l Arthur battered his conqueror until Klondike quit in round 14.

This set him for a fight in his hometown of Galveston, where his family home had been flattened by a hurricane a few months earlier. He was thrown in with one of the finest

Jack Johnson, the first African-American to hold the world heavyweight boxing title, which he won by knocking out Tommy Burns in Sydney, Australia, in 1908. In six-and-a-half years he made eight successful title defences.

Jack Johnson stands over the knocked out former world heavyweight champion Jim Jeffries. The battle, lasting 15 rounds, was staged in Reno, Nevada, 4 July 1910. Following Johnson's victory 26 people were killed in racial violence.

boxers of the previous decade, Joe Choynski, who, at 32, was ten years older than Johnson and had numbered Corbett, Fitzsimmons and Jeffries among his 70 opponents. Choynski used his skill to keep the youngster away, and knocked him out with a left hook to the temple in the third round. But, as the *Marion Daily Star* reported, 'just as the negro went to the floor, a state ranger stepped into the ring and arrested the fighters.' The black novice and the Jewish veteran spent 23 days in a jail cell together on suspicion of engaging in an illegal contest. Choynski took a liking to this bright and confident young man and gave him three weeks of intensive tuition in the fine points of defensive technique. They were helped by the sheriff, who allowed them to entertain fellow prisoners and outsiders with daily public sparring sessions, and by the end of their spell together the master told the pupil: 'A man who can move like you should never have to take a punch.' A grand jury failed to return indictments against them, so the sheriff released them on the condition they left town. Johnson rode the rails on a freight train bound for Denver, where he moved in with a community of boxers. He was joined by his common law wife, Mary Austin, and the couple then relocated to Bakersfield, California.

The new Johnson was a more mature boxer, combining his immense natural ability and strength with sophisticated technique, so that he became the most elusive big man around. His approach involved shadowing the gloves of his opponents and picking their punches out of the air or simply slipping them, while slotting in hurtful counters. He fought at a slow pace, biding his time, clinching frequently and making frequent use of his uppercut on the inside, and only when he had the other man sufficiently softened would he open up with his heavy artillery. He also developed a habit of taunting his opponents along the way, particularly if they were white.

On 5 February 1903, the 6'1¼, 180 lb. Johnson outpointed the 6'6¼, 203 lb. Denver Ed Martin to win the 'coloured' world heavyweight title in his 43rd listed fight and then knocked him out in two rounds in the return. From then on he was viewed as the leading challenger for Jeffries's world title. But the champion resolutely drew the colour line, which meant that Johnson had to make do with defending his 'coloured' title against talented men like Sam McVea, Joe Jeanette and the young Sam Langford, while occasionally fighting white contenders. One of these was his dubious points defeat against Marvin Hart in 1905 – breaking a 23 fight unbeaten streak. Another was his two round knockout victory over the faded 43-year-old Bob Fitzsimmons.

A new king seized the throne – the little Canadian, Tommy Burns, who, on beating Hart, declared: 'You're not a real contender if you duck a man because of his colour.' He added: 'I will defend my title as heavyweight champion of the world against all comers, none barred. By this I mean black, Mexican, Indian or any other nationality without regard to color, size or nativity. I propose to be the champion of the world, not the white or the Canadian or the American or any other limited degree of champion.' But Tommy was a tricky fellow so he went on to say he would first 'give the white boys a chance'. Johnson followed him to France, Britain and Australia and eventually secured the fight after Burns received a record purse offer. Just in case anyone had the wrong idea, Tommy declared: 'All niggers are alike to me but I'll fight him even though he is a nigger.'

When Johnson outclassed Burns, he was nearing 31 and already a veteran of 86 fights and 15 years of professional boxing. He was approaching the end of his peak years and most of his performances as champion were uninspiring. His first defence was a six round no decision bout against the 161 lb. Philadelphia Jack O'Brien, who danced around him, making him look bad. Two more white challengers, Tony Ross and Al Kaufman, also lasted the distance in no decision bouts. Then Johnson signed to fight the big-hitting world middleweight champion Stan Ketchel in Colma, California, on 16 October 1909. Johnson, with his 34¾ lb. weight advantage, agreed to carry the little man, and although he dropped Stan once along the way, nothing else of interest happened until the bout suddenly exploded in round 12. 'The whole climax of the fight was crowded into thirty-four seconds,' Associated Press reported. 'They met in the centre, clashed and wrestled to Johnson's corner. The negro broke, and poising himself, dashed at Ketchel, who shrank to meet him. Ketchel drove his right to the black's lowered head. Johnson ducked and received the blow behind the ear and rolled to the floor. Johnson arose slowly and leaped toward the white man, landing a terrific blow on Ketchel's jaw; with his left he struck for the stomach and with his right swung again, catching Ketchel's head as it rolled from the onslaught. Ketchel dropped in a heap while Johnson sprawled across the beaten rival's legs. Johnson arose still dazed and clung to the ropes.' Johnson's right knocked two of Ketchel's teeth out, which Stan's manager made into a pair of dice.

The arrival of the world champion Jack Johnson in Chicago in 1910.

The fear of Johnson had been growing ever since he tortured Burns to defeat, and with each White Hope vanquished, it spread. It was bad enough that Johnson was black but what made it infinitely worse was that he refused to show the deference expected of him. For example, he talked for himself during the prelude to his next fight against Jeffries, prompting a reprimand from the other side of the table to leave the deal-making to the white man. He replied disdainfully that seeing as he was the man doing the fighting he would also do the negotiating, and no one would tell him what to do. That was Johnson – a highly intelligent, opinionated, well-read man with a taste for history books, whose attitudes were, in some respects at least, decades ahead of his time.

His one-sided win over Jeffries was the determining event of his career. For Jack himself it was his greatest feat of vindication. He'd been chasing the white grizzly for eight years and finally cornered and finished him off. But this feat of skill, endurance and power turned him into the premier figure of hate for the substantial section of white America who could not abide the idea that a black man was the best fighter on earth, and particularly not one who paraded his dominance. It was two years before he made his next defence, against one of his former white victims, Fireman Jim Flynn, who fouled so often and so blatantly that in the ninth round, after one head butt too many, the police stopped the fight, awarding it to Johnson. In the meantime Jack bought a fleet of fast cars, took up motor racing, started smoking cigars and drinking heavily, none of which endeared him to his white countrymen.

He was not universally popular in black America either, particularly among middle class 'race men' who felt he was setting back their integrationist cause. Johnson, they felt, was out only for himself, not for his people. He was an individualist who regularly scorned other black boxers and made no attempt to assist them, and once his relationship with Mary Austin dissolved he also began to make derogatory remarks about black women. 'Every coloured lady I ever went with two-timed me; white girls didn't,' he said.

This was the prime incendiary point in his fraught relations with white America – even more than the way he dominated their flawed heroes in the ring. It touched the rawest of racist nerves: not just beating their strongest men but taking their women too. Congress reacted by passing the Mann Act in 1910, banning the transportation of women across state boundaries 'for the purpose of prostitution, debauchery, or for any other immoral purpose'. This law was designed to combat organised vice, but the government chose to use it as a way to get internal enemy number one. One of Jack's companions was a white prostitute named Hattie McClay and they were later joined on their travels by another white prostitute, Belle Schreiber. Johnson then married a third white woman, Etta Duryea, but she committed suicide in 1912 – partly because she was a manic depressive but also because Johnson had become a heavy drinker who regularly abused her. Three months on he married another white prostitute, Lucille Cameron, after which the Feds struck. Johnson was tried for violating the Mann Act and Schreiber testified against him. He was sentenced to a year's imprisonment, after which the prosecutor acknowledged, 'This Negro, in the eyes of many, has been persecuted. Perhaps as an individual he was. But it was his misfortune to be the foremost example of the evil in permitting the intermarriage of whites and blacks.' While out on appeal Jack posed as a member of a black baseball team and skipped the border, first to Canada and later France, remaining in exile for seven years.

By this stage it is doubtful that Johnson was still the best heavyweight in the world. The three leading black contenders, McVea, Jeanette and particularly the brilliant Langford, had caught up with him, but he had no interest in accommodating any of them. Instead, six days before the Christmas of 1913, he defended his title in Paris against 'Battling' Jim Johnson, a mediocre black heavyweight from his hometown of

Galveston. Their fight was set for 20 rounds but ended as a ten round draw because Johnson broke his arm, having hurt it in a wrestling match earlier that week. He made only one more successful defence, coming in grossly overweight to outpoint yet another White Hope, Frank Moran, in Paris seven months later. Then after an exhibition tour of Argentina, he made his way to Havana, Cuba, and got his much-abused 37-year-old body back down to 205 lb. to face the huge but crude Kansan Jess Willard.

It is one of the paradoxes of boxing that the best of champions can lose to the worst and this is what happened to Johnson. If the fight had been over the usual 20 or 25 rounds, he would have won by a mile but it was set for 45 rounds in the 105 degree heat. The start was predictable enough – a slow fight with Jack in charge. He rocked Jess several times and in round nine opened a deep cut on Willard's right cheek and the giant was also bleeding from his mouth. From rounds 10 to 16 Johnson, knowing he couldn't last 45, tried for a knockout but gradually his strength drained away. At the end of round 25 he motioned to his wife to leave the arena, not wanting her to see the inevitable. The exhausted champion was slow coming out for the 26th. Willard moved forward, landing a hard right to the face and another right to the body, followed by a third one to the jaw. Johnson fell on his back, his right glove over his face and he was counted out. 'I have no excuses to offer,' he said. 'A better and younger man has taken the championship title.' Several decades later Johnson approached the editor of *The Ring* magazine, Nat Fleischer, and sold him a 'confession', in which he said he'd thrown the fight. 'I was tired of being hounded,' he claimed. Fleischer, who rated Johnson as the greatest heavyweight of them all, didn't believe him and the film of the fight backs him up. It shows Jack dominating early but fading in the later rounds, and the knockout appears as genuine as they come.

Johnson moved to Spain, then Mexico and continued boxing while making ends meet any way he could – including bullfighting – but eventually, homesick and broke, he returned to the United States, surrendered to the authorities and served a year in Leavenworth Prison in Kansas, where he was appointed athletic director and allowed to take part in several fights on prison grounds. When he was released in 1921 he tried a few alternative ideas, including securing a patent for a wrench he designed, but when he returned to Cuba two years later he resumed his boxing career with a knockout over one of Jack Dempsey's sparring partners and then proceeded to pick up wins in Canada, the United States and Mexico, while divorcing Lucille and marrying Irene Pineau. Finally in 1926, at the age of 48, he lost a fight in Juarez, Mexico, against a journeyman, when he refused to come out for the eighth round, claiming he was fouled. In the intervening 11 years he'd been unbeaten in 22 fights but neither Willard nor Dempsey had any interest in giving him another shot at the title.

Johnson made one final return to the ring at the age of 62, getting knocked out in seven rounds by a novice featherweight, although he continued boxing in exhibitions throughout the war – his last at the age of 67. He made a regular point of deriding Joe Louis's ability and intelligence and in 1946, while on his way to watch Louis preparing for his return fight with Billy Conn, he was incensed by a racist incident in a North Carolina diner and drove off in a huff, smashing his car into a lamp pole. The car crumpled and rolled and he died in hospital of internal injuries.

Jess Willard – 'The Pottawatomie Giant'

World heavyweight champion 1915–19.

'It's easier for me to hit a man after he's hurt me but with my reach it takes seven or eight rounds before he gets to me at all. When I do go after an opponent I try to finish him off as quickly as possible. I get absolutely no pleasure from punishing a man.'
Jess Willard, as world champion.

Height: 6'6¼
Peak weight: 225–230 lb.
27 wins (20 stoppages),
7 losses, 1 draw
Born: Pottawatomie, Kansas
29 December 1881
Died: 15 December 1968

Big Jess recorded 35 fights but is known for just two: winning the title and losing it. Before, during and after his reign this Kansas farm boy, who wandered into boxing in the heat of the 'White Hope' hunt, achieved little of significance. 'He was one of the poorest heavyweight champions,' *The Ring* editor Nat Fleischer declared. 'Jess was a slow moving pugilist who disliked training as much as he disliked the sport.'

Jess, the youngest of four sons, married local girl Hattie Evans and then roamed the West, looking for work. He ended up in Oklahoma City where he saw his first boxing match and decided to give it a try, fighting several exhibitions. His first official bout came at the age of 29 when he dropped Louis Fink in round three but became frustrated, belted him in a clinch and tossed him to the canvas, earning a tenth round disqualification. They fought again and this time Jess put him to sleep in the third.

The anti-Johnson campaign 'to restore the prestige of the white race' was becoming more hysterical with each fresh failure, prompting the establishment of a 'White' heavyweight title. Having beaten several would-be white champions, Willard lost to the 180 lb. Gunboat Smith. Clearly not yet up to championship level, Jess was fed a novice, 'Bull' Young. Willard landed a huge uppercut in round 11 – some reports insisting it 'drove the base of Young's jaw up into the brain'. Young died and Jess was arrested for manslaughter, and although the charges were soon dropped this tragedy haunted him for the rest of his life. He lost his next two fights but what impressed the White Hopers was his indestructibility. This gave him a chance against the 37-year-old Jack Johnson and a sixth round knockout over his former conqueror 'Boer' Rodel convinced the doubters and Jess was shipped to Cuba to fight for the title. His trainer, Tex O'Rourke, built his stamina and by fight time the 230½ lb. 33-year-old was in the finest shape of his life. He absorbed a beating for 16 rounds but outlasted Johnson, knocking him out in the 21st round.

For most of his long reign he toured America with circuses for a minimum of $1,000 per day. By the time Willard signed to fight Dempsey for $100,000 he'd been out of the ring for three years and he took a lackadaisical approach.

That Jess survived three rounds is testimony to his astonishing courage. The first was the most savage three minutes in boxing history and the violence was all from the little fellow to the big, who went down seven times suffering multiple fractures to his jaw, cheekbones and nose. There were no more knockdowns but Willard was too badly injured to come out for round four. The giant retired to his ranch but four years later, aged 41, he embarked on a brief comeback. In his second fight he took on the Argentinean Luis Angel Firpo and was knocked out in seven rounds. He died a week before his 87th birthday.

Jess Willard stalks heavyweight champion Jack Johnson in Havana, Cuba, 5 April 1915. This was Willard's only fight against a black man. He called Johnson 'that smoke' and 'that nigger' and showed no intention of fighting black contenders during his four inactive years as champion.

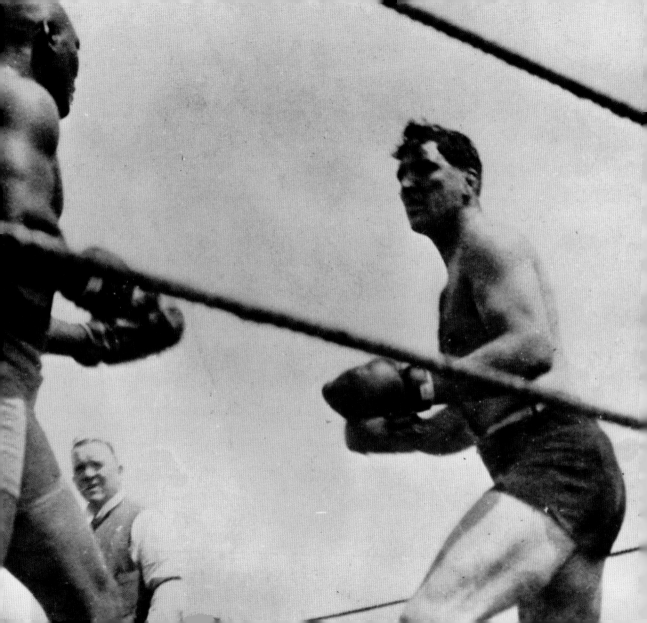

Sam Langford – 'The Boston Tar Baby'

World 'Coloured' heavyweight champion
1909–11, 1912–14, 1914–15, 1916–17, 1917–18.

'I think Sam Langford was the greatest fighter we ever had. I didn't have the experience to fight a man like that. He was a hell of a puncher, so why should I get my brains knocked out for nothing? Even at my best I don't know whether I could lick him. He was a good man, good puncher, rough, tough.'

Jack Dempsey, on why he refused to fight Langford in 1916.

Height: 5'7½
Peak weight: 160–190 lb.
197 wins (130 stoppages),
46 losses, 42 draws,
19 no decisions
Born: Weymouth, Nova Scotia,
4 March 1883
Died: 12 January 1956

There is one question that seldom attracts dispute in boxing circles: who was the greatest fighter never to win a world title? Sam Langford has no challengers. He could have won world titles in every division from lightweight to heavyweight but was too good and too black to get the chance. After moving through the divisions, he was probably the world's best heavyweight from around 1912 to 1916, and the second best for a while before and after but Dempsey wouldn't go near him, and before that Willard and even Johnson took a similar stance. While many of his heavyweight contemporaries are underwhelming on film, Langford is an exception: fast, elusive, busy, aggressive and extremely powerful. As *The Ring* magazine editor Nat Fleischer put it in 1939, 'Langford was as quick and slippery as an eel in action, highly intelligent and made up of surprising dodges from head to heels. Sam used his bulky shoulders and clever blocking arms to avoid blows and his potent punching power stayed with him until the end of his career.'

The only doubt about Sam is his age. We know he was born in Nova Scotia, Canada, a descendant of escaped slaves and the date of 4 March 1883 is engraved on his tombstone, but some sources make it 1886. We also know he was one of seven children of an abusive 'windjammer and sailor' and that he went to jail for 15 days for stealing eggs at the age of 10. A year later he took his first job, 18 miles from home, as an ox-driver and log hauler, earning $1.25 a week. He was still a child when he left home to work on a steam boat because, as he explained, 'my pa was always lickin' me.' The ship was wrecked in a storm, after which he rode the rails and learnt to defend himself against men who picked fights with black lads. He crossed the US border and travelled the eastern states with his only friend, a dog, arriving in Boston where he sought work in a drugstore because he hadn't eaten in two days. It turned out to be a fortuitous stop because the owner gave him a meal and offered him a job as the janitor in the boxing gym he ran on the side. This perpetually smiling kid with a pronounced lisp volunteered his services as a sparring partner, took his share of licks and began boxing as an amateur. He won the featherweight championship of Boston before beginning his professional career in 1902 with a fifth round knockout.

Within 20 months he'd put in 27 fights, with just one loss and was thrown in with the world lightweight champion, Joe Gans, in a 15 round non-title fight. Gans, having his 130th bout, was rated the finest lightweight champion of them all, but was knocked

Sam Langford who, despite continuing his successful heavyweight boxing career until the age of 43, never got a shot at the world title.

Sam Langford could have won world titles from lightweight to heavyweight but was denied the chance because he was considered too dangerous or because his opponents opted to draw the colour line.

down and handily outboxed by the 138 lb. Langford. The long-armed, broad-shouldered, deep-chested Sam soon grew into a welterweight and in 1904 challenged Joe Walcott (also rated at the time as the best-ever of his weight). The official verdict was a draw although the press made Sam the winner. 'Langford was willing to mix it up and gave Walcott plenty to do at the same time outboxing him,' wrote Arthur Lumley, sports editor of the *New York Illustrated News*. 'My personal opinion is that Langford was entitled to the verdict and should have been awarded the world's title.' This was to be his only world title fight in a 24-year career. He moved to middleweight and had his first experience with a top heavyweight, getting stopped in eight rounds by the talented black contender Joe Jeanette. Four months later, in April 1906, they fought a return and this time Langford won, setting the scene for a challenge for Jack Johnson's world 'coloured' heavyweight title. Langford, at 23 (or perhaps 20), had been a professional for four years and came in at 158 lb. Johnson, 28, had reached his peak after 12 years and 72 professional fights and came in at 187 lb. The youngster put up a fierce fight but was dropped twice in round nine and emerged with a broken nose. After 15 rounds there was no dispute about the winner. As Langford put it, 'Johnson gave me the only real beating I ever took.'

Sam worked his way through the heavyweights, with occasional sojourns in the lighter divisions, going unbeaten in a 56-fight spell. One of his opponents was reigning world middleweight champion Stan Ketchel, who'd lasted 12 rounds with Johnson six months earlier, dropping the champion. It was a six round non-title bout, held in Philadelphia on 27 April 1910, with ringside reports suggesting Langford dominated the early rounds before easing off – perhaps because he was angling for a title shot (he regularly 'carried' white opponents at the insistence of promoters). Ringside opinion was divided but their reports imply Langford could have won it if he'd wanted to. The *Philadelphia Bulletin* said Sam dominated behind the jab and in the third round 'shook Ketchel badly with swings to the head' while in the fourth he 'twice shook Ketchel with jaw punches and brought blood from the mouth and nose with well timed jabs'. This report concluded, 'Langford was much the stronger and cleverer and his jabs had a disconcerting effect on Ketchel. The coloured man looked to be in pretty good shape at the close, but Ketchel was tired and wild and the sound of the bell was a welcome interruption.' Stan showed no interest in accommodating Sam in a title bout after this and six months later was murdered by a jealous farmhand.

Sixteen months on, Langford fought world light heavyweight champion Philadelphia Jack O'Brien (who had held Johnson to a draw a year earlier). The 178 lb. 'Boston Tar Baby', having his 113th professional fight, took it easy for four rounds before cutting loose. *The Herald* reported, 'After feinting and dancing for a time the Negro plunged a terrific right into the pit of the white man's stomach and the latter howled from the pain of it. The Negro gave him a hard pounding and all the skill that he could marshal could not avail him. When O'Brien was bending over from the result of the impact the Negro dropped over a short left hook to the jaw and it was farewell for O'Brien. He went down on his haunches half-way through the ropes and then rolled over.'

Langford called for a fight with Tommy Burns in 1908 but was beaten to it by the more persistent Johnson. He campaigned for a return with Johnson, but was ignored by a champion in decline. Langford reached his 185 lb. peak after 1910: a far more formidable challenger for Johnson than the youthful middleweight he'd outpointed in 1906. Comparing films of the pair at that stage of their careers it is not hard to see the Boston Tar Baby getting the better of the overweight, drinking, cigar-puffing and clearly declining Galveston Giant. Norman Clark, who watched both men on their British tours (Sam visited England three times and also fought in Australia, Argentina and Mexico), said, 'Whereas Johnson would not let the heavy stuff fly until he had worn the man down, Sam always waded right in and immediately let go punches heavy enough to drop anyone.'

Any hope of a title shot disappeared when the openly racist Jess Willard won the title. Instead, Sam had to content himself with an endless series of fights for the 'coloured' world title against his premier black rivals – in particular Joe Jeanette (14 times) and Sam McVea (15 times), with Langford holding a slight edge. In 1914 a new black heavyweight entered the scene, the big and powerful Harry Wills. For a couple of years they fought on even terms, with Langford knocking him out twice and getting outpointed twice while dropping a few newspaper verdicts in no decision bouts. Gradually, as Langford closed in on his 200th professional bout, he began to slow while Wills grew stronger and more experienced, but Sam's main problem was his left eye, which 'went' when he fought Fred Fulton in 1917 (a detached retina). This meant he had trouble seeing right hands. Wills twice stopped Sam in 1918, once on a clean knockout (his first count-out defeat in 16 years as a professional). After this Langford adapted to fighting one-eyed – in five more bouts with Wills (in all, they fought 23 times) he was never stopped again – but he was not quite the force of old.

He fought future world middleweight champion Tiger Flowers in 1922 and was hurt in his good right eye. All he could see was a blur of motion before him. As he recalled of round two, 'I decided, I'll let Flowers come and get me.' Tiger closed in and Sam fired, heard a crack and then a thud. The *Atlanta Constitution* reported, 'The fatal clout was a right chop that travelled six inches.' Doctors warned Sam that the optic nerve was damaged and he would go blind if he boxed on, but he was broke He was a generous, happy-go-lucky man who gave away most of his money and had a wife, Martha, and daughter, Charlotte, to support, so he pressed on for 50 more fights. In 1924 a specialist operated to draw together a muscular fold in the retina of his right eye, which improved his vision, but it soon deteriorated again. He retired in 1926 at the age of at least 40 after suffering a first round stoppage in his 314th officially listed fight against an opponent he could barely see. He had another operation in 1935, which brought back partial sight. When he woke after the surgery and opened his right eye, he said: 'It's wonderful, just wonderful!' Later that year, however, he was run over by a taxi and suffered internal injuries, after which his general health deteriorated, and eventually his sight went completely. He was living destitute in Harlem, spending most of his time sitting on the porch of his run-down tenement block, when a *New York Herald Tribune* reporter tracked him down and wrote a series of stories on him in 1944. A sportswriters' fund was established and this kept him in reasonable comfort for the final decade of his life.

Harry Wills – 'The Brown Panther'

World 'Coloured' heavyweight champion, 1914, 1915–16, 1918–26.

'My only regret in life is that I never got a shot at Dempsey. I'm sure I could have beaten him.'
Harry Wills, after his retirement in 1932.

Height: 6'3
Peak weight: 204–212 lb.
76 wins (47 stoppages),
9 losses, 3 draws,
12 no contests
Born: New Orleans,
15 May 1889
Died: 21 December 1958

Here was a man who had 100 fights over 21 years. He lost just one out of 50 at his peak (and that on a dubious disqualification), beat most of the best men of his era and defended his title 32 times. Yet he is known for the fight he never had. Mention the name Harry Wills to all but the most dedicated of boxing pundits and they'll say, 'Ah, the big black guy Dempsey avoided.' Which may just be true, but is hardly the full story of this outstanding heavyweight's career.

Harry took to the sport while building his formidable strength as a stevedore on the docks of New Orleans and had his first recorded bout at the age of 21, winning on a first round knockout. Over the next four years he built up a 25 fight unbeaten record, including wins over two of the three best black contenders – Sam Langford and Joe Jeanette – and the white contender, Willie Meehan (who would go on to beat Jack Dempsey twice). The Langford win gave him the 'coloured' world title, but his first reign lasted just seven months. They fought a return in November 1914 and Wills dropped Langford four times in the first two rounds. But the smaller, older man gradually wore him down and knocked him out. 'I still don't know what punches Sam used to knock me out' said Wills. 'When the fourteenth began I was going easy. Sam was in a bad way. I backed him around the ring trying to set him up for a one-punch finish. His eye was bleeding and the last thing I remember was having him against the ropes just about five feet from his corner. It must have happened right then.' The *San Francisco Chronicle* reported, 'a left hook to the jaw turned the trick.'

Harry was back three weeks later against the third leading black contender, Sam McVea, and lost a 20 round decision. But he quickly regrouped, twice bettering Langford to regain his title, and once McVea. Things were going well for the 26-year-old, he was simply too powerful and talented for any other heavyweight in the world, or so he thought. He'd bought a house in Harlem and got engaged to a young woman called Edna Jones; their wedding date was set for 12 February 1916 – the day after his fourth fight with Langford. But it all fell to pieces. The fight was more intense than expected but by the later rounds Harry seemed to be getting on top. As he told it: 'In the 18th Sam was in a peck of trouble and when the bell sounded for the 19th I was after him again. I figured if I could get him in a corner I could finish the fight. That was all I could remember. He must have caught me as I rushed in. I don't know how long I was unconscious but it must have been quite a while.' The following day, shortly before noon, three hours before the wedding, Edna Jones committed suicide.

For Harry there was only one thing to do: return to work as quickly as possible. Four weeks later he fought Langford again, and outworked him over ten rounds. A month on

Harry Wills in training at Southampton, Long Island. For several years he was the best heavyweight in the world but was denied a shot at the title due to the colour of his skin.

he beat the top black light heavyweight John Lester Johnson (who, in his next fight, gave Jack Dempsey a sound beating). Wills repeated the trick against Langford and finally regained his 'coloured' heavyweight crown by knocking Sam out in six rounds in 1918. Aside from being big and exceptionally strong, he was a sound defensive boxer who was adept at range or up close. He was a master of holding and hitting and was rough and tough with reasonable speed, but most of all he was an exceptional puncher. There is little doubt he was the world's best heavyweight by the time he reached his peak in 1916.

It was Wills, not Dempsey, who deserved the 1919 world title fight in Toledo, but Tex Rickard wasn't interested. Despite regularly promoting black heavyweights (including Wills later in his career), with no qualms about black versus white fights, Rickard did everything in his power to prevent Dempsey fighting an opponent as dangerous as Wills. 'A black heavyweight champion would not be worth a bucket of warm piss,' he sneered. And again, 'If a nigger wins the championship then the championship isn't worth a nickel.' And it has to be said that Dempsey himself was no innocent in this plot – at least not in the early part of his reign. A few days after winning the title he was quoted in the *New York Times* as saying he would 'draw the colour line and pay no attention to Negro challengers.' Wills responded by venting his frustration, 'I'll take on Dempsey at any time in any street he wants to name,' he said. 'I'll knock him out for nothing.' Much of the mainstream press in the Midwestern and eastern states felt the same way. Several white reporters took a liking to Harry, seeing him as mildly eccentric in a polite way – very different from Johnson. He would, for example, avoid all solid food and drink only water for one month a year 'to burn off impurities'.

Some publications campaigned for the fight. Quoting Wills's desire to challenge Dempsey, *Time* magazine wrote, 'Besides being a substantial citizen between fights he is even more substantial in the ring. It is the generally accepted opinion that he is the only man in the game who can stand at Dempsey's level. Wills deserves his chance.'

In the wake of this pressure Dempsey insisted he was willing if a promoter could be found to put up enough money. Rickard responded with his usual guile – making a deal with Wills to fight under his banner, with the promise of a fight with Dempsey in 1924 – a promise he had no intention of fulfilling. Instead he promoted a fight between the 35-year-old Harry and the 29-year-old Luis Angel Firpo, who'd won three knockouts since losing to Dempsey. It was a 12 rounder with Wills dominating every round and earning his highest-ever purse of $150,000. The *Beloit Daily News* reported, 'No decision is permitted by the boxing law in New Jersey, but a decision never was so unnecessary. Not even the partisan followers of the South American champion felt that Firpo could win after he had been dropped with a long right to the jaw in the second round.' Yet Wills was clearly slower and more lethargic than a few years earlier. After 14 years as a professional and 93 fights he was on the slide.

Meanwhile, the pressure on Dempsey to accommodate his top contender had become intense while his relationship with his manager and, for a while, his promoter, was deteriorating. He therefore tried an alternative route for the promise of a million dollars, by agreeing to take on the ageing Wills in a ten round, no-decision contest in Michigan City, Indiana in 1926, under the banner of the well-connected Midwest promoter, Floyd Fitzsimmons – who promised Dempsey $100,000 and Wills $50,000 if it never took place. Rickard worked hard to ensure precisely this outcome. Immediately after the contract was signed he told *Time*, 'I think Dempsey must be crazy,' adding ominously, 'a lot of things can happen between now and the fall of 1926.' Kearns also threatened to block the fight, and with strings being pulled all over the place, it fell through. Meanwhile, Rickard tried to justify his stance by claiming his friend the New York governor opposed the fight, while at the same time placing new obstacles in Wills' path. One of these was a $150,000 offer to fight Gene Tunney in a final eliminator, but Wills's protective manager Paddy Mullins declined, pointing out that Harry had already eliminated all the leading contenders. This gave Rickard the excuse he needed to promote a Dempsey Tunney fight in New York. At this point the New York Commission, the most powerful control body in world boxing, cracked down, insisting that Dempsey fight Wills and no-one else. The only effect of all this was for Rickard to move the Dempsey-Tunney fight to Philadelphia.

After this final disappointment, the 37-year-old Harry, who had been out of action for a full year, went into a fight with the extremely lively young Jack Sharkey. Wills, at 214½ lb. was too slow for the 188 lb. 24-year-old and was handily outboxed, resorting to frequent clinching, headbutting and other fouls. After suffering a bleeding mouth and a swollen eye he was disqualified for throwing a backhand blow. Wills was knocked out in four rounds in his next fight, against the Spanish contender Paulino Uzcudun, and retired soon after, but made a brief comeback at the age of 43, winning his 100th listed professional bout on a third round knockout. He lived his last 26 years away from boxing, moving into a successful real estate business in Harlem. He was admitted to hospital on 8 December 1958 for a series of exploratory tests and died of diabetes 13 days later, with his daughter, Gladys, at his bedside.

The 35-year-old Wills in his last big win – over the 'Wild Bull of Pampas' Luis Angel Firpo in Jersey City, on 11 September 1924. The bout was officially a 'no decision', but Wills scored two knockdowns, outclassing the 220 lb. Argentinian. After the fight Firpo faced deportation on charges of bringing a female manicurist from Argentina 'for immoral purposes' and committing perjury on his immigration papers.

Jack Dempsey – 'The Manassa Mauler'

World heavyweight champion 1919–26.

'He had great truculence, pugnacity and aggressiveness, a valuable and unlimited fund of natural cruelty, tremendous courage, speed and determination and good, though not extraordinary, hitting powers. His protection was aggression. Dempsey's entire reputation was based on two fights, the one when he knocked out gigantic Jess Willard and the thrilling, atavistic brawl with Luis Angel Firpo. But they were sufficient, for they marked Dempsey as a giant killer, a slayer of ogres.'

Paul Gallico, who once sparred with Dempsey, getting fouled and flattened in 20 seconds.

Height: 6'1
Peak weight: 185–92 lb.
61 wins (50 stoppages),
6 losses, 8 draws,
6 no-decision
Born: Manassa, Colorado,
24 June 1895
Died: 31 May 1983

William Harrison Dempsey was a force of nature who burst through by brutalising Jess Willard and reigned supreme for seven years during the jazz era. With his menacing scowl, intense black eyes and unshaven chin, he would stalk opponents with frightening intensity, fighting out of a crouch, always ready to pounce, and the public couldn't get enough of it – loathing him at first, then, at the end of his career, adoring him. Along the way he became America's first international sporting hero, drawing the first-ever million dollar gate, the first two million dollar gate and his biggest fights, attracting crowds of up to 120,000, were screened in many countries, so that his legend spread.

Starting life in a log cabin as one of 13 children of Mormon converts Hyrum and Celia Smoot Dempsey, he grew up as hard as it came for white boys in the American West. His father had been a teacher, landowner and local politician, but by the time William was growing up they had fallen on hard times. He took his first job as a dishwasher at the age of 11 and from there, whatever work he could find – shoe shining, crop picking, mining, cattle herding – while riding the rods of the freight trains, moving from town to town. In a world of desperate and violent men, this skinny teenager with an unusually high voice – as he put it, 'I sounded like a girl' – learned to fight with savage intensity, determined never to be a victim and becoming a bully in the process. Explaining his route into boxing he said 'You'd go to a saloon, fight anybody in the house for "pass the hat". Sometimes you got licked, sometimes you'd run like hell, sometimes you'd get a little money.'

The lad was full of fire but there were hard lessons along the way. He was occasionally bettered by more experienced battlers but usually learnt from his errors. He was dropped and beaten by Jack Downey, but a year later knocked Downey out. He was dropped nine times in one round by a journeyman called Johnny Sudenberg in one of two fights officially called 'draws' but a year later flattened Sudenberg in two. The one conqueror he never fought twice was the black light heavyweight John Lester Johnson who broke three of his ribs in 1916. Johnson was, in fact, the last black man Dempsey would ever face. Soon after he refused to tangle with Sam Langford, admitting, 'I wouldn't fight him. I knew he would flatten me.' He kept clear of the top black heavyweight, Harry Wills, and his manager admitted doing the same with the top black light heavyweight, Kid Norfolk.

Dempsey worked as a sparring partner, bouncer, bowling alley skivvy and pimp and was even accused of being 'a professional rapist of virgins' (who would then be sent to

The twelfth round as Gibbons stands up to Jack Dempsey on 8 July 1923. Dempsey won on points over 15 rounds in a fight that virtually bankrupted the town of Shelby, Montana, because the town's men were taken in by the promise that the fight would make a mint. They built a new stadium and agreed to all the financial demands of the Dempsey camp. In the end only 7,702 people paid to watch the fight, forcing four Shelby banks to close down.

KINGS OF THE RING

brothels). He married a prostitute, Maxine Cates, who accused him of beating her regularly and of living off her earnings. But his luck changed in the autumn of 1917 when he met the publicity-hungry and extremely wily former pilot, wrestler, gambler and boxing manager, Jack 'Doc' Kearns. They later linked up with the clever and powerful Tex Rickard, who liked what he saw of the 22-year-old and shared some of his ways.

The fighter was still far from invincible – late in 1918 he lost for the second time to Willie Meehan – but mostly he was winning in spectacular style. His bobbing, weaving style, constant aggression and willingness to trade punches made him a popular attraction, allowing Kearns and Rickard to steer him towards a title shot against Jess Willard in the hot sun of Toledo, Ohio on 4 July 1919. Dempsey's blend of speed, ferocity and power in that first round, when he tore into Willard and dropped him seven times, still looks mightily impressive, but by the end of the third Jack could hardly hold his hands up and was taking a few in return from the disabled champion. He was fortunate Jess was so damaged from his multiple injuries that he couldn't make it out for the fourth.

Anyway, Jack 'the Giant Killer' was heavyweight champion of the world – a wild and compelling character who could make millions for himself and his backers. Together they ensured that his title would never be placed under severe threat. For starters, Rickard and Dempsey each made what they claimed was a principled decision about keeping the title as the preserve of the white man. Jack regularly used black sparring partners and years later expressed a willingness to fight Harry Wills (although Rickard had no intention of permitting it), but in the end, for the last 11 years of his career, he never fought a black man. If Dempsey's 'no Negro challengers' quote was a one-off aberration we might be able to explain it away, but it wasn't. When Harry Greb lost his world middleweight title to Tiger Flowers in 1926, Dempsey commented, 'I don't see why Greb gave that nigger a chance.' And when the Nazi-backed Max Schmeling stopped Joe Louis in 1936, Jack declared this triumph of white over black 'the finest thing to happen to boxing in a long time'. There is little doubt that the young Dempsey's attitudes to race were antediluvian, but the tougher question is whether this racism affected his choice of opponent, and the answer is hard to determine because he also avoided the best white fighter of his era, the same Harry Greb, who avoided no one.

This extraordinarily fast, slippery, unorthodox, dirty and hard-headed man was a perpetual motion fighting machine who seldom weighed more than 165 lb. but had no trouble beating some of the best heavyweights in the world. In their first three round public sparring session on 1 September 1920 Greb 'went into him like a hurricane, piling up points with his rapid, erratic style, and eluding the champion's retaliatory efforts with ease', according to a newspaper report. They sparred again the next day when Greb nailed Dempsey with 'a crushing right'. For their third session Jack's people asked Harry to ease off because the champion's defence against Billy Miske was a week away. When they sparred again in 1924 Greb was reported to have cut and dominated Dempsey, with a local paper running with the headline 'GREB MAKES DEMPSEY LOOK LIKE A KITTEN' – enough to convince Kearns to turn down an offer for Jack to fight Harry.

Instead they provided Jack with a soft but compelling passage. His first challenger, Miske, had given him hell in an earlier fight but was now suffering from a terminal illness. It was essentially a favour for a friend, who was despatched in three rounds. Next came former

Jack Dempsey drives Jess Willard to the ropes corner during the heavyweight boxing championship at Toledo, Ohio, on 4 July 1919. Willard's cheekbone was broken in 12 places, his jaw in 13 and he suffered eight avulsed teeth and two cracked ribs. He claimed Dempsey fought with 'loaded' gloves – a charge Jack denied.

Dempsey and Greb victim Bill Brennan who managed to outbox and rock Jack, tearing his ear before getting stopped by body blows in round 12. By his third defence Dempsey had become a public villain because of allegations of draft dodging. He claimed he'd supported his wife's family during the war, but she claimed that, in fact, she was supporting him through prostitution. Jack used a publicity photograph showing him labouring in a shipyard for the war effort. On closer inspection, however, it emerged that underneath his overalls a neatly pressed pair of trousers and a shiny pair of patent leather shoes were poking through. Although eventually acquitted of draft evasion, the trial exposed him to ridicule and to the epithet 'slacker', but Rickard wasn't worried. He used Jack's disgrace to promote his next fight against Georges Carpentier, the declining light heavyweight champion who happened to be a bona fide war hero. Drawing a record gate of $1.63 million, it pitted the debonair 172 lb. Frenchman against the 188 lb., scowling, swarthy American. The result was inevitable. Georges rattled Jack twice and wobbled him once with a right cross that landed a bit high, before being overwhelmed in four rounds.

Two years later he outpointed the light heavyweight Tommy Gibbons and then he took on a raw Argentinean novice Luis Firpo, whom Rickard had brought to America for the sole purpose of serving as a fall-guy. For most of the first round of their fight he played his designated role to perfection. Dempsey took a knee from a big right, after which he tore into the slow, clumsy visitor, dropping him seven times. But Firpo clambered up each time and kept swinging. One of his haymakers caught the lighter man (by 24 lb.) flush and

Dempsey (*centre*) taking a break from training at Frank Welch's farm at Summit, New Jersey, to play cards. It was not unknown for Dempsey to assault his sparring partners and his wife, Estelle was said to have 'lived in constant terror of him'.

Preceding pages: The Jack Dempsey vs Carpentier fight watched by over 80,000 spectators in boxing's first million dollar gate. Dempsey's promoter, Tex Richard, built up the Frenchman, Carpentier, as a war hero to counteract Dempsey's image as a draft dodger.

knocked him flying through the ropes and into the crowd. Had the pressmen not pushed him back into the ring he would have been counted out. In fact he may have been out of the ring for over ten seconds – Rickard was said to have ensured this bit of the fight film was cut and spliced, to prevent proof of the long count emerging. Anyway, Dempsey stood on wobbly legs and survived until the bell. A minute's rest was enough and in round two he dropped Firpo twice in quick succession before landing a left hook to the jaw, following through with a right as Firpo was falling, and this time he failed to beat the count.

After that he put his title on ice for three years, taking part in 44 exhibition bouts, acting in the odd movie, marrying the film star Estelle Taylor, making celebrity appearances, bed-hopping, breaking up with manager Jack Kearns, fighting legal battles, getting a nose job and gradually transforming his reputation from bad guy to diamond in the rough.

If it could be argued he'd never before taken on the best in the world, he certainly made amends in the final year of his career. His last defence was against the handsome, defensively minded, Shakespeare-quoting former marine Gene Tunney, who also happened to be one of the toughest, most calculating and determined men to lace on a pair of mitts. Jack, in contrast, was distracted by Kearns's legal suits and was over-confident, having taken the fight over the smaller Tunney as a way of avoiding the bigger and supposedly more dangerous Harry Wills. Facing the 'Fighting Marine' in the pouring Philadelphia rain, in front of 120,557 astonished fans, he took a one-sided ten round shellacking, losing nine out of ten rounds. When it was over, his face a mess, Estelle was said to have asked, 'What happened, Ginsburg?' (her pet name for him), to which he supposedly replied 'Honey, I forgot to duck.'

After a spell of prevarication Dempsey became desperate to earn his return. The best around was the erratic Jack Sharkey and the early beating Dempsey received was as one-sided as against Tunney. The frustrated, hurt and desperate Dempsey resorted to type – going for the groin and landing rabbit punches behind the neck. But unlike the resolute Tunney, Sharkey did not cope with changes to the script. And so, after two more low blows in round seven, he dropped his guard to protest. Dempsey promptly teed off with a massive hook, and instead of disqualifying one, the referee counted-out the other Jack.

This took Dempsey to the most famous of all his 80 fights, his return against Tunney, known as 'The Battle of the Long Count', before 105,000 fans in Chicago on 27 September 1927. It was Dempsey's third fight in a year and this time he had a clear idea of the scale of the task ahead of him. And yet for the first six rounds it followed the original script, with Gene jabbing, moving to his right, stepping in with quick rights, and slipping out of range, and Jack hitting the night air and landing the occasional low blow. But in the seventh Dempsey finally connected with his payoff left hook, and followed up with seven of the hardest punches he ever threw, continuing to batter Tunney as he fell. Before the fight Jack's team had insisted on a new rule, requiring a boxer scoring a knockdown to retire to a neutral corner, but in the heat of the moment Dempsey forgot. He hovered over Gene until referee Dave Barry ordered him to retreat, losing five seconds. By the count of eight, 13 seconds had passed and Tunney was alert, sitting on his haunches, ready to rise, after which he put his well-practised back-peddling routine into operation. This delay was one of the most controversial in boxing history, and Dempsey dined out on it for years to come. It was, in fact, the final step transforming him from villain to hero. In round eight it was Dempsey's turn to get dropped, although this time referee Barry forgot the neutral corner rule. Jack rose in good time but he had little left and by the end of the tenth, his face was a mess and, once again, he was wobbling precariously.

Dempsey retired four months later, in January 1928, at the age of 32, claiming he was having trouble with a left eye muscle, but like so many ex-champions he found life outside the ring unsatisfying at first, particularly after losing $3 million in the stock exchange collapse of 1929. He tried boxing management and promotion, did the odd acting gig and whatever else he could find. He also married again, this time to the showgirl Hannah Williams, with whom he had two daughters. Finally, in 1931, over three years after his retirement, he decided on the idea of challenging Max Schmeling for the world title and worked his way into shape with a stream of exhibition bouts. He went through 104 of these in eight months and felt he was nearing the stage when he could fight for real again. But in exhibition number 87, watched by 23,322 fans, he chose a better class of journeyman, King Levinsky, and found himself on the wrong end of a four round hiding. His confidence shattered, he completed a final month of his exhibition tour and gave up the plan. Eight years later, in 1940, he fought four more exhibition bouts before retiring forever.

Instead he was absorbed by the war effort, serving on USS *Arthur Middleton* and taking part in active combat. After this he worked his way more deeply into the hearts of sporting America. In 1935 he had opened 'Jack Dempsey's', a restaurant in Broadway, with the bidding card 'COME IN FELLOWS, here's where you'll MEET – THE FIGHTERS, THE MANAGERS, THE WRITERS'. This became his base and pilgrims would come from all over the world. Age, adulation, contentment and testosterone reduction mellowed the 'Manassa Mauler', who died of a heart attack in his New York apartment three weeks before his 88th birthday.

Gene Tunney – 'The Fighting Marine'

World heavyweight champion 1926–28.

'Don't let anybody tell you Tunney wasn't a great fighter. I should know. Let me say that Tunney may have defeated me at any time in our careers. I had one consolation: I lost to a great fighter – one of the greatest.'

Jack Dempsey

Height: 6'0½
Peak weight: 180–192 lb.
62 wins (47 stoppages),
1 loss, 1 draw, 1 no contest,
19 no decisions
Born: New York
25 May 1897
Died: 7 November 1978

James Joseph Tunney may well have been the best heavyweight of the 1920s and certainly stands out as one of the sport's all-time greats. He was one of the world's top light heavyweights for several years; then stepped up to box rings around Dempsey. Along the way he suffered only one official loss (subsequently avenged) in 84 bouts. He retired as champion, was a decorated Marine officer and enjoyed a highly successful business career. But he is still known principally for one thing: a 14 second count for which he was blameless.

Tunney was derided for being a know-all who made friends with George Bernard Shaw and regularly quoted Shakespeare, which hardly endeared him to American sports writers like Paul Gallico who felt such affectations were best left to men like themselves, and that the business of fighting was for hard, rough men like Dempsey. Tunney's cerebral approach to boxing and his prissy behaviour beyond the ropes – banning swear words in the gym, for example – were a turn-off to those who desired simple brutality.

Gene, as he was called, was a working-class lad from Greenwich Village who grew up in conditions not unlike those faced by other boxers. The second of seven children of Irish immigrants, his stevedore father presented him with a pair of boxing gloves at the age of 10, after which he fought with great enthusiasm in the ring and the streets. At 16 he took a job as a butcher's boy while continuing his studies, and later as a shipping clerk, but his spare moments were devoted to perfecting his boxing skills in the amateur ring. What marked him as special, aside from his good looks, was his blend of high intelligence and single-minded determination. Nothing would distract him from his ambitions, and once those settled on the world heavyweight title he built methodically until achieving his goal.

Weighing 152 lb. he had his first fight for pay shortly after his 18th birthday, stopping an experienced veteran in the seventh round for $18, and after three years of boxing he had 15 fights without defeat. He volunteered for the US Marines and won the armed forces light heavyweight title. When he returned home he began to obsess about one day beating the new world heavyweight champion, Jack Dempsey, and, soon after, met him for the first time. 'It wasn't his words that interested me so much, it was his hands,' he recalled. 'They looked big to me – terrible weapons. He had been pickling his hands for a time and in places the skin had cracked into a hard scaly substance'. A debilitating injury to a knuckle of Gene's right hand and a broken thumb prompted him to take six months off to work as a lumberjack and as a manual labourer while concentrating on a variety of hand and wrist exercises. 'It was something that could not be shirked,' he said. 'I had been given a glimpse of Dempsey's powerful mitts and I knew I was going

Gene Tunney after ten rounds of sparring at Speculator, New York, July 1928. Tunney's trainer Lou Fink is seen wrapping the heavyweight in a few extra towels to prevent the possibility of Tunney catching a cold. He was training for his final fight with New Zealand's Tom Heeney, who was stopped in 11 rounds.

KINGS OF THE RING

The tenth round of the Tunney vs Dempsey heavyweight title fight on 22 September 1927. Tunney had Dempsey wobbling – on the verge of being stopped.

to need good tools for that party.' In January 1922 he felt ready to make his move, taking on the former world light heavyweight champion, Battling Levinsky, who was having his 248th recorded professional fight. Their fight, for the US title, went the full 12 rounds, and Tunney won all of them, outboxing and outpunching the heavier veteran.

The man who turned Tunney from a good boxer into a great one was Harry Greb, who has a strong claim to being the finest fighter the world has known. A natural middleweight, who held that world title for three years when past his best, he beat five world light heavyweight champions and had 40 fights against heavyweights, beating the lot. When he met Tunney he was blind in one eye and past his peak and was more than 12 lb. lighter and four inches shorter. It made no difference, he dished out a terrible beating. Tunney could not cope with Greb's phenomenal speed, unorthodox skills and non-stop, swarming attack. As Tunney recalled, 'I had never bled so much before, nor have I since. For most of the fight, I saw Greb as a red-filmed phantom bouncing before me. When the 12th round ended, I believed it was a good time to take a swallow of orange juice and brandy. I had no sooner done so when the ring started swirling around. I had never taken anything during the fight up to that time. Nor did I ever again. When the thirteenth round started, I saw two bobbing red opponents rushing in at me. I don't know to this day how I ever survived…'

'Fighters who lose fights have cut eyes, broken noses, torn lips and broken bones,' Damon Runyon wrote. 'Tonight Gene Tunney simply had a broken face. He had no business being around for the full fifteen rounds, but he was and you have to take your hat off to this boy. He has the kind of courage of which great champions are made.' He fought again a month later – one of nine wins in nine months before the return fight. Greb had declined and Tunney had improved, so the return at New York's Madison Square Garden was a closer affair. William Muldoon, the New York boxing commissioner, commented, 'The decision in Tunney's favour was unjustifiable' and even Gene admitted: 'No one was as surprised as I was when Joe Humphreys lifted my hand in token of victory. Greb relentlessly battered me about the ring from the sixth to the eleventh round. They told me in my corner I was losing, that if I wanted to win I would have to capture the remaining rounds or knock him out. In sheer desperation I came out at the start of the twelfth and luckily hit Greb with a long right on the cheekbone that had everything I had in it. It knocked him to the ropes. He slowed up considerably. Fight, fight; hit, hit. I kept on repeating to myself – and did. Realizing there was some justice in his claim of a bad decision, I offered him a return engagement.' So they fought for a third time ten months later and this time Tunney won clearly.

Greb shaded their fourth fight and their fifth and final bout took place in March 1925 – the 270th bout of Harry's 12-year career. Greb had two broken ribs by the end of the third round and in Tunney's bowdlerised version, Greb's post-fight comments went like this: 'You've become a helluva good fighter, Gene. Tonight you hurt me more than I was ever hurt before and I'm lucky I was still around at the end of ten rounds. You'd stop me for sure the next time. I'm satisfied to call it quits as far as fighting you is concerned.'

After wins over George Carpentier and Tommy Gibbons the chance came to fight Jack Dempsey. Gene had no doubts: 'I've seen Dempsey fight and I was impressed by his lack of knowledge of boxing,' he said. 'He is a great natural fighter but I'm certain that I can outbox him. He's got to hit you to beat you and he won't hit me… I know I'm a faster and straighter hitter than Dempsey. Jack never was much of a stayer. By that I mean he fights so fast in the early part of the bout that he tires quickly.'

Greb commented: 'I fought them both – Dempsey only in the gymnasium but for the kill – and Gene's too smart for him. He'll counter-punch him silly. He's tough as hell, too, and the best body puncher I ever fought.' To the astonishment of the rest of the boxing fraternity, he was right. Tunney went to work with his jab, cross and body attack and made no complaint when Jack went low or rabbit punched and seemed not to notice the pouring Philadelphia rain or the noise of over 120,000 spectators or anything else but the job at hand. Had the fight gone any longer than the 10 rounds Dempsey insisted on, he would surely have been stopped. So Gene's best-laid plan had worked just as expected – in his 82nd fight. The public thirst for a return suited Tunney, who was paid boxing's first million dollar purse for the return, held before 105,000 excited fans at Soldiers Field, Chicago, on 22 September 1927.

This time Tunney had been out for a year while Dempsey had tuned up against Jack Sharkey, arriving in mint condition. But, once again, the New Yorker had no trouble outboxing him – circling to his right, landing stiff jabs and stepping in with hard crosses or draining body blows, while parrying or avoiding most of Dempsey's swings. But suddenly Tunney found himself on his back in round seven. He later speculated that the reason he missed the first of Dempsey's seven hooks was an impediment to his lateral vision – the result of an eye injury sustained in sparring nearly two years earlier. In any event he

THE GREATEST GATHERING THAT EVER ASSEMBLED TO SEE A BOXING MATCH: THE VAST CROWD OF ABOUT 150,000 PEOPLE WAITING IN THE STADIUM AT PHILADELPHIA TO WITNESS THE FIGHT BETWEEN JACK DEMPSEY (THE HOLDER) AND "GENE" TUNNEY FOR THE HEAVYWEIGHT CHAMPIONSHIP OF THE WORLD—SHOWING THE ILLUMINATED RING IN THE CENTRE.

THE FOURTH ROUND, WHICH PROVED THE TURNING-POINT: DEMPSEY (RIGHT) TRYING IN VAIN TO PENETRATE TUNNEY'S DEFENCE.

THE FALLEN CHAMPION EMBRACES HIS CONQUEROR: DEMPSEY (WITH BACK TO CAMERA) PUTS HIS ARMS ROUND TUNNEY'S NECK AFTER THE FIGHT.

The victory of "Gene" Tunney over Jack Dempsey in the fight for the Heavyweight Championship of the World, on September 23, was one of the most sensational events in the history of boxing. It was a terrific contest which went to the full ten rounds, and was decided on points, Tunney winning eight rounds and the other two being drawn. Dempsey, who was not up to form, was outboxed and suffered heavy punishment. After the decision he put his arms round his opponent's neck and congratulated him. Later, Dempsey asked that a return match should be arranged. The match attracted the largest crowd ever seen at a championship meeting—about 150,000 people, including 20,000 women. Rain fell as the fight began and everybody was drenched. The receipts were estimated at £400,000, of which it was said that Dempsey got £200,000 and Tunney about £70,000. The new champion, whose name is really James Joseph Tunney, is twenty-eight, and of Irish descent, though born near New York. He was formerly a railway clerk, but in 1917 he enlisted in the U.S. Marines and served in France. Among other famous boxers whom he has defeated in the course of his career is Georges Carpentier.

fell, used the ropes to pull himself into a crouching position, watched the referee's count and leapt up. Dempsey ignored the referee Dave Barry's instruction to retire to a neutral corner, with the result being that Tunney was down for 14 seconds. 'Realizing that the first nine seconds of a knockdown belong to the man on the floor, I never had any thought of getting up before the referee said "nine",' Tunney explained. 'Only badly dazed boxers who have momentarily lost consciousness, and show-offs, fail to take that nine seconds that are theirs. No boxer that I have ever known has carried a stopwatch on his wrist going

into the ring. Boxers always go by the referee's timing; whether 25 seconds or nine seconds had elapsed when the referee said "nine" would have made no difference to me. My signal to get off the floor was the count "nine".' This was the only knockdown in Gene's career and he certainly seemed alert for several seconds before he rose. Dempsey claimed he was robbed after the fight but when the bitterness left him he reconsidered. 'I look back on the fight, he wasn't hurt too bad,' he admitted years later. 'Tunney would have got up.' Dempsey chased, but couldn't catch, until, in desperation, he beckoned Gene to fight. Shortly before the end of the round Tunney landed a hard right under Dempsey's heart. The former champion admitted this blow took everything out of him and he took a bad beating over the final three rounds. Tunney dropped him with a right in the eighth round (the 17th knockdown of Dempsey's career, incidentally) and, once again, had him wobbling in the final round. But the long count controversy forever stamped Tunney as a man who only survived through the favour of a biased referee while it confirmed Dempsey's heroic status.

On 31 July 1928, five days after the eleventh round annihilation of the New Zealander Tom Heeney, Tunney announced his engagement to the steel heiress Polly Lauder while saying goodbye to boxing. 'I have fought my way to the goal of my ambition,' he said. 'I became a professional fighter because I realized it afforded me the quickest way to earn a fortune and now that I have it I shall retire.' He and Polly had three boys and one girl – with one of his sons, John, going on to become a US Congressman and then Senator for California. Gene made another fortune in business and served as a Commander in the US Navy during the war. In 1970 he heard that his 31-year-old daughter, Joan, had murdered her husband while in England – attacking him with a chopper while he was asleep. She was ordered to be detained at Her Majesty's pleasure at Broadmoor top security hospital. Gene took to drinking heavily, descending into severe alcoholism. He died in his sleep while in Greenwich Hospital as a result of blood poisoning at the age of 81. When Dempsey learned of his old rival's death he said: 'We were as inseparable as Siamese twins. As long as Gene was alive I felt we shared a link with that wonderful period of the past.'

Tunney faces Greb in the fourth of their five fights. This one in Cleveland, Ohio, on 17 September 1924, was a no decision bout in which Greb won the newspapers' verdict. Despite being blinded in one eye in a fight with Kid Norfolk in 1921 Greb held his own with the bigger Tunney. He also dominated Dempsey in competitive public sparring sessions. Tunney was one of the pall-bearers at his funeral in 1926.

Opposite: The 'Long Count' controversy, the return fight between Gene Tunney and Jack Dempsey.

Jack Sharkey – 'The Boston Gob'

World heavyweight champion 1932–33.

'Sharkey's the best fighter in the world – from the neck down.'
William Muldoon, New York boxing commissioner.

Height: 6'0
Peak weight: 188–198 lb.
37 wins (14 stoppages),
14 losses, 3 draws,
1 no decision
Born: Binghamton, New York,
26 October 1902
Died: 17 August 1994

What Muldoon meant was that when it came to physical ability, Sharkey was hard to top. He could be a brilliant boxer-puncher – quick, clever, elusive and extremely accurate with both hands. Promoter Tex Rickard said of him: 'I've seen 'em all, big and little, but Jack Sharkey stands out because he's the fastest heavyweight in the ring, with a left like a piston and a right straight and hard as a ramrod.' Look at the men he bettered and you sense the quality but look at the 17 blemishes on his record and you wonder. The truth is that no heavyweight champion could match Sharkey when it came to inconsistency. One night he could be the best in the world and the next he'd box like a journeyman. His problem was from the neck up. On an off night, or an off moment within a fight, he could fold when fouled, or fight as dirty as they come, or burst into tears, or whine to the referee.

No fight typified Sharkey's odd blend of strength and weakness better than his battle with Jack Dempsey at New York's Yankee Stadium on 21 July 1927. For six rounds the 196 lb. 24-year-old not only handed Jack a comprehensive boxing lesson, he also hurt him – staggered him a few times, cut him up and even outfought him up-close. The 194½ lb. Dempsey managed to land some good body blows, a few distinctly low, but he was taking a beating. As Nat Fleischer put it: 'Dempsey could not possibly last through to the limit. His legs were showing signs of weakening and he was slowing up considerably.' Then in round seven he hit Sharkey once on the leg and once in the groin. He'd done the same to Tunney who just ignored it, but Sharkey complained to referee Jack O'Sullivan and when that was ignored he raised his eyes and dropped his guard in exasperated protest. Dempsey needed no second invitation. 'I turned to the referee to complain I was getting hit low, and I got hit with a haymaker,' said Sharkey. 'That was that. I was out on the canvas.'

Josef Paul Zukauskas grew up in Binghamton, New York, the son of Lithuanian immigrants. His father, a mechanic, lost his job, so Josef left school in the eighth grade to work in a shoe factory before becoming a construction worker, glassblower and railroad brakeman. Already useful with his fists by the time he joined the navy in Boston, he heard of a boxing show needing warm bodies. He lied to the promoter, claiming a 39-fight record, and was offered $100 for four rounds. 'For $100, I would have fought the entire navy,' he said. When he told the man his name he received the reply, 'You can do better than that', so he borrowed his surname from the turn-of-the-century heavyweight Sailor Tom Sharkey and his first name from world champion Jack Dempsey. As Jack Sharkey, the 21-year-old won his first professional fight in Boston on a first round knockout on 29 January 1924.

He proved to be a natural. Every so often he would lose a fight but invariably he would win the return and by late 1925 he had lifted the American Legion heavyweight title

Jack Sharkey, the Boston heavyweight, hard at work getting into shape for his forthcoming bout with Harry Wills, whom he beat on a thirteenth round disqualification in 1926.

Primo Carnera slowly rises at the count of six as the referee holds off Jack Sharkey during their heavyweight bout at Ebbets Field, New York, on 12 October 1931. Sharkey went on to defeat Carnera on points over 15 rounds but 20 months later he lost on a controversial sixth round knockout to the Italian giant.

and was earning a reputation as an outstanding prospect. A ten round points win over the huge hitting, 220 lb. black contender George Godfrey, followed by an even more impressive 13th round disqualification win over the rapidly declining 37-year-old Harry Wills, set him up for his 34th professional fight against Dempsey. Sharkey was on a 13-fight winning streak, but the Dempsey loss seemed to weaken his desire, drawing one fight and losing another before returning to his winning ways. But these setbacks gave Gene Tunney an excuse to avoid him. A few months earlier Tunney said of Sharkey, 'He is as good a fighter as I've ever seen. He has everything.' But when it came to choosing his final opponent he focussed on other considerations: 'With Sharkey anything can happen. He can go berserk, hit me low and get away with it.' And so instead he beat up Tom Heeney and then announced his retirement. *The Ring* magazine said it was 'sorry to see him go without having fought Jack Sharkey. That match would have brought out the best in Tunney's boxing skill and it possibly would have developed into a grand fight as well as a test of skill and craft.'

Sharkey pressed on, knocking out two former world light heavyweight champions, Jack Delaney and Tommy Loughran, while outpointing heavyweight contender Young Stribling and then in a final eliminator, took three rounds to knock out the British and European champion Phil Scott, who kept collapsing whether hit fair or foul. Sharkey looked like he was on his way to beating Max Schmeling when he finally got his world title shot on 12 June 1930, but he was not given the same leeway as Dempsey and was disqualified for a low blow in the fourth.

He came back to face former world welterweight and middleweight champion Mickey Walker, who had previously lost to Loughran and Harry Greb. But the 5'7, 167 lb. Toy Bulldog gave the 6'0, 198 lb. Boston Gob hell, boring in, holding ring centre, catching him with quick hooks. Sharkey used his jab and cross effectively, landing the cleaner, harder blows, but it was Walker who delighted the crowd and they booed when a draw was announced after 15 rounds. This embarrassment was offset in his next fight when he handily outboxed the 6'5¾, 261 lb. Primo Carnera, setting him up for a return with Schmeling. But in the two years since their previous fight he had declined, and wasn't helped by coming in overweight, at 205 lb. Jack entered the ring wearing an American flag over his blue robe and felt that as local boy and a navy veteran he deserved the backing of the crowd. But it was the German who was cheered. Instead of being inspired to prove his point, Jack gave a depressed performance, refusing to take chances against the more purposeful and harder hitting champion. For once, however, the luck was with the Bostonian, who emerged via an undeserved split decision as the new heavyweight champion of the world.

A year on, Sharkey made the first defence of his title against Carnera, whose previous opponent, Ernie Schaaf, had died after being knocked out in the 13th round. Sharkey was in Schaaf's corner and was shaken by this tragedy. The Sharkey–Carnera return, at Madison Square Garden on 29 June 1933, went predictably enough for five rounds, with the 201 lb. American easily outboxing the 260½ lb. Italian. Then, late in round six, it turned, with the giant going on the offensive. As the *New York Times* reported, 'Carnera rocked Sharkey with a left and right to the head. At close range Carnera whipped two long rights to the body. After Sharkey missed a right to the jaw Carnera crossed a hard right to the jaw. Sharkey landed a right to the jaw, but Carnera came back with a right uppercut to the chin and floored Sharkey for the full count.'

Carnera had taken part in several fixed fights, and many assumed the worst – a jibe Sharkey faced for the rest of his life. As he explained: 'I had no trouble with him in the second bout, but all of a sudden – and I can't convince anybody of this, even my own wife has her doubts, I think – I see Schaaf in front of me. The next thing I know, I'd lost the championship of the world.' The film of the fight shows Sharkey, who did not have the hardest chin, getting his head rocked back by Carnera's uppercut before falling. His emotional fragility, renowned inconsistency and the clear signs of decline might all have played a role in a result that, on balance, seems genuine. In any event it finished him as a serious force in boxing. He won just two of his last seven fights, finally bowing out when knocked out in three rounds by Joe Louis. Asked who hit him the hardest, Dempsey or Louis, he replied, 'Dempsey, because he hit me $211,000 worth, while Louis only hit me $36,000 worth.'

Sharkey had a largely happy retirement. He used his money to open a huge bar and restaurant in Boston which he sold seven years later, and then moved with his wife, Dorothy, and their three children to Epping, the New Hampshire village of Dorothy's childhood. He spent most of his spare moments on fly fishing, giving exhibitions all over America, and also refereed wrestling and boxing matches and entertained troops in North Africa during World War II. They had 14 grandchildren, 21 great-grandchildren and one great-great grandchild. Dorothy died in 1974 and over the next twenty years Jack placed a red rose on her grave, or in bad weather on her portrait. He died of respiratory arrest in a Massachusetts hospital at the age of 91.

Max Schmeling – 'The Black Uhlan'

World heavyweight champion 1930–32.

'If we'd been found in Max's hotel apartment that night I would not be here tonight and neither would Max.'

Henri Lewin, Jewish hotel owner, telling how Schmeling smuggled him out of Nazi Germany in 1938.

Height: 6'1
Peak weight: 187–193 lb.
56 wins (40 stoppages),
10 losses, 4 draws
Born: Brandenburg, Germany,
28 September 1905
Died: 2 February 2005

Maximilian Adolph Otto Siegfried Schmeling is remembered as a boxer not for his inconsequential title reign but for three other events: winning the crown while groaning on the canvas, pulling off one of the upsets of the century by knocking out Joe Louis and then getting brutalised by Louis in their two minute return. As a symbol he is known principally for his role as a Nazi poster boy in the two years between those two Louis fights. But as a man there is more to commend him: from refusing to sack his Jewish manager to smuggling Jews out of Nazi Germany, to providing financial support to his old rival Louis when he fell on hard times. He lived longer than any other heavyweight champion, dying in his 100th year, still as sharp as they come.

To start with his finest moment in the ring: that victory over Louis at Yankee Stadium on 19 June 1936. The Brown Bomber, a ten-to-one favourite, was rampaging through the division in apparently invincible style: 27 fights, 27 wins, 23 knockouts in 23 months as a professional. Schmeling, however, was unperturbed, simply saying in his quiet way: 'I have seen something.' What he'd seen, watching Joe's fights from ringside and via his suitcase of 8mm movie reels, was that the Brown Bomber was open to a right hand counter because he dropped his left after throwing a jab.

Nothing would deter him from his quiet calm. For three rounds the upright 192 lb. 30-year-old was outboxed and outpunched by the shuffling 198 lb. 22-year-old, but there was always hope because, just as predicted, Max's own right was landing. Then in the fourth he struck with full force: a short overhand right cross counter that caught Louis flush at the high point of his vulnerable chin. Max followed up and pounded him, driving him to the canvas, and although the Bomber was up at the count of two, from then on he fought in a fog and seemed unable to avoid that deadly right. Finally, in the 12th round, Schmeling caught him again and then opened up until one last right cross put Joe down and out.

Max was born on a farm on the outskirts of Berlin. After watching a film of the 'million dollar' Dempsey–Carpentier fight in 1921 he turned to boxing. 'I was a complete failure in everything I did before I turned to boxing,' he said in typically self-deprecating style seven years later. 'It is the easiest means of a livelihood, so I would like to be world champion because the title is worth a fortune – and I will be, if they give me the chance.'

After winning the German middleweight and light heavyweight titles as an amateur he turned professional shortly before his 19th birthday in 1924 and six months on boxed a two round exhibition with Dempsey, when the world champion was on a European tour. He won the German light heavyweight title in 1926 and the European title a year

German heavyweight contender Max Schmeling pictured in fighting pose during a training session for his fight with Paolino Uzcudun of Spain on 28th June, 1929. He won impressively on a 15 round points decision and was cheered enthusiastically by the 40,000-strong New York crowd.

later, developing a reputation as a sound defensive boxer and outstanding counter-puncher, using a stiff jab to make openings and a potent cross to exploit them. His weakness was that he did not respond well to intense pressure and his chin was only so-so. In February 1928 he was knocked out in one round by the British and Commonwealth champion, Gypsy Daniels, whom he had previously beaten. Five weeks later he won the German heavyweight title.

Max came to the conclusion that earning a decent living meant looking abroad. He took on an American manager, the tiny, sharp-tongued, cigar-puffing New York Jewish hustler, Yussel 'Joe' Jacobs and began campaigning in America. Between fights he returned to Berlin where he was adopted by an avant-garde circle that included actors Marlene Dietrich and Emil Jennings, playwrights Bertolt Brecht and Heinrich Mann, the artist George Grosz, the sculptor Rudolph Belling, the composer Kurt Weill and filmmaker Fritz Lang. Some were moving into exile in America; others clinging on in Berlin, partying desperately as the threat from the Nazis grew more terrifying. They liked this black-haired, beetle-browed Adonis. He once said he felt like 'yet another exotic presence for them – a kind of mythical animal', but still posed for Grosz and Belling, attended their parties and bedded their women.

Arriving in New York in late 1928, he picked up five wins in seven months under Jacobs's direction. He received a wild ovation in stopping the contender Johnny Risko in nine rounds, setting him up for a world title eliminator against the Spaniard Paolino Uzcudun at Yankee Stadium on 27 June 1929. Max 'cut the Basque's face to ribbons and had him blinded, bleeding and groggy at the finish,' UP reported. 'Most of the crowd of 40,000 roared its approval of the black-haired Teuton terror as he left the ring unmarked and fresh as a daisy.' This made Max number two contender, although it took another year to meet Jack Sharkey for the vacant title.

Their fight at Yankee Stadium on 11 June 1930 attracted 80,000 fans eager to see the crowning of Gene Tunney's successor after a long drought. For three rounds the 197 lb. 27-year-old Bostonian outboxed the 188 lb. 25-year-old German and then in the fourth he sunk a huge left into the groin. 'Schmeling was writhing in pain, helpless, incapacitated by an illegal punch and had to be carried to his corner,' the *New York Times* reported. Joe Jacobs leapt into the ring, demanding Sharkey's disqualification. He was supported by the equally vociferous Hearst Group editor Arthur Brisbane. Two of the judges did not see the low blow but the third did, and this persuaded referee Jim Crowley to disqualify Sharkey. 'I didn't want to win this way,' was all Max could say after being carried to his corner. The decision prompted the introduction of the no-foul rule where the boxer who lands low is deducted a point and the fouled boxer is given up to five minutes to recover.

The New York Commission stripped Schmeling of his title when Jacobs refused their demand that Sharkey be granted a return, but he was still recognised by the rest of the boxing world. In those days lighter weight boxers fought frequently (Harry Greb, for instance, had 46 fights, going 445 rounds in one year) but heavyweight title fights were rare events – just 17 between 1916 and 1937. Schmeling followed this tradition, making one successful title defence in two years as champion. Twelve months later Max finally agreed to face Sharkey again, at New York's Madison Square Garden on 21 June 1932. It was a

Joe Louis is shown squaring off with Max Schmeling for the benefit of the camera at the weighing in ceremony in Madison Square Garden, New York, 22 June 1938. The German received a cable from Adolf Hitler conveying Germany's best wishes. It began – 'To the coming world champion'. But this time time Schmeling lasted just 124 seconds.

boring fight, with the negative challenger slower and more lethargic than previously. The more aggressive Schmeling seemed to shade it with his cleaner, harder punches. One judge gave Max 10 of the 15 rounds, which seemed about right, but to the astonishment of the crowd and the ringside press, the referee and second judge gave it to the American, prompting Jacobs to unleash his most famous quote: 'We wuz robbed.'

The now former-champion returned to his cultural circle in Berlin where he met and married the actress Anny Ondra, who was about to start work on Alfred Hitchcock's *Blackmail*. Anny was appropriately blonde and blue-eyed but she was Czech rather than German and despite Hitler's infatuation with her, Nazi officials later suggested it would be best to divorce her – a request Schmeling ignored. Max was flattered when summoned to the Reichstag to see Hitler, Goebbels and Goering at a private dinner three months later where the Führer asked Max to promote the Nazi cause in America. For several years Schmeling made a point of highlighting to the foreign press the pro-boxing stance of Hitler's *Mein Kampf*. The relevant text says, 'No other sport is its equal in building up aggressiveness, in demanding lightning decision and in toughening the body in steely agility.' But it also says that if more Germans boxed, 'the seduction of hundreds of thousands of girls by bowlegged, disgusting Jew bastards would be quite impossible.'

Max managed just one fight in the next two years – a thrilling eighth round stoppage over former world middleweight champion Mickey Walker. His next opponent, at Yankee Stadium on 6 June 1933, was the part-Jewish Californian Max Baer who was determined to have his way with this Nazi-backed German. Wearing a Star of David on his trunks, he surprised the 53,000 crowd by dominating Schmeling, stopping him in round 10.

Schmeling was allowed more leeway than most Germans because of his crucial role in the Nazi propaganda campaign, which is perhaps why Jacobs was allowed to remain his manager until his death in 1941. Max was an emissary for Hitler in the Nazi campaign to offset the boycott of the 1936 Berlin Olympics, and this role was expanded after his surprise victory over Louis (an event Goebbels opposed beforehand, assuming Max would lose). When Louis was counted out the German radio commentary gushed, 'All America is enchanted by the great achievement of the German. How much this has accomplished for the German cause should not be underestimated.' Max received a telegram from the Führer: 'Most cordial felicitations on your splendid victory. Adolf Hitler.' And another from Goebbels: 'Your victory was a German victory. Heil Hitler', while the Nazi weekly *Das Schwarze Korps* added, 'Schmeling's victory was not only sport. It was a question of prestige for our race.' When Max returned home he was paraded as a symbol of Aryan superiority. He spent a weekend at Berchtesgarden with Hitler, years later explaining: 'What can you do if your president invites you to tea? Of course you must accept.'

German heavyweight champion Max Schmeling pictured in training near Hamburg for his fight with former British Empire heavyweight champion Ben Foord in 1938. Schmeling won on points.

But Max's attitude to Joe Louis was devoid of bigotry. At the Berlin Olympics he met the great black sprinter Jesse Owens, saying he hoped Jesse would win some gold medals, before talking about Louis. 'Joe is a great fighter and man – I would like to become friends with him one day.' However, by the time of their return, at Yankee Stadium on 22 June 1938, the climate had changed. However reluctantly, Max had become a vehicle for Nazi propaganda. 'The black man will always be afraid of me – he is inferior,' the German press quoted him as saying. He later denied saying anything of the sort and when he met Joe again 17 years later, the first thing he said was, 'I hope you never took account of some of the things that got put in the papers when we fought.' But Max could not openly contradict his political masters – he had a family to worry about – and this affected his image. One American report referred to a Nazi uniform in the training camp closet of Max's trainer, Max Machon. Another, written by Paul Gallico, described Max's house in Germany, mentioning a basket of flowers with a red swastika ribbon (sent to Anny by Hitler) along with a photograph of Hitler with a personal inscription from the Führer, hung over Max's trophy case.

He might have been distracted by the pickets outside his hotel but he was in superb condition when he met Louis again, yet he was up against a far superior fighter from the under-trained, over-confident, inexperienced version of two years earlier. Spurred on by the roar of 70,000 fellow countrymen, with 70 million listening on the radio, 'The Brown Bomber' overwhelmed the 'Black Uhlan'. Max liked space to move, think and counter but he was at his weakest when forced backwards, and Louis gave him no room to breathe. In the two minutes and four seconds it lasted Schmeling took four counts

KINGS OF THE RING

and received a terrible beating – aside from his bruised ribs and face, two bones were fractured and he screamed in agony when one of his lumbar vertebrae punctured his kidney – from a right to his lower back after he half-turned his back on Louis. Max Machon threw in the towel after the third knockdown and when referee Arthur Donovan ignored it he climbed into the ring and the massacre ended. By then a Nazi official had already pulled the plug on the radio broadcast to Germany.

'Looking back, I'm almost happy I lost that fight' he said many years later. 'Just imagine if I would have come back to Germany with a victory. I had nothing to do with the Nazis, but they would have given me a medal.' It was 13 months before he could fight again – knocking out Adolf Heuser before 70,000 fans at Stuttgart's Adolf Hitler Stadium on 2 July 1939. But by then he was superfluous to requirements, which meant previously overlooked sins were remembered. Max was summoned by Goebbels and reprimanded for meeting Jewish friends, 'What are you thinking, Herr Schmeling? You come to the Führer, you come to me, and you still socialise with Jews!' His bravest stand came on *Kristalnacht*, 8 November 1938 – when Nazi thugs smashed and burned Jewish shops and synagogues across the country, murdering hundreds of Jews. Max hid the two young sons of a Jewish friend in his hotel. He used his artistic connections to smuggle the boys to China and then to the United States.

Max's defeat to a black man, his friendships with Jews and his continued refusal to join the Nazi party prompted Hitler to punish him – ensuring he was conscripted into the paratroops. In 1941 he was dropped into Crete, but badly injured his knee on landing and aggravated the back injury sustained in the second Louis fight. The *Daily Telegraph* reported: 'Max Schmeling … has been shot dead in Crete while trying to escape his New Zealand captors.' In fact, he was being treated by a captured British army doctor. At the end of the war tried to win favour by visiting Prisoner of War camps, handing out pictures of himself, although these weren't always well-received. A sergeant was quoted in a despatch: 'When he left we took the picture he'd given us and did our duty on it in the latrine.' But another despatch called Max a 'genuine anti-Nazi who helped American prisoners in German camps.'

Penniless at the end of the war, he mounted a comeback, winning a couple of fights and losing others until on 31 October 1948, at the age of 43, watched by 25,000 fans, he was outpointed by the German light heavyweight champion Richard Vogt and retired. He bought a Coca Cola franchise and, partly through his links with the former American boxing commissioner Jim Farley (later the US Postmaster General), he was appointed chief executive of the Coca Cola Corporation in Germany. He was already a rich and successful businessman when he visited Joe Louis at his home in Milwaukee in 1954. They hugged and cried and became close friends, with Max twice paying for Joe to visit him in Hamburg. He later paid Louis's hospital bills and contributed to the costs of his funeral.

He also set up the Max Schmeling charitable foundation to raise money for the poor and elderly. 'That's my hobby – making money with one hand and giving it away with the other,' he once said. Asked what he thought was the most important quality in life, the old man replied:'Tolerance, then tolerance again and finally, tolerance.'

Max died in his sleep at his home in Hollenstedt, Germany, at the age of 99 and was buried next to Anny, his wife of 54 years (who died in 1987). They had no children.

Primo Carnera – 'The Ambling Alp'

World heavyweight champion 1933–4.

'There is probably no more scandalous, pitiful, incredible story in all the record of these last mad sports years than the tale of the living giant, a creature out of the legends of antiquity, who was made into a prize fighter. This unfortunate pituitary case became the heavyweight champion, yet never in all his life was he ever anything more than a fourth-rater at prize fighting. He must have grossed more than two million dollars during the years that he was being exhibited, and he hasn't a cent to show for it today.'
Paul Gallico, Novelist.

Height: 6'5¾
Peak weight: 250–263 lb.
88 wins (70 stoppages),
15 losses
Born: Sequals, Italy,
26 October 1906
Died: 29 June 1967

The Ambling Alp – also known as Old Satchel Feet and The Gorgonzola Tower – is known for two things: as the biggest-ever world heavyweight champion and as a mob-backed Italian peasant notorious for fixed fights. But he deserves better – certainly better than fourth rate – a strong and brave champion who was more than just a victim.

The gap between perception and reality is most marked with his title-losing effort against Max Baer at New York's Madison Square Garden on 14 June 1934. The common perception is that Madcap Max had a whale of a time beating up the giant, dropping him 11 times until the fight was stopped in round 11. Some of this is true. Baer did indeed have a good deal of fun at Primo's expense but the fight was not one-sided. With his mobster manager, Bill Duffy, in prison, Primo did not have his usual corner support, which he certainly needed that night. He insisted he was a victim of referee Arthur Donovan's determination to ignore Baer's repeated fouls. In round one Max fell on Primo, who severely sprained his ankle, which meant he fought with painfully restricted movement. Some of the knockdowns were a result of Baer's mauling tactics and when Carnera fell Baer ignored the neutral corner rule and once he punched Primo while he was down. And yet the giant always rose quickly and for long spells outboxed Max. As the *Mid-Day Standard* reported, 'Carnera won the admiration of the huge crowd for the wonderful recoveries… Using a fine straight left which won him many points, he took the fourth, seventh, eighth and ninth rounds.' In fact, one of the judges had Primo ahead at the time of the stoppage.

Primo, the first son of a stonecutter, grew up in the northern Italian village of Sequals as an illiterate peasant boy known for his size, strength and gentle nature. A defect of his pituitary gland caused excess excretion of growth hormone and he weighed 24 lb. at birth. Touring Europe as a circus strongman and wrestler he was spotted by Leon See, a tiny French entrepreneur, boxing promoter and Oxford graduate, who saw the lad's earning potential. He also saw that the giant had only moderate natural ability, which meant he was fed a diet of stiffs – either so inept they had no chance or paid to take a dive. In his first 15 months he 'fought' 18 times in Europe and Britain, 'winning' 16 with two disqualification losses. See made a point of exaggerating the giant's size, power and even food consumption. One press release read: 'For breakfast, Primo has a quart of orange juice, two quarts of milk, nineteen

The towering sight of Italian heavyweight boxing champion, Primo Carnera, standing on a podium with his arm raised in a fascist salute. He took part in several fixed fights but also genuinely beat some good heavyweights.

KINGS OF THE RING

pieces of toast, fourteen eggs, a loaf of bread and half a pound of Virginia ham.'

When they arrived in America this publicity attracted a gang headed by the murderer Owney Madden, who made an offer See could not to refuse. Fixed fights continued – some victims falling without taking a punch – but now and then they took a chance with more willing competitors. One was the 33-year-old former 'coloured' world champion George Godfrey, who was one of the biggest hitters in the game despite being overweight and past his best. Godfrey bashed Primo around for four rounds before sinking his fist into the groin – for which he received his eighth disqualification defeat. 'Yes I hit him low – I admit it,' he said. 'I'm a good nigger and I always tell the truth. Primo fouled me in the third and fourth round, so we are about even.'

Primo was developing into a capable boxer with a decent jab. He lacked speed or power but mastered other tactics – standing on feet, pinning arms to sides, pinching biceps with gloved thumbs, elbowing, back-handing, punching low and using his strength to push

Primo Carnera running in St James's Park, London, with trainer Maurice Eudeline in preparation for his upcoming fight with George Cook at the Albert Hall in 1932. Carnera won on a fourth round knockout and it took several minutes before Cook regained consciousness.

and pull. He was outpointed by Jim Maloney but gained revenge in the return. He outpointed Paulino Uzcudun in Spain but was outboxed by Jack Sharkey in New York. He picked up wins over two fringe contenders but lost to the black Canadian Larry Gains before a 70,000-strong crowd in London. Then on 10 February 1933 he fought leading contender Ernie Schaaf at Madison Square Garden. The 207 lb. Schaaf had absorbed a severe hammering from Max Baer five months earlier but showed no ill-effects from that beating. The 250 lb. Primo landed a slow right in round 13 and Schaaf was counted out, but any thoughts of a fix were hastily dispelled when he was rushed to hospital for an operation to remove a blood clot and release the pressure on his brain. He died four days later. There were threats of banning the sport in New York State before boxing commissioners announced the establishment of a 'super-dreadnought' class, adding that Primo could only fight men from this class, although the proposal was never implemented.

This carried Primo to his title-winning knockout over Sharkey – viewed either as proof of foul play or proof that Primo was too damn big for normal-sized heavies. Four months later he made his first defence in Rome, against his Spanish rival Uzcudun, who held the European title. In the heaviest title pairing ever – Carnera at 259½ lb., Uzcudun at 229¼ – Primo won a 15 round decision, much to the delight of Mussolini who dressed him up in a fascist black shirt and adopted him as a giant mascot. Primo returned to Madison Square Garden on 1 March 1934 to defend against former light heavyweight champion Tommy Loughran; in a fight with the biggest-ever weight differential. Loughran, way past his best after 148 fights, could not offset the size and strength differential and grumbled after losing on a clear decision, 'The big bum kept standing on my feet.'

He went into the Baer fight as the betting favourite and despite his loss, won respect for his courage. Four wins on he was put in with the undefeated, 21-year-old Joe Louis. Mussolini, who was about to invade Ethiopia, did his best to promote Primo's cause while Owney Madden did his best to muscle in on Louis. And the quietly persuasive muscle of the 'Brown Bomber' had no trouble seeing off the heroically courageous

Ambling Alp before a 60,000 crowd at Yankee Stadium on 25 June 1935. Primo hauled himself back to his feet after being smashed to the canvas in round six but he was soon down again, up again, and down for the third time with a right cross and left hook, when referee Donovan finally rescued him. The bleeding, battered giant was 'utterly helpless, clinging to the top rope,' the *New York Times* reported.

He was back four months later, stopping the world rated German Walter Neusel in four rounds for his last big win. After a couple of bad losses to a fringe contender he retired in 1936. He tried a comeback in Europe but an operation to remove a kidney – as a result of his diabetes – kept him from boxing for eight years and the mob finally lost interest – he'd served his purpose. Gallico wrote of his fascination with the 'sheer impudence of the men who handled the giant, their conscienceless cruelty, their complete depravity toward another human being, the sure, cool manner in which they hoaxed hundreds of thousands of people. Poor Primo! A giant in stature and strength, a terrible figure of a man, with the might of ten men, he was a helpless lamb among wolves who used him until there was nothing more left to use, until the last possible penny had been squeezed from his big carcass, and then abandoned him.'

This former Italian army reservist returned home, joining the Italian Sniper Brigade to aid the Allies. He made another comeback in Italy in 1945, winning two and losing three before turning to professional wrestling. Here he finally found his niche, making decent money and becoming a star attraction. He also acted in 15 Hollywood films, winning plaudits for his villainous supporting role in *A Kid for Two Farthings*. He married Guiseppina Kovacic in 1953 and they became American citizens, settling with their two children in Los Angeles, where they opened a restaurant and liquor store. Two films were based on his life – Fellini's *La Strada* (1954, with Anthony Quinn) and *The Harder they Fall* (1957, with Humphrey Bogart and Rod Steiger), based on the Budd Schulberg novel about a giant whose fights are fixed. Carnera, who was unaware his fights were fixed, sued Columbia Pictures but lost. His health deteriorated through his diabetes, cirrhosis of the liver exacerbated by alcoholism and probably also the beatings he took in the ring, and he returned to his home village of Sequals where he built a home and a gymnasium. One leg was paralysed when he died alone at the age of 60. As Gallico put it, 'None of the carrion birds who had picked him clean ever came back to see him or to help him.'

But Primo left a more hopeful legacy. The Sequals council made a Carnera museum in his home, and organised boxing matches in his honour every summer in the square. In 1998 his children established the Primo Carnera Foundation. 'My father didn't have the opportunity to go to school,' Giovanna said. 'He used the gifts God gave him to take care of his family, but he always stressed education for us so that we would have a choice.'

Former heavyweight boxing champ Primo Carnera compares his king-size palm with the tiny hand of actress Audrey Dalton on a Hollywood movie set. Both are appearing in the new Bob Hope picture *Casanova's Big Night.*

Max Baer – 'The Livermore Larruper'

World heavyweight champion 1934–35.

'Baer was shaped to be a great pug but his heart did not belong in that immense and thrilling body. It was a clown's heart, a heart that must have been hurt by terror and fear in the years Baer was forced to pretend he as a fighter. I'm positive Baer disliked punching another man.'
Jimmy Cannon, sports writer.

Height: 6'2½
Peak weight: 200–210 lb.
71 wins (53 stoppages),
13 losses
Born: Omaha, Nevada,
11 February 1909
Died: 21 November 1959

Madcap Max's defining fight came early in his career when he faced the big-hitting West Coast contender Frankie Campbell. In round two Baer slipped and Campbell, assuming a knockdown, walked to a neutral corner. Max charged, hurt Campbell with a right behind the ear and took over. In round five he cornered his rival and landed 20 unanswered blows.

Maximilian Adelbert Baer was born in Nebraska but after the war his family moved to Livermore, California where Max worked on his father's ranch. His feats of strength impressed a boxing-mad industrialist's son and he made his fight debut on 16 May 1929 with a two round knockout. By the time this rough, aggressive 21-year-old fought Campbell, Baer was regarded as the most exciting young star in the game. But the tragedy changed Max and what emerged was a persona of a joker, all-night drinker and playboy.

Baer's record over the next year was shaky but he gained a valuable ally in Jack Dempsey and Max responded positively, beginning a 14-fight winning streak that included a return with Ernie Schaaf to whom Baer had previously lost. Associated Press reported, 'Two seconds before the fight ended Schaaf was knocked flat on his face, completely knocked out.' Four fights on the 24-year-old died after going down from a feeble Primo Carnera right but it was speculated that the real cause of death was his knockout at Baer's hands.

Once more Max responded with overt jollity but the opportunity to take on the Nazi-backed former champion Max Schmeling temporarily changed this. Baer, who had a Jewish grandfather, applied constant pressure and by round 10 the beating was becoming so one-sided that Baer motioned to referee Donovan to step in – before dropping his rival with a right cross for a nine count. Baer next took on world heavyweight champion Carnera, teasing him throughout the weigh-in and the fight before mauling the giant to take the title. Baer's first defence of the title was against the supposed no-hoper Jim Braddock. Baer, who broke his right hand in the early rounds, remarked after losing the decision, 'I was too busy clowning that I guess I forgot to fight.'

This loss broke Baer's resolve to maintain the colour bar so he agreed to fighting Joe Louis. Dempsey told him at the end of the first round, 'You doing great kid – he hasn't hit you.' To which Max replied, 'Then you better keep an eye on the referee because somebody in there is beating the hell out of me.' At the end of round four he was dropped for the second time and the crowd watched him kneeling for the full count, completely conscious. Asked why he made no attempt to rise he said, 'The fans paid to see a fight, not a murder.'

After serving in the Air Force Max settled down and opened a nightclub before growing fat from booze and bad living. At the age of 50 he suffered a heart attack while shaving.

Max Baer trains for the Primo Carnera bout, which he won in the eleventh round after dropping the Italian eleven times. But in a sense his defining fight was his 1930 victory over Frankie Campbell, who died of his injuries. Baer was charged with manslaughter – although the charges were later dropped.

KINGS OF THE RING

Jimmy Braddock – 'The Cinderella Man'

World heavyweight champion 1935–37.

'Jim Braddock is one cat you ain't gonna scare and he ain't gonna quit, either.'
Jack Blackburn, trainer of Joe Louis, prior to his 1937 title fight with Braddock.

Height: 6'2½
Peak weight: 180–199 lb.
46 wins (26 stoppages),
24 losses, 6 draws,
10 no decisions
Born: New York City,
7 June 1905
Died: 29 November 1974

Damon Runyon dubbed this Irish-American nice guy 'The Cinderella Man' and it stuck because whatever he lacked in charisma and flair, he made up for with a wonderfully inspiring storyline: basket-case family man who gritted his teeth, took his chances, paid his dues and finally won the big prize against impossible odds. Max Baer was a 10-1 favourite to beat Braddock at Madison Square Garden on 13 June 1935, which seemed about right for this failed former light heavyweight challenger. The 29-year-old bulked up to 193¾ lb. – his heaviest ever – but was still outweighed by 16 lb. and there was no comparison in strength and power. He was viewed as a time-filling no-hoper and Baer trained and played accordingly, while the superbly conditioned Braddock assured reporters, 'I may not be a great fighter but I ain't no bum.' Max spent much of the fight clowning for the benefit of the crowd. He would land a few hard punches and then step away to smile at the ringsiders, while Braddock doggedly jabbed and moved and now and then stepped in with a right cross – piling up the points. Baer assured his worried corner he could 'drop this bum whenever I want' but Jim was avoiding most of his haymakers and absorbed the rest while maintaining his stick-and-move plan. At one point he taunted the taunter: 'Hey Max, you better get going – you're way behind.' Even in defeat the tiring Max could see the joke, laughing at his failure to land. He came on strong in the 15th, attacking the body and also landing hard to the head – enough to win the round but not the fight. He was generously awarded four, five and seven of the 15 rounds by the three scoring officials, which meant the Cinderella Man was the new world heavyweight champion.

Weighing in at 17 lb. James Walter Braddock was born in Hell's Kitchen, New York, and raised in New Jersey – one of seven children of poor Manchester-born Irish immigrants. He fished in the river, played baseball, did plenty of street fighting and left school at 13 without qualifications, hoping to become a fireman or train engineer. Instead he found work as a postal messenger, printer's assistant and errand boy. The one thing he was really good at was boxing. He twice won the New Jersey state light heavyweight title before turning professional early in 1926 at the age of 20, co-trained and managed by the diminutive, cigar-puffing, ever-loyal Joe Gould. He excelled at first, going 36 fights without defeat, sometimes coming in as light as 162 lb. but beating heavyweights with his skill and hard right cross. Early in 1928 he dropped a pair of decisions, but bounced back to beat light heavyweight contenders Pete Latzo (breaking his jaw in four places) and the previously unbeaten Tuffy Griffith (dropping him four times). A disputed points loss to top contender Leo Lomski hardly set him back and *The Ring* magazine put him on their cover with the caption 'Jimmy Braddock, One of the World's Greatest Light Heavyweights.'

James 'Jimmy' Braddock was not one of the great heavyweight champions, nor one of the great personalities of the division, but his Horatio Alger story of honest, blue collar persistance eventually prevailing against all the odds remains a source of inspiration 70 years on. He held the title for two years and never successfully defended it, but eventually secured his pension by agreeing to take on Joe Louis rather than Max Schmeling, and surprised 'The Brown Bomber' by dropping him in the first round before going down in the eighth.

He proved his worth by stopping former champion Jimmy Slattery, setting him up for a shot at Tommy Loughran's world title at Yankee Stadium on 18 July 1929. The 24-year-old, 170 lb. Braddock was on his 47th fight, with just three losses, but he faced an extremely elusive champion, who was having his 120th, and lost on a clear, unanimous decision. His fortunes slumped – just in time for the 1929 Stock Market collapse, which swallowed all his savings. He was soon reduced to taking fights at short notice, often with broken hands, and came out on the wrong end of several disputed decisions. During a four-year spell he won only nine out of 31, usually for a pittance. Desperate to provide for his wife, Mae, and three young children he would walk up to 15 miles a day, looking for piece jobs loading ships on the docks, working double shifts when possible and also doing bits and pieces as a bartender and casual labourer. But work was scarce and they often had to survive on a $24 monthly welfare cheque and were forced to move out of their flat and into the basement, with Jim as janitor.

His boxing career ground to a halt after a couple of wins in late 1933, partly because his right hand broke whenever he landed it. But nine months of enforced retirement gave time for his hand to heal while his body grew strong from his periodic shifts as a longshoreman. When Gould found him another fight – on the Carnera–Baer undercard – he was in decent shape. His opponent was Corn Griffin, an army boy who made his name outfighting Primo Carnera in public sparring sessions. 'I had about two days' notice that I was going to fight Griffin,' Braddock said. 'Two hours would have been enough.' Jim was dropped in the second round but he rose, knocked Griffin down and then finished him in the third – for a purse of $250. This led to a return with the top light heavyweight John Henry Lewis, who'd beaten him two years earlier. Braddock won a clear-cut decision for a purse of $700. Four months on he fought leading heavyweight contender Art Lasky and despite giving away 15 lb., romped home again. 'They figured Lasky'd lick me but I hit him with everything,' Jim recalled. 'Wherever his kisser was, I had a punch there – a left hook, a right cross. It was one of those nights.' He paid $300 from his $2,000 cheque to the state relief fund to compensate for his spell on welfare, paid off his rental, gas and electricity arrears and for once had enough left to eat and train properly.

When Max Schmeling turned down an elimination fight against Braddock, the Baer fight went directly to the 'bum' and the title changed hands. Braddock agreed to make his first defence against Schmeling in New York on 30 September 1936, but it fell through when he broke his hand in training and was rescheduled eight months later. By then Joe Louis's promoter, Mike Jacobs, was working closely with the Anti-Nazi League to convince Jim to bypass Max and instead defend against 'The Brown Bomber' for a higher price ($300,000 plus ten percent of Jacobs's share of the net purse receipts over the next 10 years if Joe won). It helped that unlike most of his predecessors, Jim had no respect for colour bars or racial stereotypes and was convinced the Schmeling fight would be hit by a boycott. He ignored an order from the New York State Commission and signed to fight Louis, accepting his $1,000 'mosquito bite' fine with a shrug. 'I'm not ducking Schmeling at all,' he said. 'I'm ducking poverty. I got my nose broken, an eardrum busted and my eyebrows laid open in a fight that paid me eight lousy bucks. I can't miss three hundred grand for this one and nobody will ever tell me that Louis is three hundred thousand tough.'

The first round at Chicago's Comskey Park on 22 June 1937 suggested the 32-year-old was right on that score. A crowd of 46,000 watched in astonishment as the 5-2 underdog landed a hard right uppercut on Louis's shaky chin, dropping him. Joe sprung up too quickly and wobbled, but survived. As champion Jim had boxed a few exhibitions but mostly he'd taken it easy, quietly drinking and smoking with his friends while he waited for the big offer to secure his retirement. Still, he was superbly conditioned and showed no sign of rust as he continued winging hopeful rights while poking out his jab. The crouching 23-year-old challenger boxed cautiously behind his own jolting jab before bringing out his heavier guns. He cut Braddock above the right eyebrow, bruised his face and body and took over completely in round six. A right cross split Jim's upper lip and he was shaken with quick, hard, accurate combinations. The slow-moving champion had no real answer but he fought back hard. At the end of round seven Gould wanted to stop it: 'I want to go out like a champion,' Jim said. 'I want to be carried out.' He started the eighth with another right but Louis blocked it and countered with his own jolting cross, followed by a hard left to the body. A jab opened a cut under the left eye but Jim bored his way in, still swinging, only to be met by a decoy hook followed by a perfectly timed right cross to the edge of the jaw. Braddock fell on his face and was counted out at one minute and ten seconds, but received a prolonged ovation as he left the ring. As the New York *Daily Mirror* put it, 'The exhibition of courage the gallant Anglo-Irishman gave before that final bolt of lightning struck him on the side of the jaw awakened admiration and compassion for him in the heart of everyone in that vast crowd.'

In his 86th and final fight, at Madison Square Garden six months on, Jim went up against another man who gave Joe Louis a hard time, Tommy Farr. The picture of these two blue-collar battlers – the cigar-puffing Irish-American longshoreman and the cigarette-smoking Welsh mineworker – chatting amiably to each other at a pre-fight event, captured an era quickly to pass. Braddock escaped with a split decision and retired. He continued boxing in exhibition matches and refereeing big fights and his share of Louis's winnings (over $150,000 in his first decade of retirement) helped him through hard times. Gould and Braddock both enlisted when America entered the war. The manager, an army captain, was convicted by court martial of conspiracy to defraud the government and was fined, jailed and dismissed. The boxer served honourably as a navy stevedore and merchant marine and after the war opened a marine-army surplus business and also serviced generators and welding equipment.

At his best James J Braddock, as he was called (although his middle initial was actually W for Walter) could be a solid boxer with a hard right, sound defensive skills and a big heart, but his lack of speed, fragile hands and unexceptional strength meant he was by no means one of the division's great champions. Nor, for that matter, was this quiet, straightforward and modest family man one of the sport's most flamboyant or entertaining characters. But the tale of his dogged refusal to lie down, and his eventual triumph against the odds, served as an inspiration to many American working people in Depression era America, told over and over in comic books, newspaper articles and radio shorts. When he died of a heart attack at home in New Jersey at the age of 69, he was an almost forgotten champion but, more than three decades on and against all odds, the story of the 'Cinderella Man' once again became a source of inspiration in an era of social and economic uncertainty.

Joe Louis – 'The Brown Bomber'

World heavyweight champion 1937–49.

'Joe, we need muscles like yours to beat Germany.'
President **Franklin D Roosevelt** prior to Louis's 1938 return with Max Schmeling.

Height: 6'1¾
Peak weight: 197–207 lb.
68 wins (54 stoppages),
3 losses
Born: Lafayette, Alabama
13 May 1914
Died: 12 April 1981

To white Americans like President Roosevelt, Joe Louis was an inspirational totem of their country's fight against fascism and a symbol of an integrationist future. To black Americans he was so much more: he represented hope. 'The Brown Bomber' carried their aspirations on his sloping shoulders like no other African-American public figure of his time and certainly like no other boxer.

It all came together – the symbolism, inspiration and hope – in 1938 when Joe fought his return with the Hitler-backed Max Schmeling who had stalled the plan two years earlier. They were representatives of two worlds set to collide and their fight was served up as a prelude of what was sure to come. When they first met it was simply another big fight and a fair proportion of white America backed the German over their black countryman. But the world changed in two years and this time Louis took most of white America with him. When Joe won the world title by beating Jimmy Braddock a year earlier, his first words were, 'Don't call me champ until I lick Smellin'.' When he finished the job at Yankee Stadium on 22 June 1938, his first words were, 'You can call me champ now.' Those two minutes transformed Joe into a hero available for all America and much of his country, and the world embraced him.

Never before and never again did Louis approach a fight with such intensity. He'd heard about Schmeling's supposed remarks about the Negro's innate fear of the white man and about Hitler's backing and it produced a frightening will to destroy. 'I am out for revenge,' he said. 'I'll give him enough to remember for life and make him hang up his gloves for all time.' His trainer, Jack 'Chappie' Blackburn, changed their usual approach which involved bombing out sparring partners for public consumption and concentrated on tightening the Bomber's defence and impressing on his charge the need to pace himself for 15 hard rounds, maintaining steady pressure throughout. But, for once, Joe had other ideas. 'I'm scared,' he said on the afternoon of the fight. 'I'm scared I might kill Smellin'.'

Caught by two jabs and a hook, the first move from the 193 lb. German was to clinch. They broke and the American sprung at him, a short left followed by a rapid-fire one-two-three from the finest combination puncher in heavyweight history. Max missed with a right and a few jabs and Joe paused to draw his enemy's fire, then belted him in the body, followed by a combination to the head. An uppercut, short left and right cross landed with frightening force and Max wobbled before grasping the top rope. Joe ripped a hook into his stomach, and the next punch – the one that released a terrible scream from Max's lungs and left him with lower back problems for the rest of his life – caused a moment's hesitation before more monster punches thudded home. With Max draped over the ropes, referee Arthur Donovan waved Joe to the neutral corner. By the count of two Schmeling was upright. Louis led with a single right to his exposed jaw and down

Joe Louis posing before his defence of the title against Max Schmeling of Germany at the Yankee Stadium, 22 June 1938. Louis won in 124 seconds, putting his former conqueror in hospital. 'You can call me champ now,' he said when it was over.

he went. When he rose a five-punch combination dropped him again. Once more he forced himself up. Joe measured with his left, hammered first the body with a right and left, then the jaw with a devastating right and down he went again. Donovan ignored the white towel and began counting for the fourth time. And then, with Schmeling still on the canvas and his trainer coming to the rescue in the ring and the timekeeper saying, 'seven, eight…', Donovan finally spread his arms above his head: enough! 'To be honest, on that night nobody could have beaten Louis,' Schmeling later admitted.

Joseph Louis Barrow was born in a small cabin in rural Alabama, the seventh of eight children of Munroe and Lillie Barrow. Three grandparents were slaves, the fourth a Cherokee Native American. When Joe was two, 56-year-old Munroe – a 6'3, 220 lb. cotton picker and sharecropper – was committed to the Searcy State Hospital for the Colored Insane. 'You don't forget a thing like that,' Joe said. Two years later the boy was told his father was dead (only to discover, 20 years later, he was still alive – dying in 1938). His mother Lillie scraped through by washing clothes, and the children, who slept five in a bed, sometimes went hungry, so she merged assets and families with Pat Brooks, a widower with five children of his own. In 1926 the family were surrounded by a Ku Klux Klan lynch mob on horseback, but they were saved from the worst when a Klansman recognised Brooks and announced he was 'a good nigger'. Soon after, when Joe was 12, they all moved north, making a 22-day trek to Detroit.

This shy boy had his first experience of schooling but showed no interest and was placed in a 'special' class. When he dropped out at 16 Lillie sent him for violin lessons but a friend took him to the Brewster Recreation Centre and he began using the money for boxing classes. Lillie discovered when the teacher asked why the boy was always absent. 'At first Momma looked unhappy,' Joe said. 'But she said if any of us kids wanted to do something bad enough, she'd try to see that we got a chance at it.' Joe filled in the form for his first fight but there wasn't space for his surname, so he stepped through the ropes as Joe Louis – and was dumped on his back seven times. But, trained by a prodigiously talented teenage welterweight, Holman Williams, he improved rapidly, ending up with an amateur record of 50 wins (43 stoppages) and four losses.

He turned professional in 1934 under two black managers, John Roxborough, a professional gambler, and Julian Black, a Chicago numbers operator and nightclub owner. Towards the end of Joe's amateur career Roxborough hired Jack 'Chappie' Blackburn to be his trainer. This scar-faced 51-year-old former lightweight spent four years in jail for murder and was as hard as they came: no one dared cross him and he was allowed free reign to tutor Joe as he saw fit and soon had him ready. Weighing 181 lb. Joe earned $52 for knocking out the 175 lb. Jack Kracken in the first round in Chicago on 4 July 1934 and his career took off at astonishing speed. His 23rd victim – after 11 months as a professional – was Primo Carnera and by then Louis, who earned over $100,000 for this fight, was the most talked-about boxer in the world and a hero for black America.

Joe later recalled his first meeting with his future promoter Mike Jacobs in 1934. 'He told me then there was a colour line – a gentleman's agreement – that there wouldn't be another coloured champion.' Roxborough was determined to change this and did his utmost to win over the white public, portraying his charge as the polar opposite of Johnson in every respect. Joe's orders were to get on with the fighting while his managers

did the talking. For those who needed an excuse his silence and 'poker-faced' approach opened the way to descriptions of him as a robot devoid of emotion.

On 24 September 1935, the 21-year-old Joe married the main love of his life, 19-year-old Marva Trotter. He adored her but he was an inattentive and unfaithful husband. His inability to keep his sexual appetite under wraps was kept out of the press but the truth was that he would abandon his wife while sleeping with hundreds of women. They had a daughter, Jacqueline, got divorced, remarried, had a son, Joe Jr, and divorced again. His stream of women, along with his new obsession for golf, meant he was unfocussed when facing Max Schmeling in 1936. It seemed a low-risk assignment but Joe's lack of condition, his vulnerability to the right cross and his chin let him down. 'I was sitting on the dressing table and crying like I don't think I ever did before,' he said of that first defeat. 'It seemed at that moment I would just die.'

Mike Jacobs put him on a reputation-rebuilding fight programme, starting with a three round knockout over Jack Sharkey, but he did not always shine, until his victory in the Schmeling return erased the doubts and he came to dominate his division until he ran out of viable challengers. At the end of 1940, in his third year as world champion, Joe embarked on his 'bum of the month' campaign. Between these quick knockouts he slacked off training and stepped up womanising. After each fight he would entertain women in 15-minute hotel room slots for hours on end. Inevitably, his form suffered. He was knocked out of the ring by Max Baer's 237 lb. brother, Buddy (before winning on a disqualification) and was then outboxed for twelve rounds by the 174 lb. Billy Conn, before stopping the Irish-American late in round thirteen.

Not long after, 'Chappie' Blackburn died while John Roxborough was jailed for racketeering and Joe opted not to renew his contract with co-manager Julian Black. He

Louis stops the 233 lb. 'Two Ton' Tony Galento at New York's Yankee Stadium on 28 June 1939. Galento made a string of racist statements about Louis and lewd suggestions about his wife, prompting the enraged champion to fight less cautiously than normal. He dropped Galento in round two but was rocked several times and dropped in round three. Galento required 23 stitches to his face after the fight was stopped in the fourth round.

agreed to Mike Jacobs's proposal to donate his purses from return fights with Buddy Baer and Abe Simon (which he won more easily than first time around) to the army and navy relief funds and then joined the army. Most of his four years as an army sergeant was spent on PR missions, including a couple of army films, scores of exhibition bouts and visits to veteran hospitals. On one occasion he and his friend, Sugar Ray Robinson, took on three armed white military policemen who called Joe 'nigger' after ordering him to leave a whites-only bus shelter – Joe's only recorded street fight. His complaint led to the reprimand of the MPs and a ban on segregated facilities in American army camps. When he returned to civilian life his transformation as an all-American hero was complete. In response to a patronising quip that Joe was 'a credit to his race', the pro-Louis sportswriter Jimmy Cannon said, 'Louis is a credit to his race – the human race.'

He returned in 1946 to knock out the seriously faded Billy Conn in eight rounds and hard-hitting Tami Mauriello with a monstrous hook. His next defence 15 months later was against his former sparring partner, Jersey Joe Walcott, a seemingly easy outing since Jersey Joe was 17 lb. lighter, at least four months older and had 11 losses on his record. But the cagey, hard-hitting, hard-to-hit old man had turned his career around, reaching his peak when Louis was on the slide. Walcott dropped him with a right in the first round and again in the fourth and although the champion won the later rounds he seemed a clear loser by the final bell. He left the ring before the official verdict but to the astonishment of the Madison Square Garden crowd, emerged with a split decision. In the return Louis was once again dropped and outboxed but this time he caught Walcott in round 11 and unleashed a combination that sent him down for the count. Louis then took the microphone: 'This was for you, Mom,' he said. 'This was my last fight.' Eight months later, after eleven years and eight months as champion and a record 25 title defences, he officially announced his retirement.

He tried promoting new world champion, Ezzard Charles, but his free-spending lifestyle and crippling debt forced him back, so two years and three months after stopping Walcott he returned to Yankee Stadium to challenge for the title. Ezzard bulked up but still gave away 33½ lb. to the podgy, balding former champion, who came in at his heaviest ever of 218 lb. The brilliant Charles had no trouble with this slow 36-year-old version and by the later rounds Joe's left eye was cut and swollen, his nose and lips were bleeding and his body covered in welts. In round 14 Charles wobbled him with an uppercut and he had to grab the top rope to stay upright. Louis's cornermen had to lift him from his stool for the last round and he was wobbled again, but Charles eased off to spare his hero from a knockout.

Two months later Louis was back. He'd lost power and speed and no longer had the reflexes or conditioning of old. The right side of his body felt strangely weak and he was finding it harder to avoid rights, but he was winning. After his eighth win in nine months Louis accepted a fight against the rising Rocky Marciano. He eased off in training, believing this crude slugger was nothing special but Rocky had a relentless, crowding style that would always have troubled Joe. Joe made Rocky miss, dug in with his right, raked him with jabs, marking up the young man's face, but he kept coming, banging away at that tired old body. From the sixth Marciano took over. In the eighth he raised the pace and landed flush with a left hook. Joe rose at the count of eight and Rocky jumped on him, driving him back with a barrage of hooks and then ending it with a brute of a right. Louis collapsed, legs caught up in the ropes, head suspended over the edge of the ring as referee Ruby Goldstein waved it off, sparing Joe the indignity of being counted out again.

He retired again, never to return. His tax bill rose to $1.5 million and the government was starting to devour his assets including his children's trust fund. He worked in a circus, as a wrestling referee, casino host and even advertising cigarettes. He paused to marry a beautician and businesswoman, Rose Morgan, on Christmas Day 1955 but when the IRS went for Rose, he accepted a $100,000 one-year deal to become a professional wrestler. But he soon had to retire again – after one of his 'opponents' mistimed a rehearsed move, cracking three of his ribs and inducing a mild heart attack. Increasingly paranoid about being jailed for tax evasion, he turned to cocaine, then to smoking heroin and by the late 1950s started mainlining. Once he had spent time hanging out with his close friend Jesse Owens, but now he turned to the darker world of new world champion Sonny Liston, who also had his troubles with drugs and drink. He divorced Rose and married a lawyer, Martha Jefferson, who managed to secure a deal with the IRS in 1965 – from then on the IRS would only tax future earnings.

He was hired as Muhammad Ali's advisor but they fell out – Joe critical of Ali's boxing style, his conversion to the Nation of Islam and his stand on the Vietnam war; Ali calling Joe 'Uncle Tom'. His drug addiction continued and his paranoia was transferred to the Mafia and particularly to an imaginary mob hitman he called 'The Texan' who, he believed was intent on hunting him down. He collapsed on a Manhattan street in 1969 while on a publicity tour and a year later he was committed to a psychiatric hospital in Denver but with the help of therapy, psychiatric drugs and the absence of cocaine and heroin Joe made a substantial recovery and was discharged after five months, relocating to Las Vegas to become a greeter at Caesars Palace.

Joe Louis suffered a heart attack and the first of three strokes in 1977, after which he was confined to a wheelchair and fitted with a pacemaker, unable to speak or see properly. On 11 April 1981 he was wheeled to ringside for Larry Holmes's world heavyweight title defence against Trevor Berbick. The crowd gave him a standing ovation and he raised his hand to wave back. He collapsed at home and died the next morning, a month before his 67th birthday. 'Usually the champion rides on the shoulder of the nation and its people,' said Reverend Jesse Jackson in his eulogy. 'But in this case, the nation rode on the shoulders of its hero.'

Joe Louis holds onto the ropes after a punch from Tami Mauriello but he came back with a monstrous hook which lifted the challenger off his feet for a 129 second knockout. This was his second fight after a four year absence because of war service.

Ezzard Charles – 'The Cincinnati Cobra'

World heavyweight champion 1949–51.

'I would have to put Charles up there with the greatest fighters of all time. He gets too little credit from boxing critics. I think he would have beaten Rocky Marciano in his prime.'
Archie Moore, who lost three times to Charles and once to Marciano.

Height: 6'0
Peak weight: 168–186 lb.
97 wins (59 stoppages),
25 losses, 1 draw
Born: Lawrenceville, Georgia,
7 July 1921
Died: 27 May 1955

When it comes to assessing the best champion pound-for-pound, Moore's view is hard to dispute. Charles was one of a group of outstanding black middleweights and light heavyweights frozen out of a world title picture by the politics of the game in the 1940s, when the all-powerful promoter Jim Norris held sway through his mob-backed International Boxing Club. But it is as a heavyweight that he is usually rated – as a good but not quite great champion who ruled with a light touch and engaged in some memorable battles. It is perhaps fitting for a man whose prime was so undervalued that the Charles fights lingering in public memory are not his trio of one-sided victories over Moore, nor even the comprehensive beatings he handed out to Joe Louis, Jersey Joe Walcott and the rest of his eight world heavyweight title challengers, but rather the pair of defeats at the hands of Rocky Marciano when six years past his peak.

In their first meeting at Yankee Stadium on 17 June 1954 Charles, 'The Cincinnati Cobra' no longer had the legs of old, so he boxed more aggressively than usual, constantly beating Rocky to the punch and claiming the early and middle rounds. But the youth and strength of the 187½ lb. champion began to tell on the face and body of the 185½ lb. former champion. As Rocky put it, 'I was bleeding from my eye and nose, but this was one time I could honestly say, "You shoulda seen the other guy."' As the fight entered the last stretch the gap closed although it was still evenly poised going into the final round. Marciano went all out for a knockout in the 15th and final round, landing huge hits, but Charles remained defiantly standing shooting back until the final bell. It was a close fight, with Rocky winning eight rounds on two cards and nine on the third. 'I couldn't put you down and I don't think anybody can,' Rocky told him.

In the return, three months later, Charles tried a hit-and-run approach, although after being dropped in round two there was more running than hitting. At 33, on his 100th fight after 15 years as a professional, he lacked the sharpness of old but managed to slice Marciano's left nostril open in round six. By the end of the seventh Rocky was gushing blood from his nose and left eye and was told he'd be pulled out by the doctor after one more round. He had no option but to go all-out for a knockout but, oddly enough, Charles decided the same thing. They met ring centre and exchanged hard hooks. Ezzard shot a quick right that landed smack on that cut eye, sending the blood flying. Rocky fired back with a heavier right. Ezzard bent at the knees and whacked him to the body, blocked two big swings, and came back with a cracking hook to the jaw. But the desperate, blood-soaked champion just didn't stop coming. A heavy left and an even heavier right bounced off Charles's head and finally he began to wilt. Another bomb of a right put him down but instead of waiting for the count of nine the courageous

Ezzard Charles fights Jersey Joe Walcott for the world heavyweight title in Chicago, Illinois, 1949. Giving away 14 lb. he outboxed Walcott and knocked him down to win a unanimous decision – the world's number one light heavyweight had become the world heavyweight champion.

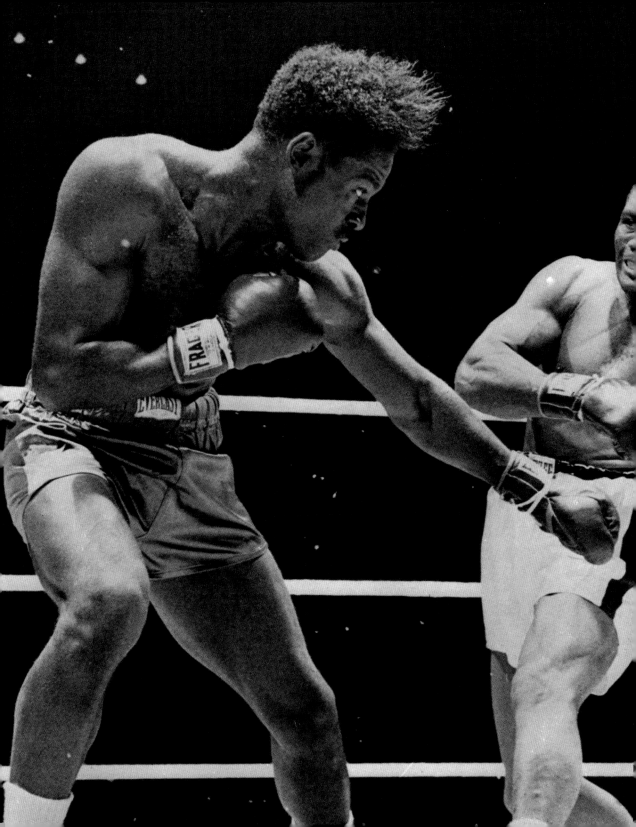

veteran was up at three. Marciano sprung at him and after several monstrous blows, ending with a left hook to the jaw, Charles went down again, collapsing on his hands and knees where he took the full count – 24 seconds short of salvation.

Ezzard Mack Charles – named after the doctor who delivered him – spent his first nine years in Lawrenceville, Georgia, but when his parents divorced he moved to Cincinnati, Ohio to live with his grandmother and great-grandmother. They raised him to be a devoted Methodist, who never swore and kept clear of alcohol and tobacco. A capable student and high school athlete he took to boxing in his mid-teens and immediately made his mark, winning a string of titles at welterweight and then the US national championship at middleweight, to end his amateur career with the perfect record of 42 wins in 42 fights. In a little over a year as a professional he racked up 21 wins in a row, with 15 knockouts.

Still only 19 he lost a close one to Ken Overlin, who'd just lost his world middleweight title on a dubious decision, but when they fought again eight months later Ezzard earned a draw. He beat two other former world champions, Teddy Yarosz and Anton Christoforidis but no one gave him a chance when he came in as a late substitute against the best middleweight in the world, Charlie Burley. At 24 Burley was a 57-fight veteran on a 20-bout winning streak, but Charles, who'd been a professional for just two years, won seven of their ten rounds. Burley trained harder for the return, coming in light at 151 lb. (to 160 lb. for Charles) but again the 20-year-old dominated. The world title was 'frozen' by Tony Zale, who was serving in the US Navy, so Ezzard acquired the habit of beating up bigger men like future world light heavyweight champion Joey Maxim (who outweighed him by 19 lb.). It didn't always work and he got his first real shock when world-rated Lloyd Marshall, who never got a title shot despite beating eight world champions, dropped him eight times before stopping him in round eight.

When Charles returned after three years in the US Army he'd grown to 170 lb. and soon proved himself the best man in a division packed with talent. Working under Ray Arcel, one of the finest trainers in boxing history, he displayed a blend of speed, reflex and technique that made him the complete boxer – masterful at any range, with the power and timing to take his man out with just one punch. He quickly secured a return with Marshall and this time outboxed his conqueror before tucking him away in round six. They did it again and Ezzard knocked him out in two. The 171 lb. Charles also trounced the 174 lb. Archie Moore in 1946, sealing his dominance by dropping him for a nine count in round nine with a left to the stomach. They fought again a year later and, as Associated Press reported, 'Charles floored Moore for nine in the seventh and slowed him to a walk the rest of the way.' Their third fight in January 1948 saw Ezzard knocking Moore out cold with a right in round eight, having won the previous seven.

Ezzard had reached his brilliant peak when he reluctantly accepted a filler fight against a 20-year-old fringe contender, Sam Baroudi, in Chicago on 20 February 1948, knocking him out in ten rounds. Baroudi never woke up and the devastated winner donated his purse to the victim's family. Ezzard never quite got over this tragedy and became more reluctant to unleash his power. His attentions were now restricted to the big men.

A third victory over Maxim made him the top contender and Joe Louis nominated him to fight Jersey Joe Walcott for the vacant title in Chicago on 22 June 1949. The 181¾ lb. Charles was in a different league from the 195½ lb. Walcott, using his left hook to drop him for a nine count and his speed and skill to box rings around him, earning a unanimous decision and National Boxing Association recognition as world heavyweight champion. Over the next 14 months he picked up three stoppage wins but it was only after he beat Louis at Yankee Stadium on 27 September 1950 that he achieved universal recognition as champion. Despite the 33½ lb. weight discrepancy he elected to fight the Brown Bomber at close and middle range, confident that his reflexes and tight defence would keep him clear of the big guns. Ezzard's compassion in holding off over the last few rounds saved Louis from being stopped. 'I didn't want to knock him out,' he said. 'It was like beating my father.' But it did not protect Joe from the most comprehensive beating of his career.

Much like Gene Tunney in relation to Jack Dempsey, Ezzard Charles was resented for beating a much-loved hero and kept facing the charge that it 'would have been different when Joe was in his prime'. His response was to prove himself over and over again. He squeezed in four more defences, including one against Walcott, before accepting a third meeting with Jersey Joe in Pittsburgh on 18 July 1951 – his ninth title defence. At the age of 30, after more than two years as champion, and having his sixth fight in eight months, he was stale and lacked focus. Having handled the old man twice before he saw no risk, but he'd lost a fraction of a second in his reflexes and his timing was off. In round seven Walcott suckered him with one of the sweetest and hardest left hooks ever thrown and in ten seconds Ezzard joined the ranks of the former champions.

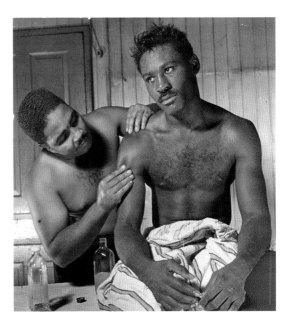

Charles saw this defeat as an aberration and quickly returned with an impressive 11th round stoppage over top contender Rex Layne. Two more wins secured a fourth meeting with Walcott, at Philadelphia's Municipal Stadium on 5 June 1952 – a hard, close encounter with a majority of the ringside press giving it to Charles while the three scoring officials felt Jersey Joe shaded it. Still, an impression of decline was reinforced when he dropped a decision to Layne in his next fight. He bounced back with nine wins, including victory over Layne in their rubber match, but defeats to the heavyweight contender Nino Valdes and the light heavyweight contender Harold Johnson proved he was well past his best and he was not given much chance when he challenged Marciano for the title.

Co-trainer Jimmy Brown gets Ezzard Charles ready to fight. 'The Cincinatti Cobra' moved up to heavyweight after killing young prospect Sam Baroudi in the ring in 1948 and became more reluctant to unleash his power after this tragedy. He was the fifth world heavyweight champion to kill a man in a boxing ring – the others being Fitzsimmons (twice), Willard, Carnera and Baer.

He went heroically close and in the return came within seconds of a stoppage victory but these 23 rounds of pain took everything out of him and were followed by unmitigated decline. Having squandered his money he boxed for another five years and lost 13 of his remaining 23 fights until he finally retired at the age of 38. By 1961 the man who had earned $2 million in his career was broke – his home and car seized by creditors, his phone disconnected. In the mid-1960s he was diagnosed with the crippling illness amyotrophic lateral sclerosis (Lou Gehrig's disease), confined to a wheelchair and spent his final years silent and paralysed, dying in Chicago shortly before his 54th birthday.

Jersey Joe Walcott

World heavyweight champion 1951–52.

'I just got hit. Did I hear the count? I guess I heard "five"… I don't know what it was tonight but he seemed more aggressive than ever.'

Ezzard Charles minutes after losing his title on a seventh round knockout to Walcott.

Height: 6'0
Peak weight: 191–196 lb.
53 wins (32 stoppages),
18 losses, 1 draw
Born: Camden, New Jersey,
31 January 1914
Died: 25 February 1994

Jersey Joe is a kind of patron saint for those looking for inspiration after one failure too many. It took him more than 17 years before he had his first crack at the world title and he was robbed blind. He tried again, and again, and again, and each time fell short. And then finally, after 21 years in the game, at the age of 37-plus, on his fifth try, he pulled it off with a mighty left hook. Without that punch, Jersey Joe would be a minor footnote in the history of the heavyweight division. Instead, he became one of the kings.

He had twice fallen short against Ezzard Charles but the 182 lb. champion was complacent. Meanwhile the ancient 194 lb. Jersey Joe seemed rejuvenated. 'I could have gone on and on,' he said. 'I knew it was going to be my night…' Coming out for the seventh round Charles was behind but there was no urgency in his work. Walcott landed a left to the jaw but Charles came back with a right to the body before sliding away. Jersey Joe walked forward, rolling both gloves as if offering a choice. Ezzard watched the right, retreated and threw a jab, but the old man slipped it and at that moment launched a perfect left hook counter, bringing it up from his hips and landing flush on the side of the jaw. Charles staggered, eyes vacant, mouth open, and flopped forward on his knees. Jersey Joe stepped back and Ezzard collapsed onto this stomach. When referee Buck McTiernan reached 'ten' tears began to drip down Jersey Joe's cheeks as he realised what had happened and then he looked up and a huge grin spread across his face. 'I got him with the left hook,' he said.

Arnold Raymond Cream was born in Camden, New Jersey – probably in January 1914 although there were rumours that he was older. His father died when he was 14 and he had to quit school to work in the Campbell's soup factory. He found his way to Battling Mac's boxing gym and decided he needed a sharper name. So, in honour of his West Indian father, whose favourite boxer was the great Barbados welterweight Joe Walcott, he became Jersey Joe Walcott. He started boxing professionally at middleweight, at the age of 16 picking up four knockout wins, but packed it in to go looking for more reliable sources of income, got married and started a family.

He returned at light heavyweight in 1933 and linked up with Jack Blackburn who invited him to be part of a stable managed by John Roxborough. 'We're gonna take a trip to find out if you're the one,' Blackburn said. Just before departure Walcott was rushed to hospital, suffering from typhoid. It took a year before he could box again and by then Blackburn was training another extremely promising prospect, Joe Louis. He eventually secured the consolation prize of an invitation to serve as Louis's sparring partner for his 1936 fight with Max Schmeling, but was a bit too keen. In a prelude to what would happen against the German, Walcott dropped Louis in the first round and was promptly told to leave.

Jersey Joe Walcott grazes the head of Elmer 'Violent' Ray with a hard right during their 10-round bout at Madison Square Garden on 15 November 1946. Ray won a much-disputed split decision but in the return on 1 March 1947 Jersey Joe gained his revenge – a win that helped secure his first world title shot against Joe Louis.

Jersey Joe Walcott a week after winning the title by defeating Ezzard Charles. The champion addressed his local congregation with tears in his eyes, giving thanks for his good fortune during church services.

Jersey Joe soon slipped into the also-ran role – good enough to beat journeymen and novices but invariably losing to world-rated fighters and the better prospects. With six children to feed he had to take whatever work he could find – usually in the New Jersey shipyards. He took fights at short notice and sometimes came out on the wrong end of disputed decisions. He was knocked out in six rounds by the 256 lb. contender Abe Simon in 1940 after which he managed just three fights in five years. But in 1945 two things changed: first, passable heavyweights were in short supply after the war; second a New Jersey sports club owner and gambler, Felix Bocchicchio, had the foresight to see his potential and offered to take over as manager. At first Jersey Joe declined. 'Fightin' never got me nothin' and all I want now is a steady job so my wife and kids can eat regular,' he said. But Bocchicchio persisted, winning his favour by buying food for the family and having coal delivered to his bin.

Eating and training properly, he pulled off a major upset by outpointing the world-rated Joe Baksi in August 1945 and followed this with a points win over another world-rated boxer, Jimmy Bivins. This set him up for a main event fight at Madison Square Garden against the popular Chicago heavyweight Lee Oma. Jersey Joe dropped him in round one, was dropped in round four, and then boxed his way to a unanimous decision. There were blips later that year when he came out on the wrong end of disputed decisions to Joey Maxim and Elmer Ray but Bocchicchio secured him return fights and he outpointed Maxim, then Ray, then Maxim again. This last win was his 14th out of 16 post-war bouts.

Louis's promoter Mike Jacobs needed to ease him back after 15 months out and Walcott seemed like an easy option. Jacobs played up the fact that Jersey Joe had dropped Louis in sparring 11 years earlier. Walcott, a 10-1 underdog, wasted no time in making nonsense of the odds. The challenger had reached his peak at a time when the rusty champion was declining: quick, elusive, cute and extremely awkward, with serious power in both hands. Then there was also the 'Walcott shuffle' which involved a little shift of the feet and pivot of the body so that Louis had no idea where the next punch was coming from. It was only in the ninth round that the champion came into the fight, attacking relentlessly. After this Walcott fought in retreat but by the end the Bomber's bruised and bleeding face told the true story. It seemed clear that Jersey Joe had won and the crowd erupted into boos when the result was announced: 'the winner and *still* champion…'

Louis granted him a return six months later and it followed the same pattern with Walcott ahead on two of the judges' cards going into round 11. For two minutes Jersey Joe stuck to his plan – jabbing, staying out of range, darting in with hard rights and left hooks. But he came too close and Louis bombarded him with a combination of lefts and rights that drove him into the ropes. Louis planted three jolting jabs, followed by a wounding right to the body. Walcott sagged and Louis drove him back to the ropes and opened up with his biggest guns. Walcott's legs could no longer hold him and he fell, rolling over on his back, forcing himself onto his knees while trying to push himself up but when referee Frank Fullam counted ten his gloves were still on the canvas.

It looked like the end at the age of 34 but when Louis announced his retirement, Walcott found himself in his third title fight in a row, against Ezzard Charles in Chicago on 22 June 1949. The younger, speedier Charles coasted to victory. This time Jersey Joe *knew* it was over and announced his retirement but Bocchicchio persuaded him to reconsider. After five wins he dropped a decision to Rex Layne and, again, it seemed hopeless, but he was offered another shot at Charles – and lost by an even wider margin. And still he held on. Four months later he found himself as a filler opponent for Charles – his fifth for the world title – and this time his left hook turned it all around. He narrowly beat Charles in his first defence nine months later before making his second defence against the 29-year-old, unbeaten Rocky Marciano in Philadelphia on 23 September 1952.

Discarding his usual style of sliding or walking out of the way, Jersey Joe fought aggressively. Forty seconds into the first round a beautifully timed left hook had 'The Rock' down. Gradually Marciano found his range, with his head as well as his fists. Walcott, however, had little trouble staving him off and when pinned, he countered with interest, extracting a heavy price. Rocky used his head to open a nasty gash near Walcott's left eye in round six, but two rounds later he complained he couldn't see properly after astringent solution dripped into his eye. After this Jersey Joe carved him up. Midway through the 11th, he turned aggressor, landing six consecutive blows to the head and face.

The end was unexpected. In the 13th Walcott backed into the ropes, preparing to launch a counter right cross but Rocky beat him to it, firing the sweetest right cross of his career – a punch that landed flush on the jaw, twisting Walcott's head around and distorting his features. Jersey Joe slowly slumped and collapsed on one knee before tipping forward and landing on his face.

Walcott tried again in Chicago on 15 May 1953, but this time, after 72 fights and 23 years as a professional, there was nothing left and he was embarrassed to find himself knocked out in the first round. He tried his hand as a boxing referee – a career that ended when he lost the count and the plot during the only round of the second Muhammad Ali–Sonny Liston fight in 1965. He was elected to the office of Sheriff of Camden County in 1971 and also served as the chairman of the New Jersey State Athletic Commission. He died as a result of diabetes at the age of 80 – in Camden, New Jersey, where he was born.

Rocky Marciano – 'The Brockton Blockbuster'

World heavyweight champion 1952–56.

'The Rock didn't know too much about the boxing book, but it wasn't a book he hit me with. It was a whole library of bone crushers.'

Joe Louis, who had his final fight against Marciano, getting knocked out in eight rounds in 1951.

Height: 5'10½
Peak weight: 185–188 lb.
49 fights, 49 wins
(43 stoppages)
Born: Brockton, Massachusetts,
1 September 1923
Died: 31 August 1969

Rocco Francis Marchegiano was small, short-armed, crude and slow on his feet. He cut if you breathed on him. He routinely resorted to foul tactics, had some lucky breaks and fought in the weak, post-war era – his best opponents old men, small men or both. But there is no doubt he belongs among the gods – not least because he ended his career undefeated: 49 fights, 49 wins, 43 stoppages. No one else can make that claim. And he had far more to boast of: an unrelenting, fearless intensity of a kind never seen before in his division, and on top of this, with his crouching style, he was not as easy to hit as he appeared and he could take a helluva punch when the occasion demanded. But his greatest asset was that pair of extraordinarily heavy hands that never stopped pumping until the resistance was tamed or overwhelmed. As his trainer, Charley Goldman, put it, 'I gotta guy who's short, stoop-shouldered, balding, got two left feet, but God, how he can punch. He aint pretty; he's just devastatin'.'

A 12 lb. baby, he grew up as a chubby but powerful good-time kid. Living in a mixed Italian and Irish neighbourhood he got involved in ethnic street fights and developed a reputation for being the toughest kid around, but his ambitions centred on baseball rather than brawling. He quit school early and took a job as a 'shoot man' in an ice and coal factory before following his father by working in a shoe factory, but an allergy to leather dust forced him to quit. He was once asked if it was the hated memories of this grueling work that inspired him to fight with such intensity. 'Not really,' he replied, explaining his desire was to keep his parents away from that kind of life. 'Even after I was knocked down, or badly cut, and was losing a fight the one thing I thought about most was the hardship my father and mother faced throughout their lives. I well knew that, if I didn't overcome the challenge at hand, both I and they would certainly never get another chance to escape poverty and oblivion.'

Rocky was inducted into the army at 20 – spending eight months in England at the end of the war. While home on furlough in 1946, he heard of a club offering money for fights and so, for $30, he volunteered, only to discover his opponent was a Golden Gloves champion. It was a total mismatch. An overweight chain smoker, Rocky was out of shape and knew nothing about boxing. Trying to land haymakers he took a beating before kneeing Lester in the stomach, earning a disqualification. 'I learned something from this fight,' he told his younger brother. 'If I ever get into the ring again, you can bet I won't be out of condition.' He gave up smoking and drinking, took up training and made it to the finals of an amateur tournament in Portland, Oregon but was beaten again after severely dislocating a knuckle in his left hand. After another loss and another hand injury, Rocky was demobbed from the army and signed up to fight for pay in his

This was the big punch that weakened challenger Ezzard Charles for his eighth round defeat. In this, their return fight, on 17 September 1954 at the age of 33 Charles was six years past his peak but had come close to victory by cutting Marciano's eye and nose.

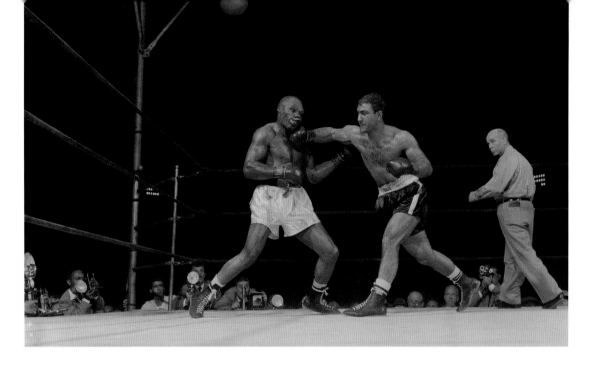

Joe Walcott's face is a misshapen mass under the force of a blow from Rocky Marciano. Rocky was losing on points when he knocked out Jersey Joe with this right to win the heavyweight crown in the thirteenth round on 23 September 1952 in Philadelphia, Pennsylvania. Walcott at 38 (and perhaps older) was the oldest man to hold the world heavyweight title.

hometown of Brockton. Using the name Rocky Mac to keep the plan from his mother, the 190 lb. novice had his first professional fight in May 1947, winning on a three round knockout. After this, he drifted for a year. Living on a government war veterans' allowance, he had a go at professional baseball (throwing his arm out while trying out for the Chicago Cubs farm team) before returning home to resume his amateur boxing career. Three knockout wins were followed by a points loss to an unbeaten amateur called Coley Wallace (who later starred in the title role of the 1953 feature film, *The Joe Louis Story*). Rocky won his final two fights in a pre-Olympic tournament but a severely broken thumb prevented him from going any further and so, in July 1948, with a paltry amateur record of eight wins and four losses – one of those losses occurring *after* he first turned professional – he returned to prize fighting.

It took three more victories before he acquired his first proper trainer, Charlie Goldman – a former top bantamweight who was helped by Rocky's friend Allie Colombo. Goldman took a look at this stocky lad (his reach was 67 inches – shorter than some flyweights), tried him jabbing and moving but saw his talent lay elsewhere. He changed the stance, improved the balance and taught him to cut off the ring, stay close and get the most out of his enormous power. He also instilled a strict training regime that allowed Rocky to throw punches non-stop for as long as it took. Managed by the mob-connected Al Weill and promoted by the straight-as-a-corkscrew James Norris, he fought under the name Marciano (Weill couldn't pronounce Marchegiano, and assumed no one else could). Sometimes weighing as light as 178 lb. he invariably gave away height and weight but his power, fitness and tenacity saw him through. His first real test came in March 1950 when put in at Madison Square Garden with fellow Italian prospect, Roland La Starza, a slick boxer, unbeaten in 37 fights. Rocky dropped Roland in round four but lost a point for low blows in round eight and was outboxed for long

KINGS OF THE RING

stretches. One judge gave it to the brawler by a point, another to the boxer by a point. The referee made it a draw but he had the deciding vote and gave it to the Massachusetts lad, with La Starza claiming he was robbed. Some said Weill's influence secured the result, but, whatever the cause, Rocky remained unbeaten.

He went into his next big fight, against leading contender Rex Layne, as a 9-5 underdog and was well behind after four rounds. But he found his range in the fifth and ended it in the sixth with a right that sheared Layne's front teeth off at the gum. Three and a half months on he was pitted against his childhood hero Joe Louis, who was well into his 38th year and was only fighting because he owed a fortune in taxes. Rocky didn't want the fight because Joe had always been his idol, yet he was really given no choice because he needed the win in order to get a title shot. In his dressing room prior to the bout he said, 'This is the last guy on earth I want to fight.' The 212 lb. veteran bore little relation to the 200 lb. coiled spring of a decade earlier and by the halfway mark it was clear he couldn't discourage the 187 lb. 28-year-old. In round eight Rocky landed several huge hooks to drop Joe and then he moved in to finish it, smashing the old man through the ropes and onto the ring apron to end his career. 'It hurt to bump into him,' Louis said when he'd recovered. 'He hits harder than Max Schmeling. This kid is tough enough to beat anyone.'

Eleven months later Weill felt his prospect was ready to take on a more lively old man, Jersey Joe Walcott. The world champion, at an official 38 years and eight months, may have been past his peak but he was still an extremely formidable fighting force who felt sure of victory. 'If I can't beat this bum, take my name off the record books,' he sneered. It took him just 40 seconds to dump Rocky on his back with a perfect left hook, but to his surprise, the 'bum' sprung up and kept coming. It was an intense battle rather than the one-sided boxing lesson of some subsequent recreations, but the old man was getting the better of it. Rocky was bruised and battered, his vision was impaired by astringent solution in his eyes, he was shaken by unanswered blows in the later rounds and he was behind by three rounds on two judges' cards, and two on the third. And still he kept coming until finally he reached Walcott's jaw with that single, Susie Q right cross in round 13 and there was no need to count. After 43 fights his apprenticeship was over and he had finally reached his goal – heavyweight champion of the world. As always, it was easier second time round. Eight months later, with Walcott well into his fortieth year, Marciano whacked him out in a single round, after which old Jersey Joe said, 'He was a man of courage inside the ring. Outside, he was kind and gentle.'

Next up was his old rival, Roland La Starza, who always maintained he was robbed in their first fight. The 184½ lb. La Starza frustrated the 185 lb. Marciano with slick movement and well-timed combinations. When pinned he would fight hard off the ropes and then slide away. Rocky became frustrated and resorted to his usual array of foul tactics until ordered by Goldman to take a different approach: 'Bang his arms until he brings them down.' Rocky beat Roland's arms and upper body until visible bruises and welts appeared. La Starza could barely lift his gloves above his shoulders after ten rounds. Rocky, now leading on two of the official cards, tore loose in round 11, ripping in huge punches and sending his rival down and through the ropes before the referee waved it off. La Starza had chipped bones in his elbows, ruptured blood vessels in his forearms and required surgery to repair the damage.

Joe Louis goes sprawling backward on the canvas, sent there by a looping right to the chin from Rocky Marciano in the eighth round of their scheduled ten-round bout at Madison Square Garden. At the count of eight he was up again, but Marciano backed the ex-champion up against the ropes, and under furious pounding, Louis went flying through the ropes, giving the Brockton slugger a technical knockout in the eighth round on 26 October 1951. It was the tenth knockdown and second knockout defeat suffered by 'The Brown Bomber', who then retired.

Rocky Marciano's hands are being wrapped by his trainer Charlie Goldman. They remained together throughout Rocky's career but Marciano's relationship with manager Al Weill was more fraught. Rocky later accused him of stealing his money.

Marciano's next two bouts were the toughest and most painful of his career – both at New York's Yankee Stadium against the fading but still formidable Ezzard Charles. In their first fight Charles put in his last great performance, boxing more aggressively than usual to win the early rounds before fading under Rocky's onslaught to lose a close but unanimous decision. By the time of their return the 33-year-old Cincinnati Cobra was clearly on the slide, having lost six out of 20 fights over the previous three years (after a four-year, 25-fight unbeaten run). But the combination of Ezzard's elbows and fists brought Rocky within seconds of losing his title. At the end of round seven the champion learned he had only three minutes because of the severity of the bleeding from his grotesquely severed nose. His final instructions from Goldman were, 'Get him now or you'll bleed to death!' Rocky got him, pouring it on until the old man went down and then out, with just 24 seconds to go. These fights finished Charles as a serious contender and also seemed to take something out of Marciano. It was eight months before he fought again; this time against the chubby, light-fisted but extremely brave Englishman Don Cockell, who was given no chance and had none. But despite absorbing a series of blatantly low blows among a variety of fouls, he fought on until the ninth when the myopic referee stopped the one-sided battering.

For over a year Marciano's leading contender was the big-hitting 6'3, 210 lb. Nino Valdes, but this erratic Cuban was a man Rocky's backers preferred to avoid. He was unbeaten in two years and had won his last 11 fights with several top contenders among his victims, including Charles. The problem was solved by former heavyweight champion Jim Braddock, who was the referee and sole judge when Valdes fought world light heavyweight champion Archie Moore in Las Vegas in May 1955. It was a bloody, dirty bout with the bigger Cuban dominating the early rounds before fading down the stretch. Braddock gave Moore the nod prompting the crowd to boo and toss cushions into the ring and Valdes to complain, 'They don't want me to fight Rocky Marciano. I won the fight, but now I can't fight Marciano.' So Rocky's final outing, at Yankee

Stadium on 21 September 1955, was against Moore, who was either 38 (his mother's view) or 41 (his own).

The Old Mongoose, who had 178 fights and 148 wins to his name, had little trouble outboxing Marciano, using clever feints and neat footwork. He landed a perfectly timed right cross in round two and Marciano went down for the second time in his career. He rose at four from a slow count and was given extra seconds to recover by referee Harry Kessler. 'I took the fight because I was sure I could put Rocky away – and I would have if Kessler hadn't saved him,' said Moore. 'He got up and put his hands on the ropes looking out, glassy-eyed. All I had to do was take two steps, clobber him, and lift the title. But the ref rushed over to him, got in front of me, chased me and got Marciano by the gloves and jerked his arms. Now what do you think that's for? To snap him out of it. He knew it. He knew I knew it.' But Marciano had impressive recovery powers. He swarmed over Moore, absorbing his best shots as he threw his own immense hooks. Moore was dropped in the sixth round and twice in the eighth. Ringside physician Dr Vincent Nardiello asked Archie if he wanted to continue. 'I too am a champion, and I'll go down fighting,' the old man replied. After a sustained battering, ending with a left hook to the heart, a right to the face and a left to the jaw, Archie collapsed in his corner and was counted out 1 minute 19 seconds into round nine. Asked the silly question which of Marciano's punches hurt him most, he replied, 'Man, they all hurt.'

Marciano announced his retirement seven months later, saying he wanted to spend more time with his wife, Barbara, and children. 'No kind of money can make me fight again,' he declared. His decision was prompted by the sour knowledge that Weill was taking an extortionate 45 percent of his purses while skimming an undeclared $10,000 per fight from each promotion. But his final years were not contented. Rocky became obsessively paranoid about money – refusing to deal with banks, insisting on being paid in cash, stashing it in mattresses and doing his own heavy-duty debt collecting. When Ingemar Johansson won the world title in 1959, Marciano was offered the fight and began working towards it but it fell through when Johansson lost his return bout with Floyd Patterson in 1960. So he never fought again, or at least not officially.

In 1969, however, he accepted a $10,000 offer from a Miami impresario for a faux fight with the now-inactive Muhammad Ali, who had been stripped of his world title for his stand on the Vietnam war. There was enough ignorance about information technology at that stage for the public to buy the daft notion that a computer could work out who would win a mythical contest, prompting the idea of a choreographed 'computer fight'. The outcome of this money-spinning farce depended on where you watched it. In most of the American versions, Rocky won by a 13th round knockout, but the British version had Ali winning on cuts. But Rocky never got to see it. On the Sunday evening of 31 August 1969, three weeks before the film's launch, he and his friend Frank Farell took a night flight from Chicago to Des Moines. He wanted to get to Fort Lauderdale to celebrate his 46th birthday the next day, but had also promised Frank's father he would turn up at ringside in Des Moines to watch a young fighter. He decided to make a quick appearance in Des Moines and then fly home. After nearly three hours in the stormy air the pilot radioed Radar Approach Control requesting assistance. Ten minutes later the plane collided with an oak tree in a cornfield. Rocky, Frank and the pilot all died instantly.

Floyd Patterson

World heavyweight champion 1956–59; 1960–62.

'A man of peace whose life has been devoted to beating men with his fists.'
Pulitzer Prize winning sportswriter **Walter 'Red' Smith**, describing Floyd Patterson.

Height: 5'11¾
Peak weight: 182–194 lb
55 wins (40 stoppages),
8 losses, 1 draw
Born: Waco, North Carolina,
4 January 1935

Patterson is often viewed as an after thought among the heavyweight champions but he deserves more respect when you consider his skills and all he achieved – the youngest man to win the world heavyweight title and the first to regain it, the fastest hands in the division's history, one of the finest left hooks and the heart to tangle with far bigger men.

The fight that encapsulates the best of Patterson was his second encounter with Sweden's Ingemar Johansson. A year earlier the heavy-handed European champion not only relieved him of his world title, he demolished him. 'A prize fighter who gets knocked out or is badly outclassed suffers in a way he will never forget,' Floyd said. 'The fighter loses more than his pride in the fight; he loses part of his future… It's easy to do anything in victory. It's in defeat that a man reveals himself.'

After a period of depression it was time to reveal himself. Floyd was not out for revenge, but rather for personal redemption after a year of humiliation. On 20 June 1960 he stepped through the ropes before 31,892 spectators at New York's Polo Grounds with a mixture of terror and determination in his heart. He had bulked up to 190 lb. but he had lost none of his speed. He trained to avoid Ingemar's potent right, boxing aggressively but never recklessly. For four rounds he kept the Swede away with his jab while stepping in with quick combinations. Then, 49 seconds into the fifth, Floyd found his conqueror's chin with a wonderfully fast, well-timed and perfectly placed left hook. Johansson fell but managed to haul himself up at the count of nine. There was no respite. Floyd opened up with both hands until he found that chin with another perfect left hook. Ingemar fell on his back, his leg twitching, and was counted out. Patterson, who gently cradled his victim's head as he came round, had succeeded where Corbett, Fitzsimmons, Jeffries, Dempsey, Schmeling, Louis, Charles and Walcott had failed – in regaining the world heavyweight crown.

Floyd was one of 11 children born into a poor family in Waco, North Carolina. They moved to the Bedford-Stuyvesant district of Brooklyn where his father worked as a sanitation truck driver but the boy struggled to adapt and became an extremely shy, insular and insecure child. Regularly arrested for stealing and playing truant, he was sent to a reform school in upstate New York at the age of ten and four years on went to the nearby Grammercy Gym where he came across the New York trainer Cus D'Amato, who had a mission for transforming the lives of boys like Floyd. He proved to be a phenomenally talented boxer, winning 40 of his 44 amateur bouts. He was extremely quick, with dazzling hand speed and impressive power and developed a style that held the crowd in suspense – he would leap forward with unexpected punches, catching opponents by surprise. His weakness was his chin but to cope with this deficiency D'Amato taught him to fight behind an unusually high, peek-a-boo guard with both gloves cupped in front of his face and plenty of head movement. He won the city and regional Golden Gloves titles before

While in training for the return fight with Ingemar Johansson, Floyd Patterson was attacked on the street by a knifeman. He blocked the stab thrust with his right, sustaining a cut in the process, and knocked the man cold with his left hook, after which he drove to camp, telling his trainer he had hurt his hand in an accident.

representing the United States at middleweight at the Helsinki Olympic Games in 1952, becoming the youngest-ever Olympic boxing gold medallist.

A month later, still only 17, he made his professional debut in New York and won 13 in a row in 20 months. He took a step up in fight number 14, taking on the former world light heavyweight champion Joey Maxim, only to lose to a questionable decision. In his next fight, against a journeyman called Jacques Royer-Crecy, he was dropped for the first of 21 times in his career, reminding Cus of his vulnerability around the whiskers. His defence was tightened even further in preparation for another adjustment in late 1959. Realising they had more to gain at heavyweight with Rocky Marciano's impending retirement, and that Floyd's body would soon struggle to make light heavy, D'Amato decided it was time to take on the big boys. In June 1956 he secured an eliminator for Floyd against the crude, tough and extremely courageous 193¾ lb. Tommy 'Hurricane' Jackson and at the end of 12 rounds Patterson emerged with a split decision victory.

Floyd, who by then had a wife and baby daughter to support, went in as an underdog to face Archie Moore for the newly vacated world title, at Chicago Stadium on 30 November 1956. It was 14 months since Moore had given Marciano hell and he was considered too experienced and tough for this 21-year-old greenhorn. But the fight proved to be surprisingly one-sided as Patterson used his speed to make the veteran miss while picking up the points with rapid-fire combinations. In round five he landed a left hook on Archie's chin that had a delayed effect – Moore took a step forward and then fell on his face, struggling to make it up by the count of nine. Floyd landed another hook and Archie dropped to his haunches, where he was counted out by referee Frank Silora. Patterson had beaten Joe Louis's record to become the youngest-ever world heavyweight champion.

The two best potential challengers were the slick, quick 27-year-old Eddie Machen who was unbeaten in 24 fights and the equally skilled and hard-hitting 27-year-old Zora Folley who had lost just two out of 40 fights and was unbeaten in his last 18. They were both bigger and more seasoned than Floyd and D'Amato was accused of avoiding them. Under pressure, he insisted Folley and Machen fight to determine who was most worthy. They agreed, but when their April 1958 fight ended in a 12-round draw, D'Amato claimed they had eliminated each other. Machen fought the European champion Ingemar Johansson and was surprisingly knocked out in one round while Folley fought British and Commonwealth champion Henry Cooper and lost a questionable decision. D'Amato then committed his man to a defence against the powerful but crude Johansson at Yankee Stadium on 26 June 1959, which ended after Floyd was dropped for the seventh time in the third round. After regaining his title a year later Patterson agreed to a third match with Johansson, which took place at Miami Beach on 13 March 1961. Ingemar knocked Floyd down twice in the first round, but from then on he was handily outboxed before being put away with a left and an overhand right in round six.

His number one challenger, and in fact the world's best since 1958, was the ex-convict Charles 'Sonny' Liston, a mob-backed heavy with an unbeatable air. D'Amato wanted nothing to do with him and even President John F Kennedy tried to persuade Floyd to stay away. 'I'm sorry, Mr President,' he replied. 'The title is not worth anything if the best fighters can't have a shot at it. And Liston deserves a shot.' On 25 September 1962 he stepped into the ring to take on this monster. Giving away 25 lb. and 13 inches in reach

he was overwhelmed in the first round and once again he resorted to the dark glasses, false beard and moustache he always kept in reserve, and once again, after a depressed spell, he steeled himself for a return, held in Las Vegas on 22 July 1967 and again Liston used his size, strength and power to overwhelm Floyd. The former champion was dropped twice before being put down and out by a heavy right and left to the jaw in the first round.

Strangely enough, this defeat had a rejuvenating effect. It was as if there was nothing to fear anymore. and after five wins, including one over Machen, he set himself up to challenge the new world champion, Muhammad Ali, for the world title in Las Vegas on 22 November 1965. Floyd entered the ring with crippling back pain, which seriously affected his ability to resist the younger, faster, bigger world champion who tormented him with his jab, knocked him down and finally stopped him in round 12.

Three months short of his 38th birthday, Floyd fought Ali again. He put up a courageous fight, surprising the 30-year-old Ali with his speed and skills, but in round seven the referee stopped the fight because of severe swelling around Patterson's eyes.

This time he retired for good. In 1976 he adopted an 11-year-old orphan, Tracey Harris, who went on to win two world titles at super bantamweight, but they eventually fell out over a dispute about money and management. 'He listened to the wrong people,' the older Patterson said, crying over the fall-out. 'But he's my son and I love him.' In 1998 Floyd discovered he was suffering from significant memory loss. On hearing this Tracey drove to his father and told him he loved him. Although his memory continues to deteriorate, Floyd remains in good physical health.

Floyd Patterson (*right*) throws a left to the head of Archie Moore in the first round of their title bout on 30 November 1956. Patterson knocked out Moore in the fifth round to become the youngest heavyweight ever to win the title.

Ingemar Johansson

World heavyweight champion 1959–60.

'In these days when so many contenders are half-baked, he fought Patterson coolly and shrewdly with the poise of a genuine professional, nullifying the champion's speed of hand with his own speed of foot, staving him off with a relentless barrier jab, saving the big right hand for the right big moment…'

Martin Kane, in a 1960 *Sports Illustrated* cover profile, making 'Ingo' Sportsman of the Year for 1959.

Height: 6'0¾
Peak weight: 195–200 lb.
26 wins (17 stoppages),
2 losses
Born: Gothenburg, Sweden,
22 September 1932

A likeable Swede with the 'Hammer of Thor' in his right hand, Johansson became an afterthought in the annals of world heavyweight champions – a European fighter who got lucky, just once, against a glass-jawed champion. But the record also shows he was an Olympic silver medallist and an outstanding European champion, with a good jab and a great right. He cleaned up the best of Britain and the Continent before flattening the top-rated American contender and then the world champion. Only one man beat him in a career that spanned more than a decade and, unusually, he ended it on a two-year winning note.

Cus D'Amato, Floyd Patterson's manager and trainer, sighed with relief when he heard top contender Eddie Machen had fallen to Johansson. It meant he could legitimately arrange a defence against the European champion without accusations of taking the soft route. Johansson seemed a lot less dangerous than the other leading options, Zora Folley or, God forbid, Sonny Liston. The difference in training regimes gave D'Amato increased confidence. Johansson trained in the open air at a luxurious resort hotel and spent his evenings at nightclubs, dancing with his pretty 'secretary' (later his fiancée) Birgit Lundren while Patterson trained in a barn, spending his evenings playing poker with his sparring partners. The fact that Ingo stopped training almost a week before the fight – unheard of at the time for boxers – meant Johansson was installed as a 5-1 underdog when meeting Patterson at Yankee Stadium on 26 June 1959.

For two rounds the oddsmakers seemed to have it right. The quicker Patterson was making Johansson miss while scoring freely – so freely that he began to sense he was in for an easy night. Instead of bobbing under Johansson's jab he started blocking it with the right, hoping to fire a left hook counter. In the third round, Floyd moved his right glove from its peek-a-boo position to block a left hook. This was the moment Ingo had planned with trainer Nils Blomberg and his response was well-practised: a short, heavy right cross to the jaw. Dramatically Patterson collapsed and rose on rubbery legs. He was so dazed that he wandered over to the neutral corner, under the impression that he had scored the knockdown. The Swede moved in again, and hammered Patterson time and again. The American was down seven times before referee Ruby Goldstein stopped the massacre two minutes and three seconds into the round.

Seven years earlier, at the 1952 Helsinki Olympics, the 19-year-old with a record of 61 wins and nine defeats delighted his countrymen by making it to the final. Earlier a 17-year-old middleweight caused a sensation by becoming the youngest-ever gold medal

Ingemar Johansson lands his 'Hammer of Thor' – on his way to dropping Floyd Patterson seven times in the third round to become the first post-war European heavyweight to win the world title.

winner and the Swedes hoped Ingemar would emulate Floyd Patterson's achievement. Against huge American Ed Sanders Johansson's strategy was to hold back and then explode with the punch he affectionately called 'Toonder and Lightning' in a surprise attack in the third round. The referee saw it differently and after two warnings disqualified the passive Swede at the end of the second for not trying. The crowd booed Johansson, branding him a coward, and Ingo was refused his silver medal – a decision that most of the Swedish press and the Swedish Olympic Committee backed.

It is hard to imagine a worse end to an amateur career but he tried to erase the memory with a quick professional start, opening with a fourth round knockout in his hometown of Gothenburg on 5 December 1952. After five wins he paused for military service but resumed professional boxing in late 1954. His first big test, after 12 fights, came against British-based Jamaican Joe Bygraves, who had won 30 out of 37. Johansson won on points. Then he travelled to Italy to face European champion Franco Cavicchi whose record boasted just three defeats in 45. Ingemar knocked him out in 13 rounds. In his first title defence he flattened Britain's Henry Cooper with a fifth round right cross. Nine months later Ingemar defended his title against British and Commonwealth champion Joe Erskine, who had just one loss out of 34, again with a round 13 KO. Johansson ran out of credible European opposition after a fourth round knockout of Germany's former European champion Heinz Neuhaus and had to look across the Atlantic. He accepted a home bout with Machen, who was unbeaten in 25 fights. The American arrived confident but had a fright early in the first round when Johansson found his chin with that killer right. Machen rose at the count of nine but Johansson dropped him again, and then finished it with another right. Still the Americans, including D'Amato, dismissed Johansson's win as a lucky fluke.

Ingemar gives an impromptu skipping demonstration in New York prior to beating Floyd Patterson for the world title. Hard training, however, was not one of his strong points.

Johansson followed the same strategy for the world title as he had for the Olympics, and when he emerged victorious his countrymen forgave him. After a year out of the ring he had to fulfil his contractual obligation for a return fight with Patterson and was installed as 8-5 favourite. Ingemar told reporters that next time he hit Patterson with 'old Toonder' the referee might as well count to 1,000. Patterson put his previous humiliating defeat behind him and outboxed the Swede. He withstood Johansson's famed right hand, then produced two quick, sharp masterstrokes. He followed a perfect hook with a right early in the fifth round and sent Johansson down for a nine count. Patterson, cool and calm, stalked his prey and finished it with a hook which arced on to the Swede's jaw. Ingemar was out for several minutes, the twitch of his right leg and the trickle of blood from his mouth suggesting brain trauma. He was still visibly unsteady when escorted out of the ring.

Another return-fight clause brought a third encounter with Patterson in Miami Beach on 13 March 1961. Johansson

sparred at the Fifth Street Gym with 19-year-old Olympic light heavyweight champion Cassius Clay, who danced around him, jabbing him at will while taunting him and forcing Johansson's handlers to call it off after two rounds. Against Patterson, the overweight Johansson was out of shape and despite scoring two first round knockdowns, he was dropped at the end of the round and then knocked out in round six.

Ingemar took a year off before returning to KO Bygraves in seven rounds, then regaining the European crown by knocking out Britain's Dick Richardson in eight rounds. While negotiating to challenge the new world champion, Sonny Liston, he squeezed in a European defence against Britain's Brian London on 21 April 1963. In an uninspired performance he was ahead until, four seconds from the end, London dropped him with a right to the chin. He was saved by the bell although it was said he was the only one in the arena not to know it. The referee's decision in Johansson's favour was booed and Ingemar took this as a signal to retire at the age of 30.

He became a successful business executive while singing and acting on the side and remained close friends with Patterson. In 1982 they completed the New York Marathon together. The same year, a 30-year wrong was righted when the International Olympic Committee finally presented him with the silver medal. In 2002 he was inducted to the International Boxing Hall of Fame but was too ill to attend. It seems likely his boxing career played a role in Ingemar's Alzheimer's disease and dementia. Now in his 70s, his health continues to deteriorate.

A terrific right from Sweden's Ingemar Johansson puts down America's Eddie Machen for the count after 2 minutes 16 seconds of the first round fight.

Sonny Liston

World heavyweight champion 1962–64.

'A boxing match is like a cowboy movie. There's got to be good guys and there's got to be bad guys. And that's what people pay for – to see the bad guys get beat … In the films the good guy always wins, but this is one bad guy who ain't gonna lose.'

Sonny Liston, before his 25 September 1962 fight with Floyd Patterson.

Height: 6'1
peak weight 204–215 lb.
50 wins (39 stoppages),
4 losses
Born: probably in Sand Slough, Arkansas, date unknown.
Died: 30 December 1970

That Sonny Liston was a bad guy is hardly in dispute. He was arrested 19 times and had two spells behind bars. He was a 'leg breaker' – perhaps worse – for the mob. He was alleged to have raped at least two women, probably more. He had problems with alcohol and perhaps drugs. He was sullen, surly, mean, rude, arrogant and nasty. But Sonny was a victim himself: of poverty; of a violent father; of racism and perhaps, at the end, a murder victim too. A more endearing human being occasionally emerged as he adored children and old people. But in his main line of work there was no question: he lived up to the bad guy image he cultivated. As trainer Johnny Tocco put it: 'In the ring, Sonny was a killing machine.' He was an immensely powerful and highly skilled boxer with perhaps the hardest jab in boxing history and right and left hooks that were frightening weapons. With his 84-inch reach he was effective at any range.

Sonny's life was shrouded in mystery – from his birth date to the cause of his death. But nothing excited more heat than the controversy surrounding his second fight with Muhammad Ali in Lewiston, Maine on 25 May 1965, when Ali, the 23-year-old arm puncher, dropped Sonny, the old man with the iron chin, with a single flick of a blow he called his 'anchor punch'. It all happened within 48 seconds, after which the inept referee, Jersey Joe Walcott, lost control. With Ali standing over him, screaming at Sonny to 'get up and fight', Liston got on his knees and collapsed again. Finally, after 17 seconds, he rose to cover up against a renewed assault until Nat Fleischer, *The Ring* editor, called Walcott over to inform him that Liston had been down for over 10 seconds so the fight was over. This was actually incorrect because Ali had not retired to the neutral corner, so the count should not have started. The bamboozled Walcott then called it off. The official result was a first round knockout for Ali, and the official time was changed by the Maine boxing authorities from one minute to two minutes 12 seconds, although even that was wrong (1:48 is probably correct). Forty years later the lines of division remain.

To start with the dive school: as with the first Liston–Ali fight 15 months earlier, there were strong pre-fight rumours the mob had muscled in and that Sonny was going to take a dive. Really, you need look no further than the physical evidence: that little reflex tap was palpably lacking in beef and it landed on the chin of a man who had taken flush hits from proven punchers without budging. Walcott's ineptitude made it more obvious by forcing Sonny to stay down for 17 seconds. He felt compelled to fill time by improvising and boxers don't make good actors. His pathetic play at attempting to rise was followed by a melodramatic collapse, before it all became too absurd and he rose to his feet. The

Close-up portrait of heavyweight Sonny Liston, Las Vegas, Nevada on 25 May 1967. He was officially listed as 35 at the time but some sources claim he was born as early as 1927, making him 40.

only question is who put him up to it? Ali's Nation of Islam backers had the motive of removing the most dangerous obstacle in the way of their man's future legacy, and we know Liston was scared of them. Sonny's criminal backers had an even stronger motive for protecting their investment in Ali's future (they secured a share of his future purses before the first fight). It is also possible Sonny himself took a high odds bet on a first round knockout defeat. These are questions worthy of debate. What is beyond dispute, however, is that Liston took a dive. As his widow, Geraldine, put it: 'I think Sonny gave that second fight away to Ali.'

The counter-argument is that if the first Ali–Liston fight was on the level (as all but the most rabid conspiracy theorists accept) why fix the return? By 1965 Ali was taller and stronger and had the confidence of a world champion who believed he was invincible and had already overcome his ageing adversary. There were fix rumours because this was Liston. Whenever he fought there was talk of subterranean intrigue, but that hardly amounts to evidence. Liston trained hard until November 1964, when Ali was rushed to hospital for a hernia operation. Depressed by the six-month delay, there were claims Sonny started smoking heroin and he definitely had a drinking problem. It is possible that when he climbed into the ring Liston saw the bigger, more manly, version of the youth of the previous year and became despondent. Then he was surprised by the 'anchor punch' which was fast, accurate, thrown with the added propulsion of bouncing off the ropes and with sufficient steam to cause his left foot to lift involuntarily – certainly enough to drop him. Sonny's decision to stay down related to his resigned mental state, his fear of Ali's supposed madness, combined with the fact that his opponent was standing over him. Walcott had not started to count, so Liston was entitled to remain there until Ali retired to the neutral corner. Fleischer's interference and Walcott's confusion ended the fight prematurely – a mess, sure, but not a scandal.

Charles 'Sonny' Liston would give conflicting answers about his birth date but his backers settled on 8 May 1932, which made him a good deal younger than he actually was. Some sources say January 1927; others, 1928, 1929 or 1930. What we can be fairly sure of is that when stopped by Ali in Lewiston he was at least 35, perhaps 38. At the time he already had a grown-up daughter, Eleanor.

Sonny was the 24th of 25 children sired by a bad-tempered tyrant called Tobe Liston. The precise place of his birth is unknown but he was raised in extreme poverty in a shack near Forrest City, eastern Arkansas. As he put it: 'I had nothing but a lot of brothers and sisters, a helpless mother and a father who didn't care about any of us. We grew up with few clothes, no shoes, little to eat. My father worked me hard and whupped me hard.' These 'whuppings' involved the buckle side of the belt and left Sonny with scars down his back and arms. His mother, Helen, eventually abandoned this brute and Sonny joined her in St Louis, Missouri. At first the illiterate teenager tried to go straight. 'I sold coal. I sold ice. I sold wood. I got $15 a week in a chicken market cleaning chickens. On the good days I ate. On the bad ones I told my stomach to forget it. And me and trouble was never apart. If a coloured kid's gonna get by he's gotta learn one thing fast – there ain't nobody going to look after him but him. I learned.' What he learned was 'living by my fists and strength'.

In 1950, he was convicted of armed robbery and larceny and sentenced to five years in the Missouri State Penitentiary. He was introduced to boxing by a prison chaplain and excelled. After being paroled in October 1952 he continued with his life of crime – as a mob enforcer – and also had a brief but successful amateur career. He turned professional in September 1953 under the management of St Louis crime boss John Vitale, knocking out his first opponent in 33 seconds. A year later, after seven wins, he went in with the far more experienced Marty Marshall, began clowning and stuck out his jaw, which Marshall broke with a right cross. Sonny didn't go down or give up; he sucked it up, losing a disputed split decision. Nine months later they fought again, and this time Marshall managed to put him down for a short count, but Liston dropped Marshall four times before stopping him in the sixth round. They fought once more and this time Liston won all 10 rounds.

Sonny was now a much-feared contender but he was a marked man with the St Louis police. On 5 May 1956, when a police officer confronted him, Liston lost his temper, broke the cop's knee, cut his face and took his gun. Liston was in jail for nine months but immediately on release he had another run-in with the cops (dumping one of them head-first in a dustbin), resulting in a 'leave town or else' ultimatum. In Philadelphia a shadowy group headed by the mob bosses Frankie Carbo and Blinky Palermo took over Liston's contract.

Liston's career resumed in January 1958 and he rapidly made a big impression. In his fourth comeback bout he stopped Cuba's Julio Mederos in three rounds in Chicago and a local newspaper reported: 'For all his 204 lb., Liston displayed poise, grace, power, confidence and a head-rocking left jab.' His most serious test came in Miami Beach on 15 April 1959 when he took on the much-feared 6'3, 210 lb. Cleveland Williams. Unbeaten since 1954, Williams's record showed 43 wins in 45 fights with 36 knockouts and he was one of the contenders being avoided by Floyd Patterson. Liston had the edge in all departments – defence, jab, power and chin. He dropped Williams three times in the third round before the referee stopped the fight. Sonny had reached his peak and his backers launched a campaign to secure a title bid. Liston responded with notable knockouts against Nino Valdes, Williams again, and top contender Zora Folley plus a unanimous points win over Eddie Machen. The jabbing and moving skills of the elusive 196 lb. Machen gave some hope to Patterson's people. He was able to frustrate the 211 lb. Liston, who was deducted three points for low blows. Machen later accused Sonny's seconds of blinding him with a chemical dabbed on Liston's gloves.

Heavyweight Sonny Liston jumping rope to his tune of choice, 'Night Train', during training in Philadelphia.

Muhammad Ali pulls away from Sonny Liston's ramrod left jab. Liston was only 6'1 tall but his reach (84 inches) was exceeded only by Primo Carnera's. When he first fought Ali he was probably 35-years-old, had a drinking problem and was undertrained and overweight. After six rounds the two men were even on points (one judge had Liston up by 58-56, the other had Ali up by the same margin and the referee had them 57 each). Liston retired in his corner, claiming a damaged shoulder – a claim subsequently verified by medical evidence.

Sonny's behaviour outside the ring was of more concern. Two more arrests – one for disorderly conduct and resisting arrest and another for impersonating a policeman – prompted his suspension by the boxing authorities. His licence was reinstated three months later but there was concerted opposition to the idea of Liston fighting Patterson – including from the National Association for the Advancement of Coloured People, who felt his reputation would damage the civil rights cause. Patterson felt Liston deserved his chance and agreed to meet in Chicago on 25 September 1962. Liston may have been in his mid-30s and probably past his peak but spectators would never have known it as he overwhelmed the terrified champion in just 125 seconds.

He was angered and saddened to find there was no hero's welcome back in Philadelphia – only a wave of cynicism – so he moved to Denver where Joe Louis's wife, Martha, became his lawyer. He began to spend much of his spare time with Joe, often taking trips to Las Vegas where a fixer was always on hand to supply them with booze, drugs and prostitutes. Liston was alleged to have raped at least one woman at this time.

His return with Patterson in Miami was postponed when Liston suffered a shoulder injury and was rescheduled for Las Vegas on 22 July 1963. Again, any signs of deterioration were disguised by the fact that Sonny simply had Floyd's number. The one round, three-knockdown win was even more impressive than the first title bout.

A week earlier he'd been confronted by the 21-year-old Cassius Clay, who shouted at him across a casino floor: 'Look at that big ugly bear. He can't even shoot craps.' In a hotel later that evening Liston slapped Clay hard in the face. 'Man, what you do that for?' the younger man asked. 'Cause you're too fuckin' fresh,' Liston snarled, and when the future Muhammad Ali walked away, he added, 'I got that punk's heart.' Clay kept up the pressure, driving to Sonny's house in the middle of the night and screaming at him: 'I'm gonna whup you, chump.' They squared up in the street on another occasion and Joe Louis had to separate them. At the weigh-in for their first fight a wild-eyed Clay tapped the champion's forehead while yelling, 'I gotcha now, you big ugly bear! I got your title now. I'm gonna put a whupin' on your butt tonight, you big ugly bear!' Liston, at 218 lb., had not trained hard for what he thought would be a quick win. Over the previous three years he'd fought just three rounds, lasting a total of six minutes and 12 seconds. In this time Clay had fought 83 rounds lasting over 240 minutes. The gap in conditioning as well as age was considerable. Clay, the 7-1 underdog, boxed circles around Liston, making him miss while jabbing and throwing rapid-fire combinations. Sonny kept pressing and landed hard body punches and hard jabs to the head but his loud-mouthed adversary was taking them and firing back, even cutting Liston below the eye. The champion's cornermen applied ointment to the cut – or perhaps applied something to his gloves – as Clay's vision became impaired. Clay managed to see enough through the stinging blur to survive and then completely dominated round six. It was an even fight and the referee had them 57-57 apiece, judge Bernie Lovett made it 58-56 for Liston and judge Gus Jacobson 58-56 for Ali. When the bell rang for round seven, Sonny refused to come out, claiming an injured left shoulder. The cries of 'fix' went up although Liston's shoulder was later found to be severely injured. In |his dressing room Sonny said of Clay: 'That's not the guy I was supposed to fight. That guy could punch!'

Losing once to Ali under questionable circumstances was bad enough but the manner of his defeat in the return made Liston a pariah. He spent a good deal of time drinking and womanising with Joe Louis but eventually opted to return to the thing he knew best – this time abroad. He won several fights by knockout in Sweden before returning to fight in America in 1968. In Las Vegas on 12 December 1969, the 219 lb. Liston outboxed the 199 lb. Leotis Martin, causing such damage to his eyes that he had to retire later with a detached retina. However, a minute into the ninth round, with Liston ahead, the big-hitting Martin unleashed his best-ever right to put Liston down for the count.

Sonny had just one more bout, reducing Chuck Wepner's face to a hideous mask of blood. This was Liston's 15th win in his last 16 bouts and he may have been as old as 43.

He never fought again but on 5 January 1971 his body was discovered in his Las Vegas home. A pathologist said Liston had been dead for at least a week, his death due to lung congestion and heart failure, apparently the result of a heroin overdose. Conspiracy theories centred on the needle marks on Liston's arm when it was well known he had a fear of needles. Some believe mobsters murdered him; others suggested the Nation of Islam was concerned he would demand a stake in Muhammad Ali's purses, now that the world champion had returned to the ring. On the other hand Sonny would have been near impossible to subdue and there was no evidence of a struggle. There had long been rumours that he was a heroin addict and perhaps the truth is no more mundane than that his addiction reached the point where it overcame his needle phobia. As with so many things about Charles 'Sonny' Liston, we'll never know but the debate swirls on and he remains no less compelling in death than he was in life.

Muhammad Ali – 'The Greatest'

World heavyweight champion 1964–67; 1974–78; 1978–79.

'I remember my father was on his dying bed and Ali went to see him. Once Ali walked through that hospital door he sat up real fast with his fists up like he was getting ready to fight. He was so weak but he just said, "Wow!" and that's what Ali does to people. He doesn't even have to open his mouth and he's the main event.'

Howard Bingham, Ali's close friend.

Height: 6'3
Peak weight: 202–216 lb.
56 wins (37 stoppages),
5 losses
Born: Louisville, Kentucky,
17 January 1942

The world heavyweight crown was essentially an American preserve before Muhammad Ali – either watched with admiration by the rest of the world, or, more usually, ignored. Right from the start, as Cassius Clay, this man was the exception. His image was built, layer by layer, over the next two decades and, strangely enough, it continues to grow. More than any preceding or succeeding champion, he is The Man: a flawed fighter and flawed human being but indisputably without equal. He could be kind, cruel, wise, visionary, self-centred and altruistic but these conundrums do nothing to detract from his immense, compelling significance as rule breaker and inspiration. More than previous holders of the crown, Ali was *world* champion – the first global sports star; the most famous face in the world.

If there was a key moment in the long ride that began with the beaming teenager winning the Olympic light heavyweight and has never stopped, it was his victory over George Foreman in a Zaire football stadium on 30 October 1974 – an event seen with disbelief and delight by the 62,000 crowd and globally on millions of TV sets. Never before had one truly great heavyweight champion at the peak of his powers been beaten by another. The Ali who outwitted George in the fight that entered boxing legend as the 'Rumble in the Jungle' was nearly 33 and well past his prime. He chanced upon Foreman's lack of stamina and obsession with finishing the job early – but he also understood his own weaknesses. Realising by the end of round one that he no longer had the legs to dance for 15 rounds in the stifling Kinshasa heat, he improvised, preserving energy by fighting off the ropes. In his corner at the end of the second round, his trainer, Angelo Dundee, berated him for the strategy but Ali replied, 'I know what I'm doing.'

He absorbed Foreman's monstrous punches to his body and head and seemed out on his feet at times. He began leaning back on the ropes, making the 3-1 favourite he called 'The Mummy' punch the night air while taunting him and then firing quick, perfectly timed left-right combinations. Ali dodged or blocked the worst of the punches and by the third round his counter-punching was having an impact. By the fifth, when Ali began to move again, it was clear that the 25-year-old Foreman's punches were more ponderous. He was weakening. Ali was also tiring but his 'rope-a-dope' tactics were preserving energy. He had spent weeks acclimatising in the African heat during a delay for Foreman to recover from a cut sustained in training. George, in contrast, had holed up in the air-conditioned Hilton hotel, and now the heat and his efforts were getting to

Muhammad Ali stopping Oscar Bonavena in the fifteenth and final round in New York on 12 December 1970 – his second comeback fight after three and a half years of enforced inaction as a result of his principled stand on the Vietnam war. Ali forced a stoppage later in the round after dropping the Argentinian three times.

Cassius Clay watches himself in a mirror at his training gym as he prepares for a title fight with champion Sonny Liston on 20 February 1964. He took the world title when Liston retired in his corner at the end of the sixth round, claiming a shoulder injury.

him. He was pushing his blows while Ali's were sharp and stinging. The end, late in the eighth round, was astonishing. Ali moved quickly off the ropes and fired four hard punches – the last of them a cracking right cross plumb on Foreman's jaw. George actually made it back to his feet by the count of nine – and should either have been allowed to continue or stopped on a technical knockout. But the referee, Zach Clayton, waved his arms and the fight was over; Ali had regained the world heavyweight title.

Legend has it that the 12-year-old Cassius Marcellus Clay got his start in boxing after his new bicycle was stolen and he turned in tears to local policeman Joe Martin, wanting to beat up the thief. He advised Clay to box and three weeks later he won his amateur debut. Growing up in Louisville, Kentucky, he inherited his father's flamboyance and flair and his mother's dedication and warmth. Preferring boxing to education he began to shine. After a few senior defeats he blossomed in 1960, winning his second American light heavyweight title, before making the US team for the Rome Olympics where he won the gold medal on speed and reflexes. His amateur record was 134 wins and seven defeats. He turned professional under the prudent management of the 11 white grandees of the Louisville Sponsoring Group. Weighing 186 lb,, he made his debut on 29 October 1960 with a six-round unanimous decision over the Virginia police chief Tunney Hunsaker.

Former world champions Sugar Ray Robinson and Archie Moore declined to be his trainer, and he settled for Angelo Dundee and his Fifth Street Gym in Miami – a partnership that lasted throughout his career. Clay's style was his own – hands low, leaning back from punches, relying on reflexes, neglecting body punching, dancing around opponents – and all Dundee did was suggest minor adjustments.

He earned his nickname 'The Louisville Lip' through his exuberant self-promotion when journalists and photographers were around and was always good for a witty quote. From his 10th fight he began predicting the round in which he would knock out his opponent, starting with a fourth round stoppage of Sonny Banks, who knocked him down in the first round. After 15 fights and two years as a professional, 20-year-old Clay took on Archie Moore, who was having his 219th bout. He introduced his first lines of doggerel: 'Archie's been living off the fat of the land; I'm here to give him his pension plan. When you come to the fight, don't block the aisle and don't block the door. You will go home after round four.' He was as good as his word.

In fights with American Doug Jones and British and Commonwealth champion Henry Cooper his poetic predictions did not always come true. Moore fought past the fourth round demise predicted for him and Clay struggled his way to a disputed points win, while Cooper landed a perfect left hook to the chin to put Clay down hard. He rose at three, still groggy, and was saved by the bell. Smelling salts and ice down his trunks revived Clay enough to carve up the Londoner before the referee called a halt.

Clay wanted Sonny Liston but his managerial syndicate were sceptical. After Cooper flooring him and Jones almost beating him, what chance could he have against the invincible Liston? With what became his standard refrain – 'I must be the greatest!' – Clay taunted Sonny. But behind all this Clay was going through a profound transition that damaged his relationships with his father, his wife and such boxing greats as Joe Louis. In 1961 he attended a meeting of the Nation of Islam which encouraged black pride and self-reliance. Charismatic leader Malcolm X cultivated Clay, who had seen the harsh edge of racism growing up in the segregated American South. He became a fully-fledged member of the Nation under the new name of Muhammad Ali. Soon after he married pretty non-Muslim cocktail waitress Sonji Roi but the Nation opposed this union and, after considerable domestic tension, Ali divorced her.

His relationship with the white public deteriorated dramatically and by the time of the second Liston fight, which he entered as a 9-5 underdog, he was cast in the villain's role because of his links with the 'Black Muslims' and his attitude to race relations. Ali grew half an inch in height between the two Liston fights while adding inches to his biceps, shoulders and thighs. The boy had become a man – stronger, more powerful, more resilient. He was reaching his brilliant peak but it was a while before the public could appreciate this. Six months after beating Liston, he toyed with Floyd Patterson, the man he called 'The Rabbit', torturing him for his condemnation of the the Nation of Islam. But Patterson was handicapped by severe back troubles and Ali was castigated for behaving like 'a little boy pulling off the wings of a butterfly' as one reporter put it. The press, which had once adored him, now derided him.

In 1964 Ali failed a mental aptitude test for army service. Two years later, however, as the Vietnam war escalated, the standards were changed, making Ali eligible. Inundated with press queries about his attitude to the war, Ali responded: 'Man, I ain't got no quarrel with them Vietcong.' He was branded a draft dodger, reinforcing his image as a hate figure for white America while enhancing his status with much of black America and also making him a hero with the rapidly growing anti-war movement. He was then placed under surveillance by the FBI and Army Intelligence.

Suddenly it became difficult to get fights in America so he went on tour. He secured a points win in Toronto over the Canadian George Chuvalo and tore apart Cooper in six rounds of a London rematch. Still in Britain, he disposed of Englishman Brian London in three rounds but in Germany the southpaw European champion Karl Mildenberger proved far trickier, lasting until the twelfth round.

Ali returned to America for the most dazzling display of his career – a three round demolition of Cleveland 'The Big Cat' Williams in Houston in November 1966. He was dazzling – his speed, anticipation, reflexes, timing and power at their absolute peak. Without taking a punch he dropped Williams three times in the second round and once in the third before the fight was stopped. 'That night he was the most devastating fighter who ever lived,' said ABC commentator Howard Cossell.

Twelve weeks later he took on Ernie Terrell, a grab-and-jab boxer who was unbeaten in five years. Ali called him, 'Uncle Tom' and promised to torture him for calling him by his old name Cassius Clay. That is precisely what he did. Terrell claimed Ali thumbed him three times in the eye and then rubbed the eye across the ropes, allegations denied by Ali. By the middle of the fight Terrell was taking a horrible beating, but Ali refused to end it, instead taunting him: 'What's my name, Uncle Tom? What's my name?' He was out to hurt and humiliate Terrell and he succeeded, for 15 vicious rounds.

His final defence took place at Madison Square Garden on 22 March 1967 when he fought the 34-year-old Zora Folley, another once-outstanding heavyweight who was stopped by a short right in round seven. Folley was full of praise for his tormentor saying boxing greats such as Dempsey, Tunney, Louis and Marciano could not have stayed with the speed, guile and power of Ali. 'There's no way to train yourself for what he does.' Ali remained the legitimate world champion until 3 February 1970 when he formally announced he would never again enter the ring as a professional boxer – a response to a slew of unconscionable official decisions. The World Boxing Association stripped him of his world title and banned him from fighting in the US for declaring himself a conscientious objector and the control bodies of 50 states followed suit. Then a Texas court sentenced him to five years in jail over his refusal of military service.

He delivered over 200 anti-war speeches, married 17-year-old Belinda Boyd and had numerous extra-marital liaisons. Then, when he expressed his desire to fight again, the Nation of Islam suspended him, calling him Cassius Clay again, but after a few months he was grudgingly allowed back. Eventually, the US Supreme Court found in Ali's favour and the state of Georgia granted him a boxing licence.

After three years and eight months away he stopped in quick succession Jerry Quarry and Argentinian Oscar Bonavena. His next outing – dubbed the Fight of the Century – was against world champion Joe Frazier at Madison Square Garden on 8 March 1971, watched live by 1.3 million via closed circuit theatre television. Ali no longer had the legs to dance, which meant he had to trade punches or try to tie 'Smokin' Joe' up by placing his glove behind the neck or cover up on the ropes. Frazier, who dropped Ali with a left hook in fifteenth round, deserved his unanimous points win.

Ali did not always train hard and was sometimes overweight but he was fighting regularly and developing the new style of boxing in spurts and then retreating to the ropes or tying his opponents up. He worked his way through contenders and near-contenders, picking up 10 wins in 18 months. He had his jaw broken by Ken Norton who outpointed him over twelve rounds but returned to his peak weight of 212 lb. to gain revenge over Norton with a disputed split decision and then Frazier on a clear-cut unanimous decision.

Then came full redemption and absolution through the 'Rumble in the Jungle' in Zaire. America's retreat in Vietnam vindicated Ali's anti-war stand and the immense courage shown in his wars with Frazier, Norton and Foreman transformed him from symbol of resistance to iconic celebrity. Ten defences in five countries helped the global spread of Ali's fame. The first saw him knocked down for the fourth time in his career, this time by journeyman contender Chuck Wepner, who inspired Sylvester Stallone's film character, Rocky. Wepner was stopped in the fifteenth round.

Muhammad Ali sits on the podium with Nation of Islam leader Elijah Muhammad while attending the national meeting of the Nation of Islam at the International Amphitheatre in Chicago on 28 August 1966. When Malcolm X split with the Nation, Ali snubbed him and followed Elijah Muhammad.

Then came the more formidable ex-con Ron Lyle, who was leading on points until Ali found the punches to stop him in the 11th. In Kuala Lumpur, Malaysia, seven weeks on he fought a return with European champion Joe Bugner, winning an easy 15 round decision. Ali's next fight took more out of him than all the previous 50. Assuming he would handle his rubber match against Joe Frazier with ease he spent his time carousing with his new mistress Veronica Porche and arrived for his 1 October 1975 date in Manila overweight and under-prepared but did not count on the intensity of Frazier's hatred, which had driven him to train with fevered intensity. Ali controlled the early rounds, but Smokin' Joe came into it from the fifth, throwing heavy hooks and forcing the tiring champion to stay on the ropes. With a supreme effort, Ali came back to close Frazier's left eye and almost close the right. Smokin' Joe's trainer Eddie Futch would not allow him out for the final round and when Ali realised he'd won, he collapsed. He said it was the closest thing to death he had known and acknowledged, 'Frazier quit just before I did.'

Belgium's Jean-Pierre Coopman was dispatched in five. Next, coming in at a fat 230 lb. he won a dubious decision over Jimmy Young and then stopped Britain's Richard Dunne in five rounds. He was followed by Ken Norton again, in New York on 28 September 1976. Although Ali got into reasonable shape at 221 lb. he could only compete in bursts. He clinched, used the ropes, leaned and wore Norton down. Coming on strong in the fifteenth and final round he took an unjust decision.

Nine months later he outpointed European champion Alfredo Evangelista, and followed this by marrying his mistress, Veronica Porche, before taking on perhaps the hardest-hitting boxer of all time, Ernie Shavers, on 29 September 1977. Watched by 70 million American TV viewers Shavers gave this tired, 225 lb. version of Ali hell, rocking

Following pages: Muhammad Ali lands a right uppercut during the sixth round of his second bout with Floyd Patterson, at Madison Square Garden on 20 September 1972. He stopped Patterson in round seven (because of swelling around the former champion's eyes). In this period Ali beat several other top men including Jerry Quarry and world light heavyweight champion Bob Foster.

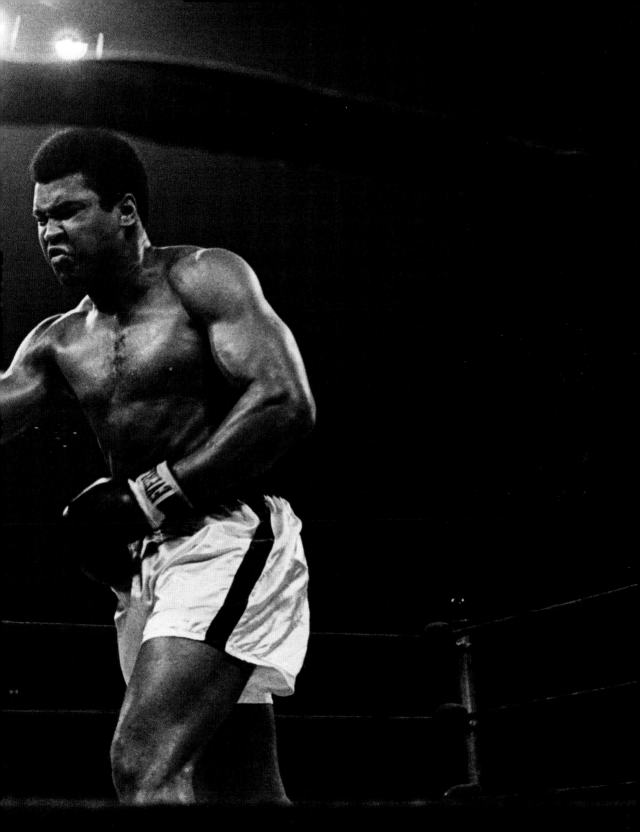

him several times with punches to the head and damaging his kidneys. After 15 rounds Ali could barely stand but won a close unanimous decision that some disputed. The man once known for his ability to avoid punches was now renowned for his ability to take punishment. He rejected the advice of his physician, Dr Ferdie Pacheco, among others, to retire and he decided to take just 'easy' fights starting on 15 February 1978 with the 1976 Olympic light heavyweight champion Leon Spinks, whose professional record showed six wins and a draw. Ali hardly trained but the challenger was in superb nick and poured it on. At 36, Ali wasn't quick enough to get out of the way or fit enough to punch consistently, and was clearly beaten even though the decision was split. Embarrassed to lose to such an inept novice Ali decided to do it again on 15 September

that year and was fortunate that Spinks's life had gone out of control. Hampered by drugs, alcohol, only 10 days of training and a thoroughly disorganised corner Spinks was facing an Ali who had trained hard. In the 15th round 60,000 fans watched him become the first man to win the world heavyweight title three times. Nine months later and at least nine fights too late he formally announced his retirement and it seemed that at last his career was over. He was used as an ambassador at large by President Jimmy Carter, although sometimes with distressing results, as when unsuccessfully lobbying African states to boycott the Moscow Olympics. Meanwhile, Muhammad and Veronica moved into a new Los Angeles mansion with their two daughters while the rest of his nine children – seven girls and two boys – lived with their various mothers. Ali continued his free-spending ways having spent, lost or given away most of the tens of millions of dollars he had earned. More had been 'borrowed' or pilfered by members of his huge entourage. Money was not the key factor in his comeback decision – he missed the thrill and adulation – and took on the new world champion Larry Holmes in Las Vegas

Muhammad Ali glares at George Foreman during their fight at the Kinshasa Stadium on 20 May 1974. Using what he later called his 'rope-a-dope' tactics (by fighting off the ropes) he tired Foreman out and stopped him in the eighth round.

on 2 October 1980, two months short of his 39th birthday. To get his professional licence back the Nevada State Athletic Commission insisted on renal and neurological examinations. It was granted despite Ali speaking more softly and slowly when tired, sometimes fluffing his consonants and evidence of a slight deterioration in coordination.

Holmes, a former Ali sparring partner, was already one of the great champions at the peak of his powers. He might have given hell to the 1967 version of Ali, but 13 years later there was no hope. Ali started training at 252 lb. and became determined to make a good physical impression by dying his hair black and taking a drug to treat an incorrect diagnosis of a hypothyroid condition which made him lose weight and energy.

Holmes handed out a horribly one-sided beating, winning every second of every round, with Ali's head and kidneys taking a terrible battering. From round seven Holmes began to ease off, concerned about the damage he was doing to his former employer.

At the end of round 10 Angelo Dundee threw in the towel for Ali.

In Ali's final fight 13 months later, against Trevor Berbick in Nassau, Bahamas, he took another beating, although he survived the ten round distance. When it was over he announced: 'Father time has caught up with me. I'm finished. I've got to face the facts. We all lose sometimes. We all grow old.'

A decade later he was diagnosed with Parkinson's disease – in his case a condition possibly caused and probably exacerbated by the punches to his head. When he took his medication some of the symptoms – slurred speech and tiredness – were eased and the diagnosis showed he was not suffering from punch-drunkenness and that his cognitive powers were unaffected. Adjusting to this new reality, and also to the loss of his profession and all that went with it, wasn't easy. He continued to be exploited by con men and chancers for his money and his name; his marriage to Veronica ended and much of the entourage evaporated. But then, it began to turn around.

In 1986 he married his fourth wife, Lonnie, who had known him since 1962 when she was six. They were already close friends and have been together ever since. He had long since moved away from the Nation of Islam to become a follower of Sunni Islam. Close friends became even closer and the visitors returned – entertained by his magic tricks, practical jokes and self-deprecating wit. His business affairs were brought under tight control, including the franchising of his name, and he began to find a wider role, travelling the world on peace and goodwill missions. His health also stabilised. Friends say Ali's mind is 100 percent and his motor function improves when he gets his rest.

He moved back into the American public spotlight from the 1990s – partly through a series of movies, television programmes and a spate of books. The Oscar-winning documentary on the Foreman fight, *When We Were Kings*, followed by the biopic *Ali*, introduced him to a younger generation. He gave his name to the Ali Act, in a bid to reform the administration of boxing in America, and remained involved on the fringes while regularly turning out at ringside to watch his daughter, Laila, who became the world's most prominent female boxer. He proudly lit the torch at the Atlanta Olympics, and at a fundraiser after the terror attack in New York on 11 September 2001 he made a poignant speech about Islam being a peaceful faith, opposed to 'killing and murder and terrorism'.

A quarter of a century after his retirement his contribution as a boxer is clear. He undoubtedly changed his sport forever – through his major stylistic influence within the ring and, far more important, through enabling other boxers and other sports stars to find their own voices. And now his wider image is also falling into place. In addition to all the other elements – his looks, flamboyance, sense of humour, doggerel, politics, religion, courage – there was an epic quality to his quest.

Unexpected victory was followed by a stand of high principle, intense adversity, exile, defeat and a long and bumpy road back to vindication. The denouement involved a slide downwards and then, finally, phoenix-like, a rebirth, ending in a different kind of triumph. Nothing before or since can compare.

Joe Frazier – 'Smokin' Joe'

World heavyweight champion 1970–73

'Man, I hit him with punches that'd bring down the walls of a city! Lordy, lordy, he's great! … Joe Frazier is one helluva man, and God bless him.'
Muhammad Ali after the 'Thrilla in Manila' in the Philippines on 1 October 1975.

Height: 5'11½
Peak weight: 203–209 lb.
32 wins (27 stoppages),
4 losses, 1 draw
Born: Beaufort, South Carolina,
12 January 1944

It was both triumph and tragedy for Joe Frazier that his career – his life even – was shaped and defined by Muhammad Ali's. More than any other champion, what we know and think about Smokin' Joe is framed by what we know and think about his premier opponent. They pitted their skills, strength and wills against each other three times, totalling some of the best 41 rounds in boxing history. For Ali, who won two out of three, Joe was one of several great opponents he faced – huge fights but once they were over he moved on. For Frazier, it was different. He was consumed by hatred for Ali and even today, he still cannot let go. Which is a shame because even without Ali he would have been one of the better heavyweight kings: a relentless, heavy-handed, bobbing, weaving threshing machine with one of the hardest hooks in heavyweight history.

The build-up to the 8 March 1971 'Fight of the Century' turned Frazier from Ali respecter to Ali hater. He knew he needed this fight to gain respect as champion and did his best to facilitate it, backing Ali's right to box and expressing respect for his stand on army service. But Ali reverted to type – promoting himself, his cause and the event by belittling his opponent. Frazier, the supposedly devout Baptist who had been prepared to serve in Vietnam but failed the aptitude test, was cast as yet another Uncle Tom. Then it got personal. 'Joe Frazier is too ugly to be champ,' Ali mocked. 'Joe Frazier is too dumb to be champ. The heavyweight champion should be smart and pretty like me.' He even derided Joe's ability as lead singer in his band The Knockouts. By the time of the fight Frazier, having seen his children teased at school as a result of Ali's campaign, was seething. The only comeback he could offer outside the ring was to call Ali, 'Clay': inside the ropes it was a different matter.

Four and a half months after Muhammad Ali's first comeback fight his physician Dr Ferdie Pacheco admitted: 'Ali's body has not yet achieved the hardness of the pre-exile years.' His reflexes and speed had slowed and he could no longer dance all night. Frazier had reached his peak and was in the finest shape of his life and all that hatred was directed into a focussed desire for victory at any cost. The first five rounds were Ali's. He went all out to weaken Frazier but he found that his bobbing and weaving adversary was harder to hit with the jab than expected. Smokin' Joe took plenty in the face but he was able to get past it and was beginning to hurt Ali's body. Ali kept landing quick punches to the face, but as the battle progressed Frazier had more success in getting inside while Ali was finding he needed to spend more time on the ropes. Joe was dictating the pattern of the fight and was even finding time to talk back to the talker.

Before the fight he commented, 'Sooner or later Ali's got to stop and fight; then I got

Joe Frazier in his prime in 1971. 'Smokin' Joe' as he was called because of his relentless, attacking style, won partial recognition in 1968 but it was only on beating Ali three years later that he was universally accepted as world champion. After that he froze the title for two years, avoiding a return with Ali – instead getting demolished by George Foreman.

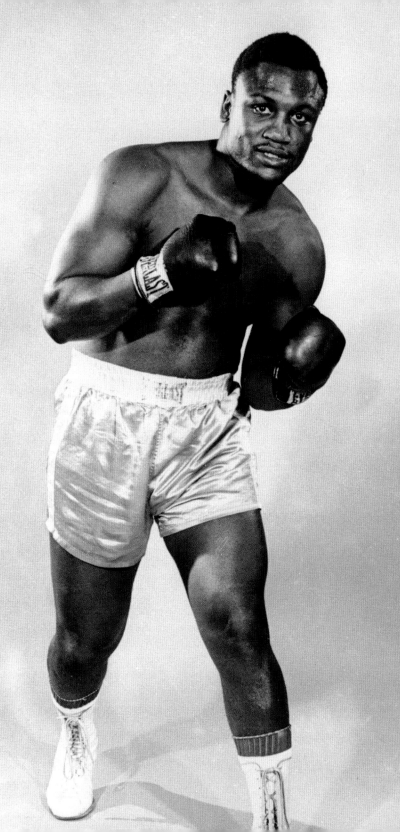

Joe Frazier knocks down Ali with a left hook in the fifteenth round to seal a victory over 'The Greatest' in their 'Fight of the Century' at New York's Madison Square Garden on 8 March 1971. Frazier won a unanimous points decision.

him.' That moment arrived in the sixth. As Joe put it, 'The truth is he couldn't move. His body was worn down. Everywhere he went, I was there. They talk about how fast he is, but he couldn't stay outta my way. I could've run past him and then come back and caught him goin' the other way if I'd wanted to. Everything I did, I was at ease, but he was strainin', because his thing is movin'. Mine is movin' *in*, and I know *how* to move in.' In round 10 there was controversy when referee Arthur Mercante accidentally caught Frazier in the eye with his little finger when trying to break a clinch. 'Goddamn, fuck man – keep your hands off me,' said Joe, adding as he walked to his corner 'Damn, I got two men beating up on me.' One of Joe's trainers, Eddie Futch, the chief strategist, had spotted that when Ali threw a right uppercut he failed to cover the right side of his face with his left glove, leaving him open, and in round 11 Frazier landed a crunching hook on the jaw. Ali's eyes glazed, his knees buckled and his jaw swelled, but his heart and brain were not to be doubted. He managed to con Joe by giving a clowning impression of a dazed boxer. Anticipating a trap, Frazier held off and Ali survived.

This allowed Ali back in the 12th but the effort meant he spent the 13th on the ropes again and in the fourteenth Joe managed a smile through his swollen lips and eyes, clearly enjoying the action. In round 15 an exhausted Ali tried a right uppercut and Frazier threw a killer left hook from his hips with all his weight behind it. It crunched into the side of Ali's open jaw and the former champion fell flat on his back, his legs in the air. Yet to the astonishment of the hitter, the referee and everyone, he was up at the count of three and by this stage Joe, his face a lumpy mess of bruises and nicks, his chest heaving, was so tired that he could not summon up the effort to finish him. Ali made it to the final bell but Frazier deservedly won the unanimous decision.

Ali went to hospital to get his jaw X-rayed and left immediately. Frazier spent over a week in hospital with high blood pressure and kidney problems but it later emerged his kidney complaint predated the fight. After this he seemed reluctant to fight Ali again and only came around to the idea after losing his world title. Their second fight was set for 28 January 1974 and this time Joe went over the edge. At a pre-fight ABC TV studio event, Ali playfully wrestled Frazier but Joe took it seriously and the men had to be pulled apart. Between the two encounters in the ring the 212 lb. Ali had been through 13 fights and more than 20 exhibitions and at the age of 32 was in better shape than he had been at 29. Thirty-year-old, 209 lb. Frazier had fought just four times in this period and had not reached the physical perfection of their first fight. Ali danced far more and kept clear of the ropes, controlling the action with his jab and throwing flurries of punches to impress the judges. By then Ali had refined his tactic of grabbing opponents behind the head and smothering them when they came too close and he used this to frustrate Frazier. Joe was fortunate not to get stopped late in the second round when Ali landed a perfectly timed right cross. He wobbled and Ali moved in to finish him but the referee, Tony Perez, thought he heard the bell and stepped in. It took 20 seconds before he realised his mistake and allowed the action to resume – by then Joe had recovered. He came back and hurt the older man but this time it was Ali who sprinted down the final stretch to win a unanimous decision.

Twenty months passed before their third match in the Philippines with Frazier in the position of world title challenger. This made him despise and hate Ali even more – a feeling exacerbated by Ali's pre-fight campaign of making Frazier look stupid. Labelling Joe 'the gorilla' pushed him to go into hiding to drive his body into the best shape possible. Ali played around with his mistress and stayed away from the gym, saying: Frazier was 'nothing but a punching bag'. The early rounds seemed to support this conclusion but Frazier kept coming and by the fifth was starting to catch Ali with heavy hooks to the head and body. The unfit world champion was already tiring in the stifling Manila heat and Joe pounded Ali for five brutal rounds. At the end of the tenth Ali muttered: 'I think this is what dying is like.' It swung again decisively in round 12. Ali wobbled Frazier, whose eyes and cheeks began to swell alarmingly. In the 13th Ali stepped it up another notch, knocking Frazier's mouthpiece out and by the 14th he had battered the stumbling, one-eyed Joe to a point where only pride was keeping the former champion upright. Despite Joe's pleadings to be allowed to fight on, head trainer Futch refused to allow him out for the final round. He placed a restraining hand on Joe's shoulder and told him, 'It's all over. No one will ever forget what you did here today.'

Joseph William Frazier was born into poverty in rural South Carolina in 1944, the 11th of 12 children of Rubin and Dolly Frazier. Rubin was a sharecropper, woodcutter and junk salesman who ran a moonshine still and grew what Joe thinks might have been marijuana. Joe became interested in boxing at nine and made his own punchbag which he pounded incessantly. He was tough and learned early how to look after himself. He recalls, 'I grew up fast – real fast. At 14, I had the mind of a 22-year-old.' The only thing that scared him was the dark.

He moved to New York at 15 to live with an older brother, Tommy, and earned his keep by stealing cars and selling them to a scrapdealer's yard. By 16 he was married with a son, Marvis, who later became a heavyweight contender himself. At 17 his first daughter Jacqui was born and she also became a boxer, as well as a lawyer. Moving to Philadelphia, Joe found work in a slaughterhouse where he pounded the sides of beef in the refrigerator room – something else borrowed from reality by Sylvester Stallone for his first *Rocky* film. Weighing a fat 220 lb. he joined the local police gym in 1961 to get in shape and was soon fighting in amateur competitions. He lost in the 1964 Olympic trials to Buster Mathis, but when Buster suffered a knuckle injury, Joe replaced him in Tokyo. Ignoring a broken thumb he returned home with the Olympic heavyweight gold medal to end his amateur career with a record of 38 wins in 40 fights.

He had cataracts in his left eye but despite this impediment turned professional under the management of a group of Philadelphia businessmen called Cloverlay Inc. making his debut with a one round knockout over Woody Goss on 16 August 1965. This 197 lb. 21-year-old, made rapid progress, although it was not always easy. He was knocked down against Mike Bruce and Oscar Bonavena (who put him down twice and held him to a split decision) but remained unbeaten, with stoppage wins over three contenders – Eddie Machen, Doug Jones and George Chuvalo. On 4 March 1968 he knocked out his old amateur rival Mathis to gain recognition in six states as world champion.

Joe had refused to take part in a World Boxing Association elimination tournament, eventually won by Jimmy Ellis, a title he defended only once – a questionable points win over Floyd Patterson – after which he was out of action for 17 months. It was finally agreed that Frazier would fight Ellis at Madison Square Garden on 16 February 1970 for the undisputed title. Frazier was far stronger than Ellis and overwhelmed him with his power and pressure, pounding him to the canvas at the end of the fourth round. Ellis did not come out for the fifth. Joe followed this with a second round knockout over the world light heavyweight champion, Bob Foster, although it was only after beating Ali four months later that the world recognised him as the real world heavyweight champion.

But the 'Fight of the Century' seemed to hurt him more than his victim – mentally as well as physically. Whereas Ali got on with the business of fighting, Frazier tried an unsuccessful European tour with The Knockouts and grew fat. When he finally got around to defending his title again, he chose two of the weakest challengers in heavyweight history. He stopped Terry Daniels, who did not belong in the world's top 50, in four rounds, then beat up the fat Ron Stander, who was not in the top 20. He waited eight months before finally defending his title in Kingston, Jamaica, on 22 January 1973 against a man considered a decent opponent, the unbeaten, 24-year-old George Foreman. Frazier, 3-1 favourite, did not expect too much trouble from this untested former street thug, and came in at a soft 214 lb. But the big Texan stood his ground when Joe came forward, winging his huge wide hooks and uppercuts – none particularly fast but all extremely heavy. Halfway through the first round one of those massive rights connected with Joe's jaw and down he went. He got up, tried again, and this time George used a series of clubbing rights to put him down. Joe rose quickly but it was clear he was dazed and just before the bell rang to end the round Foreman dropped Frazier a third time. Joe charged out for the second round and got in with a stiff left hook to the chin, but it seemed Foreman could take it as well as dish it out. He replied with a left-right combination to the chin and Joe went down again. He leapt up at the count of two and George put him down again with a pair of left hooks. Once more Frazier made it to his feet and Foreman poured it on, lifting him off his feet with an uppercut. Frazier went down for the sixth time, but when he rose he reeled so much around the ring that referee Arthur Mercante finally stopped it.

The chastened ex-champion chose London to begin his return journey – against the relatively light punching European champion Joe Bugner. It was surprisingly competitive with Frazier winning on points. After losing his return with Ali he went over old ground again – stopping Quarry in five rounds and Ellis in nine before the third and most draining of his wars with Ali. He then opted for a chance to avenge his defeat against Foreman on 15 June 1976. He shaved his head and beefed up to 224 lb. in a bid to match Big George's strength but the pattern was basically the same – although it took three rounds longer. After dominating the first four rounds Foreman, at equal weight, battered Frazier to the canvas in the fifth. After a second, more brutal knockdown – the 11th of Frazier's career – the fight was stopped. He was out of the ring for six years but returned at 37 for his swansong fight with tough Jumbo Cummings and was lucky to escape with a draw.

He looked after his money better than most previous champions and had some success as a trainer. But his health deteriorated – diabetes, a life-threatening infection to his big toe and the telltale signs of slurred speech. He seldom gave the impression of being a happy man. He had several blows to his reputation over the years. In 1998 he was acquitted of a drink-driving allegation. In 2004 he was arrested for allegedly assaulting girlfriend Sherri Gibson who had facial injuries. Joe did not deny hitting her but charges were dropped when Gibson decided not to cooperate with the police. Perhaps the most serious damage has come from the way he has expressed his feelings about Ali. In his autobiography, *Smokin' Joe*, he said he had no pity for Ali's health problems and would love to open the graveyard and bury his rival. When Ali lit the Atlanta Olympic flame, Joe muttered he would like to have 'pushed him in'. Ali told the *New York Times* he was sorry about the way he had treated Joe but Frazier was not ready to draw a line under the bad feelings. 'He didn't apologise to me – he apologised to the paper,' he complained. 'I'm still waiting for him to say it to me.' Ali's impish response was, 'If you see Joe, you tell him he's still a gorilla.' It is unlikely that proud Joe managed to share the joke.

Ali rose at the count of three and made it to the final bell of his first fight with Joe Frazier in Madison Square Garden on 8 March 1971. 'Smokin' Joe' won the decision but then spent a week in hospital complaining of high blood pressure and kidney problems. Ali won their two subsequent fights in 1974 and 1975.

George Foreman – 'Big George'

World heavyweight champion 1973–74, 1994–96.

'I've moulded a monster. I've taken the best of Joe Louis, Jack Johnson and Rocky Marciano and rolled it all into one.'

Dick Sadler, George Foreman's trainer.

Height: 6'3½
Peak weight: 217–225 lb.
235–257 lb. (during comeback)
76 wins (68 stoppages),
5 losses
Born: Marshall, Texas,
10 January 1949

The 'Rumble in the Jungle' on 30 October 1974 brought a transformation for George Foreman. Big George had been the archetype of a new generation of heavyweight: sullen, violent and with an aura of menace. He seemed enormous and indestructible until he met Muhammad Ali in Zaire. This defeat was not an easy one to live down because it just happened to be the most remembered event in boxing history, but he found a better way of dealing with this stigma than Joe Frazier. He was forever the giant who fell in the jungle but after a religious epiphany he acquired wit, wisdom and the appearance of warmth, became a preacher and waited. When he finally returned, a decade later, the old fatty still had an astonishing hand to play.

He recast himself as the humane fun guy, with the joke on himself and the world chuckled with him, delighted he had found a way of overcoming such a life-defining setback and that he had found it in his huge heart to love his conqueror. Occasionally he hinted that he was still privately seething but he slaved away in his Houston gym, building the biggest set of arms the heavyweight division had known, dragged railroad trucks to forge his strength and perfected a new, relaxed, energy-preserving style. Critics accused him of cherry-picking opponents and there were failures along the way but George was out-earning the lot of them. Then one day, a chinny champion decided he wanted an old man to play with. He beat on George for nine rounds until, finally, with one patient right cross, it was all over. George hung around for a while but eventually drifted off to make millions more selling burger-frying machines.

The event this rested on was his shot at Michael Moorer's world heavyweight title in Las Vegas on 5 November 1994. The ancient, but still immensely popular, Foreman seemed an ideal choice for a maiden defence by this small, soft-chinned champion. George had been beaten twice since starting his comeback, had been out of the ring for 17 months and was two months shy of his 46th birthday. Even his much-vaunted power seemed to be deserting him. The 250 lb. Foreman was in the finest shape possible, but for nine rounds Moorer's cynical choice was vindicated. The 222 lb. southpaw pecked and prodded away, always moving out of danger. It seemed so effortlessly easy and the bout was so one-sided referee Joe Cortez considered stopping it. In round 10 Foreman finally registered: a one-two combination which should have prompted a flight reaction from Moorer, but instead he chose to fight only to be finished by Foreman's long, slow, accurate and well-timed right cross flush on his chin. Moorer said ruefully afterwards, 'If I had ducked one more time, we'd be selling Michael Moorer grills today.'

George was the fifth of seven children of Nancy and J B Foreman. His father, a railroad worker, was born in Marshall, Texas and raised in Houston. He knew extreme

In his first life as a world heavyweight champion in the 1970s, Foreman was a sullen, menacing character who inspired terror in his opponents. When he returned in the 1980s, however, it was as an avuncular, self-deprecating nice guy – on the surface, at least.

KINGS OF THE RING

George Foreman knocked Joe Frazier down six times in two rounds in their first fight in Kingston, Jamaica, on 21 January 1973. The final knockdown lifted Joe off his feet. He beat him again – in five rounds – in 1976.

deprivation. He dropped out in the 10th grade and got into mugging, shoplifting drinking and street fighting. President Lyndon B Johnson established the Job Corps to provide work and hope for no-hope kids like George, who joined at the age of 16 in 1965 and credits the programme with saving his life. He worked in construction and forestry, earned his high school equivalency diploma and was introduced to boxing.

With his size, power, natural strength and athletic ability he was an instant success. He won his first fight in January 1967 and left the Jobs Corp after winning the national amateur title in 1968. With 16 wins in 20 fights, he represented his country at the 1968 Mexico City Olympics and won the gold medal. Trained by veteran Dick Sadler, he made his professional debut by beating Don Waldhelm on 23 June 1969. He was crude, wild and after just 24 amateur fights lacked experience. He learned his trade quickly but they were not all easy because George had trouble with elusive boxers and difficulty pacing himself – a weakness first seen in his sixteenth fight when the Argentinian veteran Greg Peralta held him to a close ten round decision. However, he was seen as big, strong and hard hitting with a powerful left jab. The contemporary, self-deprecating Foreman presents Frazier as a fearsome specimen who terrified him so much that when they did meet in Jamaica he decided to get it over early. On 21 January 1973 Foreman seemed impervious to Frazier's efforts, which resembled a child flailing at an adult. When George used his bargepole jab to knock the smaller man's head back on his shoulders and then started bouncing Joe on the canvas, the differential in size, strength and power seemed unbridgeable. Former champions Joe Louis and Jack Dempsey reckoned Foreman was the strongest heavyweight puncher they had ever seen.

For his first defence on 1 September 1973 George chose the unrated Puerto Rican Jose Roman – and the fall guy hardly helped his cause by calling George a 'Texas nigger'. It was all over in two minutes. But his second defence, in Venezuela on 26 March 1974, was against ex-Marine Ken Norton, a man with a far more serious pedigree as he had broken Muhammad Ali's jaw. He was strong, hard hitting, had a great jab and years later George admitted being terrified of Norton, but again that was not the way it looked. Foreman's huge clubbing punches dropped Norton three times in the second round before a Norton trainer leapt into the ring to halt the massacre.

He took an aura of invincibility to Zaire for his third defence against Ali and played on this by cultivating a dark, heavy image in stark contrast with Ali, who was at his most loquacious, surpassing himself when it came to doggerel. This included: 'Only last week I murdered a rock/Injured a stone, hospitalised a brick/I'm so mean I make medicine sick.' None of this seemed to bother Foreman, but eight days before the fight, a sparring partner accidentally jabbed his elbow into George's eye, cutting it, this postponing the 25 September fight to 30 October. The extra weeks in Africa seemed to increase Ali's confidence while Foreman became more introverted.

Yet when he entered the ring he was in magnificent shape and after absorbing a surprise lead right in round one he showed impressive agility and skill in cutting off the ring while pursuing his dancing adversary, and it seemed certain he'd soon catch his man. When Ali took to the ropes in the second round, it looked like a gift – just where the Foreman camp wanted him. Enough huge punches got through to hurt Ali, who was out on his feet several times, but he just wouldn't go down and kept talking to Foreman: 'Hit harder. That don't hurt. Show me something, George.'

The end, in the final seconds of the eighth round, was a thing of beauty and perfection from Ali. He caught the thoroughly exhausted George, who was officially counted out two seconds from the end of the round, having actually made it to his feet just in time. He admitted later that even if he had been saved by the bell Ali would have won.

The defeat was a devastating experience and he took 15 months before returning with a new trainer, Gil Clancy, to face the heavy-handed contender Ron Lyle in a brutal encounter. George was down twice and Ron once. No one was better than Foreman in a brawl and in the fifth he stopped Lyle. He followed this with four more wins, including a stoppage winner over Frazier, but the return with Ali seemed no closer.

George had what he described as a meeting with 'Jesus Christ himself' while lying exhausted after a points loss against Jimmy Young in San Juan, Puerto Rico, on 17 March 1977 and returned to Houston to open the Church of the Lord Jesus Christ in a poor section of the city. He became a minister and family man with ten children, calling five of his sons George, one daughter Georgette and another Frieda George.

After nearly a decade out of the ring, the lure proved too much and he announced a comeback at the age of 38 in 1987, claiming to be motivated by his church running dry of funds. At first his return was taken as a joke and the gregarious George had the grace to laugh along. After seven wins he came in at a relatively sleek 235 lb. (down from 267 lb.) to take on former WBA light heavyweight and cruiserweight champion Dwight Muhammad Qawi, stopping him in seven rounds. Fifteen months later he knocked out future heavyweight title challenger Bert Cooper in three. These, however, were small heavyweights and it was only when he fought the 6'7, 231 lb. Gerry Cooney – a big-hitting former top contender – in Atlantic City on 15 January 1991 that his comeback was taken seriously. Cooney whacked Foreman's chin with a big left hook in the first round, but George took it and came back to knock Gerry cold in the second.

By this stage George had given up trying to slim down and instead worked even harder on increasing his strength, while constantly joking about training on cheeseburgers. He came in at 257 lb. when he challenged the 208 lb. world champion Evander Holyfield in his 25th comeback bout on 4 April 1991. Holyfield comprehensively outboxed him, twice coming close to putting him down, but Foreman proved his ability to pace himself, coming on strong in the later rounds, although he lost on a unanimous points decision. A year later he fought the former contender Alex Stewart, who took a beating in the early rounds, but picked himself off the canvas to outbox Foreman, catching him frequently until his 42-year-old face began to swell hideously. Even so George squeaked home via a majority decision.

He looked more impressive in battering another former contender, Pierre Coetzer, to defeat him in eight rounds, showing a tinge of mercy by pleading with the referee to rescue the South African. Coetzer said: 'You think he's just old and slow, but he's so strong that every time he hits you, even with a jab, your whole body shudders. It takes everything out of you and he's so damn accurate.' In his next fight he took on the heavy hooking but vulnerable Tommy Morrison for the low-rent WBO heavyweight title. Morrison wisely opted to box rather than brawl, with the result that Foreman managed to win only two of the 12 rounds.

He was in a state of semi-retirement when he accepted the chance to fight Moorer, and astonished the boxing world by pulling it off at a point when his quest seemed hopeless. After this he rode on his immense public appeal but the WBA stripped him of their belt for refusing to fight their top contender, Tony Tucker. For his first defence, in Las Vegas on 22 April 1995, he chose Germany's Axel Schulz, a non-puncher of moderate skill who had never beaten anyone of note. Schulz outworked and outboxed Foreman and at the end of 12 rounds seemed a clear winner to everyone at ringside other than the judges. George emerged as the winner on a disgraceful majority decision. The experience brought home to Foreman that even men in the bottom half of the world's top 20 were too competitive. The IBF then stripped him of their version of the world title for refusing to countenance a return with Schulz. Instead George took 19 months out before outpointing the unrated Crawford Grimsely, followed by another non-contender, Lou Savarese, who held him to a split decision.

Stung by criticism that he was only prepared to fight soft white men, he settled for a novice black heavyweight, Hasim Rahman, before changing his mind. 'George Foreman's a self-serving phoney, a surly guy who unfortunately has people snowed, but you never heard me say he wasn't smart,' said Rahman's incensed manager, Robert Mittleman. Instead George chose the more vulnerable Shannon Briggs. Back to 260 lb., Foreman was slower and more ponderous than ever, but faced with an opponent who was reluctant to fight back, he did enough to deserve the verdict. Instead, in a reversal of the Schulz debacle, he emerged from his 81st bout the majority decision loser.

At almost 49 Foreman drifted out of the sport, combining his time making tens of millions selling his George Foreman Lean Mean Grilling Machine while serving as an inter-round boxing expert for HBO, doing plenty of charity work and, now and then, retreating to his 300-acre ranch in his birthplace of Marshall, Texas.

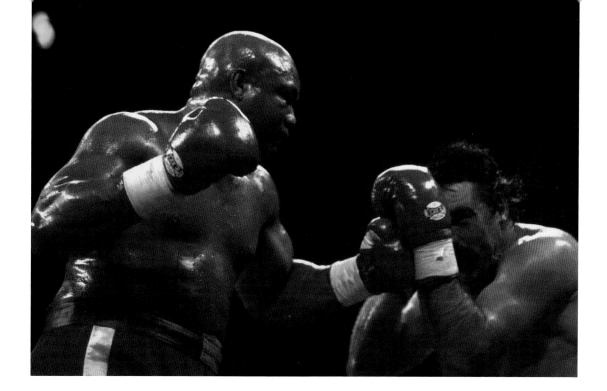

He was tempted by the idea of a final fight against Larry Holmes, originally scheduled for 12 January 1999, two days after his 50th birthday. After a couple of postponements the promoters failed to find the money and it was called off. Holmes blamed Foreman, calling him a 'total fraud who is the opposite of the nice guy he pretends to be'. He went on to say, 'Foreman tries to make fools out of people and won't enter a situation that he can't completely control,' which, he claimed, was the reason George never fought him. 'I don't think George Foreman was ever a great fighter. He was a good puncher and that's how he got to be in the position he's in. He's always hand-picked his opponents, and if you notice, he never hand-picked me.'

Foreman, however, never bothered to reply, content in the knowledge that he did not need Holmes. Enormously popular and fabulously rich, he dropped his HBO position and sort-of announced yet another comeback after Lennox Lewis's retirement in 2004 though he left himself a rather large caveat: 'I feel pretty good but I'm not going to get into the ring unless I'm 225 lb. and I haven't been that weight since 1978.'

The subject was soon dropped and today Foreman seems content to know that his reputation has been fully restored, over 30 years after the 'Rumble in the Jungle'. While Ali became a transcendent figure, George fits comfortably as an appropriate symbol for his time: the most inspired, most marketable reinvention of the century.

An ageing but still ferocious George Foreman pounds Pierre Coetzer in Reno, Nevada, on 16 January 1993, winning in eight rounds after pleading with the referee to stop the fight. He beat Coetzer more easily than Riddick Bowe or Frank Bruno had managed, helping to convince sceptics he still belonged within the leading ranks of contenders at the age of 44.

Leon Spinks – 'Neon Leon'

World heavyweight champion 1978.

'He's fast, he's aggressive, he's young, he takes a punch… After I beat him, he'll come back and win the title and he'll hold it for four or five years and he'll go down in history as one of the great heavyweights. Not the greatest but one of the greatest.'

Muhammad Ali, before his second fight with Spinks, 1978.

Height: 6'1
Peak weight: 194–204 lb.
26 wins (14 stoppages),
17 losses, 3 draws
Born: St Louis, Missouri,
11 July 1953

When boxing conversation turns to Leon Spinks, the question is always: How could such a poor excuse for a challenger beat the greatest of champions? 'Neon Leon', with his gauche smile and missing front teeth, never came close to Ali's generous prognosis about his future: too much coke, dope and booze, too little training and, in the end, not enough talent. But he made good copy during his seven months as champion and without him Ali would not have won the world heavyweight title for the third time.

Ali was supposed to defend against Ken Norton but even his most sycophantic acolytes were admitting he might get beaten. His rationalisation for choosing Spinks for a 'warm-up' in Las Vegas on 15 February 1978 was that Leon was an Olympic gold medallist, just like Patterson, Frazier and Foreman before him. So after one professional year and seven fights Spinks found himself challenging for the world heavyweight title. He was not one for hard work but his manager, Butch Lewis, took him to a camp in the Catskill Mountains to keep him away from the bars. He escaped once by climbing out of his bedroom window, but for the rest he worked like never before, for eight non-stop weeks – unlike Ali, who saw no risk and no need to train. Spinks was near to peaking when he tore a rib muscle in sparring, and was in agony whenever he threw a right. After that he got by with painkiller injections, including one a few hours before the fight.

Leon would steam forward 'kamikaze' style and pound away at whatever was in the way, a style memorably dubbed 'the roving tripod' by Hunter S Thompson ('with Leon's legs forming two poles… and the body of the opponent the third'). Ali was in poor shape and opted to stay on the ropes. For six rounds he did very little as his challenger racked up the points. As Leon put it: 'I just fought to win. Throw punches. Don't worry about what he's doing.' Ali told Angelo Dundee there was no need to worry. 'I'll get him, I'll get him', but Dundee wasn't so sure. 'I knew it was too close for comfort,' he said. 'I told him to stop fooling around. He was giving away too many rounds.' In the last third Ali tried to step it up but Spinks stayed with him. The painkiller wore off in the 11th round and he hurt every time he tossed a right, which was often, but he kept piling it on and the crowd turned in his favour. Going into the final round Ali knew he needed a knockout and, despite driving Spinks into the ropes, it was too late to prevent a clear-cut victory for Spinks. 'I knew I'd won it in the ring but you know how judges are,' said Leon. 'When the fight was close they always gave it to Ali, so it surprised me that I won.'

America's first glimpse of Leon's toothless smile came during the 1976 Montreal Olympics when he and younger brother Michael were part of a brilliant boxing squad

A toothless Leon Spinks beams for America after beating Muhammad Ali to win the world heavyweight title in 1978. By the later rounds the Las Vegas crowd turned in his favour, chanting: 'Leee-on! Leee-on! Leee-on!' The novice won a split – but well deserved – fifteen round decision over the unfit veteran, closing the fight by shaking him with a hard overhand right to the jaw.

KINGS OF THE RING

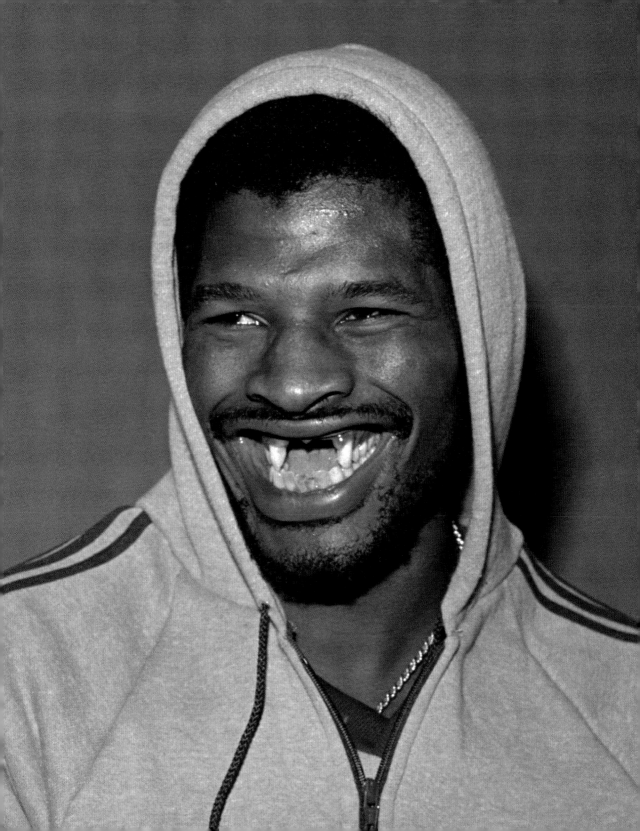

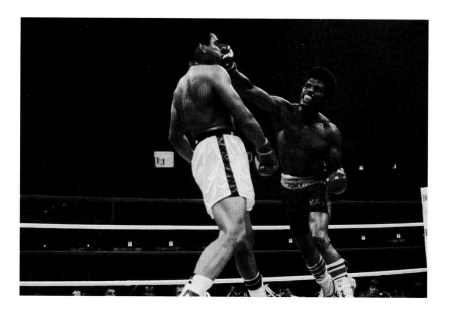

Spinks's superior fitness, his youth and 'kamikaze' style secured him victory over Ali in Las Vegas on 17 February 1978, but in the return in New Orleans on 15 September 1978, the poorly conditioned Spinks was clearly beaten by a fitter Ali.

that included Sugar Ray Leonard and five other medallists. Happy-go-lucky 23-year-old Leon, a Marine lance corporal and father of two, was regarded with particular warmth by his team mates. His more talented middleweight sibling was his rival but the pair were inseparable. They came from a family of six children and the five brothers grew up fighting each other. Leon watched with unrestrained delight when Michael pulled off an upset to lift the gold; then went into his own final against Cuba's much-favoured Sixto Soria. The *New York Times* described the fight as 'the most explosive of the night.' The relentless, perpetually attacking Leon dropped the more experienced Cuban twice before the bout was halted at 1 minute 9 seconds of round three – making Michael and Leon the first brothers ever to win gold medals in boxing at the same Olympics.

Leon had won the US light heavyweight title three years in a row, the bronze medal at the 1974 world championships, the silver at the 1975 Pan-American Games and had a record of 178 wins (133 stoppages) and seven losses. But there is a gulf between amateurs and professionals, light heavyweights and heavyweights. Leon did not have the frame to carry more than 200 lb. – making him a little guy in a growing division. Trained by Sam Solomon, he stopped 'Lightning' Bob Smith in five rounds in Las Vegas on 15 January 1977 and then flew to Liverpool to knock out the Britain's Peter Freeman in one round. Two fights later he took on the Puerto Rican champion Pedro Augusto, who had recently lasted four rounds with George Foreman. Spinks flattened him in one. In bout six he fought a ten-round draw on national TV with future world title challenger Scott LeDoux. Watching this, Ali picked Leon and the WBC boss Jose Sulaiman obligingly agreed to rate him if he bettered the unbeaten Italian champion, Alfio Righetti. Leon outpointed him and that was it: 12 weeks later he was world heavyweight champion.

His days of dedication were over and he decided the purpose of his achievement was to have an endless party. The advertising agencies lined up at his door but it was not long before Leon's habits had them running the other way – pictures of him in handcuffs appeared on front pages when he was caught with $5 bag of cocaine in his hatband. The endorsers fled and the leeches arrived, intent on separating him from his hard-fought cash, which they did with great success. He hired a bodyguard, the future actor Mr T, but even a member of TV's *A Team* had problems keeping control while Leon and his hangers-on blew his money, smoked his dope and drank his whiskey.

A month after beating Ali the WBC stripped Spinks of his title for avoiding their top contender Ken Norton. As Ali put it, 'He makes $5 million with me and $1.5 million with Norton. Who would you fight?' Spinks chose Ali but by the time of the return, before 63,532 fans at the New Orleans Superdrome on 15 September 1978, Leon had lost all his previous conditioning and the drugs, drink and partying had taken their toll. He put in two weeks' work for the fight and found himself up against a fitter Ali, albeit an older version with slower reflexes and coordination. Spinks was also hampered by the chaos in his corner with a cacophony of conflicting voices trying to instruct him. Ali stuck to his strategy of keeping away from the ropes, clinching when Spinks came close, using the jab and closing each round with a flurry. It worked, albeit in slow motion, and Ali won a unanimous decision.

Ali retired and Leon fought a final WBA elimination against South Africa's Gerrie Coetzee on 24 June 1979, and was dropped three times before being stopped in 2 minutes three seconds of the first round. He bounced back to knock out the former European champion Alfredo Evangelista and three bouts later beat the world-rated Bernard Mercado in nine rounds. This earned him a challenge for Larry Holmes's world title in New Orleans on 12 June 1981 but he caught the champion at his brilliant best and was stopped at the end of the third round. He returned at cruiserweight, was beaten in six rounds by future champion Carlos De Leon, then retired for two years. Coming back against Muhammad Qawi for the WBA cruiserweight title in 1986 he was again stopped in six.

He was declared bankrupt but with a wife and three sons to support he had no option but to fight on, losing seven of his next nine bouts. Leon retired in 1988 but made a comeback in mid-1991, picking up five wins before returning to his losing ways. In 1993 his 19-year-old son, Calvin, a professional boxer, was shot dead but Leon pressed on, losing on a first round knockout to John Carlo the following year – the only time a former heavyweight champion has lost to a man making his professional debut. A win and one loss later he retired for good at the end of 1995, aged 42. He lived homeless for a while, still plagued by alcoholism.

His two other sons, Darrell and Cory, turned professional and after a few rough years things picked up for all of them. Leon was recruited by a sports promotional company to become a headliner on their year-round, touring autograph shows. Since then, several months a year have been spent on the road, living at Marriott hotels. For the rest, he lives in Columbus, Nebraska, where he works as a cleaner at the local YMCA and volunteers three days a week in an after-school youth programme. In 2003 his son Cory, born five days after Leon beat Ali, became the undisputed world welterweight champion. As always, his father was at ringside to support him.

Ken Norton – 'The Black Hercules'

WBC heavyweight title holder 1978.

'Norton beat me today, fair and square. I tried to win but he was too tough. He was the better man. Norton whupped me.'
Muhammad Ali, after losing to Norton in 1973.

Height: 6'3
Peak weight: 205–220 lb.
42 wins (33 stoppages),
7 losses, 1 draw
Born: Jacksonville, Illinois,
8 September 1945

If you were to build a mythical heavyweight king you might choose Ken Norton and most of the time this handsome, smart Adonis fulfilled the part in reality: strong, aggressive, defensively adept with a great jab from his awkward, crouching style. He fought Ali three times and deserved to win at least two. He took Larry Holmes to the wire and beat several other top men. But he fought in the most competitive decade in heavyweight history; the judges were against him in three crucial fights; he was frozen out of the title picture in 1977 and 1978 and his punch resistance was not the best. These factors denied him the crown and he was left with the compensatory package of the WBC belt – awarded rather than won in the ring. Yet he still belongs to be called a star of the 1970s alongside Ali, Frazier, Foreman and Holmes

Muhammad Ali had won ten in a row since losing to Frazier and was running out of options for his 31 March 1973 date in San Diego when he had a minor run-in with an undercard heavyweight – Norton. As Ken recalled: 'He was down in the lounge area with a bunch of ladies. I came down and kinda stole part of his thunder. He jumped up and started yelling "I'm gonna kick your butt".' Ken had won 29 out of 30 fights, but that single blemish – a knockout loss against Jose Luis Garcia in 1970 – convinced Ali he wanted Norton. He neglected training but was up against a highly talented fighter reaching his peak after spending many hard hours sparring with Joe Frazier. Norton's strategy, devised by veteran Eddie Futch, was to block and then step in with his own hard jab. In the second round Norton drove Ali to the ropes and nailed him with a big, perfectly timed right cross, breaking his jaw. Ali did not want it stopped and fought on, in excruciating agony. As an admiring Norton later put it: 'Ali had a break that was an inch-and-a-half long and if you keep getting hit as hard and as much as I hit Ali, the pain would take over and you would pass out.' Norton seemed in control but, astonishingly, in the eyes of the judges the fight was even going into the last round, which Norton dominated to win a split decision.

When Ali's jaw healed his priority was a return and in the rematch Ali danced, stayed off the ropes and avoided being cornered. Norton was the aggressor but Ali was able to outjab him and now and then would get in something more tasty – like the hard hook to the chin that rocked Ken in the fourth round. In round six spectators could sense a change. Ali was punching hard but was beginning to tire and Norton was registering more frequently. He dominated the seventh, driving Ali around the ring and wobbling him with a left hook at the end of the eighth. They went toe-to-toe in the ninth – Norton shaken by a right cross and Ali battered on the ropes with body punches. Ken continued this treatment over the next two rounds but seemed to fade at the end of the 11th. Ali

Ken Norton on his way to a fifth round knockout over Lorenzo Zanon at Caesars Palace, Las Vegas, Nevada, on 14 September 1977. In his next fight Norton won a disputed decision over Jimmy Young, after which the WBC made him their heavyweight champion.

knew he needed the 12th and started the round with quick, accurate combination punching, followed up with a rare right uppercut that snapped Ken's head back. Norton fired back over the final half minute but the round clearly belonged to Ali. It was a hard fight to score. Norton had clearly won five of the 12 rounds, while those Ali shaded were closer. The official decision was split: six rounds to five and one even for Ali, the same margin for Norton, and, for the deciding vote, seven rounds to five for Ali.

Norton had to wait three years for his third dose of Ali – this time for the world title at New York's Yankee Stadium on 29 September 1976. He chased Ali all over the ring, belting him to body and head. The champion could no longer move like before, his timing was out and he could only fight in bursts. He did plenty of clowning, clinching and holding behind the head but it was beginning to look like a rout. Ali came back to shade rounds 9–11, lost the twelfth and edged the thirteenth and fourteenth. Norton's manager, Bill Biron, warned: 'Be careful. Stay away from him. Don't take chances because you have the fight won.' In the other corner Angelo Dundee told Ali to 'fight like hell'. The challenger coasted and despite a late rally, it was Ali who won the round and the fight. Of that final three minutes Norton said, 'I wish I could fight it again. I wasn't tired. I was in good shape. I could have fought the whole three minutes flat-out and won it easily but my corner said I had the fight won and don't take any chances. That's why I was so cautious.' He felt hurt by his treatment from the judges but in time that eased. 'I wouldn't say I had any bitterness, but I was very disappointed. In my mind I won all three fights. I would say that even though I lost those fights with the judges, I was never bitter towards Ali. We became good friends and we're still good friends. I feel he knows and I know that I won all three fights.'

Kenneth Howard Norton probably would have made it whatever path in life he chose. He excelled at athletics and basketball and earned a football scholarship at Northeast Missouri State University. After two years there, he joined the Marines and was persuaded to take up boxing. He won the All-Marine heavyweight title and finished his amateur career with a record of 24 wins and two losses. He turned professional in November 1967 and over 30 months he won 16 fights straight, with 15 knockouts. A surprise eighth round knockout defeat at the hands of the lighter Jose Luis Garcia was a devastating setback but he bounced back, winning 13 in a row, while learning the trade as a sparring partner for Joe Frazier. Norton's two fights with Ali established him as one of the division's top men, setting him up for a shot at George Foreman's world title. But the world champion's power, strength and ability to cut off the ring made him the wrong opponent for Norton, who lost in two rounds. Once again he proved his grit, coming back with seven straight knockouts. He handed out a severe five-round beating to Jerry Quarry, who taunted him with racist comments, and followed this by knocking out his former conqueror Jose Luis Garcia in five rounds. He also had parts in two movies of the 1970s, both times acting as a slave.

He bounced back from the third disappointment against Ali by knocking out former American amateur star Duane Bobick, who had won 38 in a row, in 58 seconds. Six months and another good win later the WBC offered him a final eliminator against Jimmy Young on 5 November 1977. For once Norton came out on the happy side of a questionable split decision, setting himself up for his third title challenge. But Ali chose

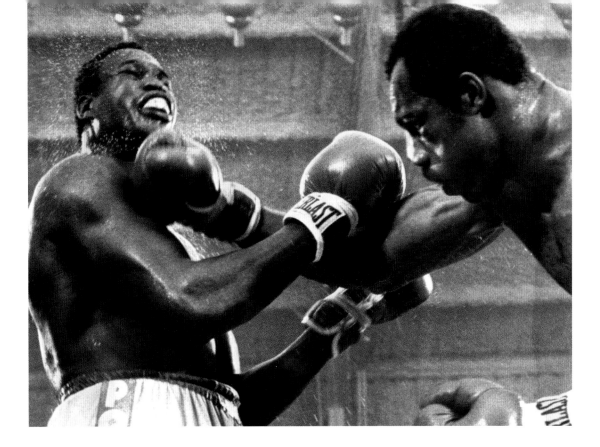

Leon Spinks as a 'warm-up', which the WBC allowed providing the winner fought Norton. Spinks made it clear he would rather grant Ali the return and as a result, six weeks after the Ali–Spinks fight, the WBC stripped Leon of their title and awarded it to Norton, retrospectively recognising his win over Young as a title bout. It was hardly the ideal state of affairs, but given that Norton had unofficially outfought Ali for the title two years earlier and was vastly superior to Spinks in every department, it was not without a hint of natural justice.

His first defence at Las Vegas on 9 June 1978 against the 28-year-old Larry Holmes was one of the great wars of heavyweight history, with Norton's strength and power offset by Holmes's speed and skill. Larry, who was suffering from a shoulder injury, dominated the early rounds and Ken came back later in the fight. The result was another split decision against Ken. Norton had delivered his last great performance and had come up short again. Nearing 33 he no longer had the motivation to drive his body but fought on until being stopped in 54 seconds by Gerry Cooney. On retirement he moved into sports management and motivational speaking. In 1986 it seemed he would never walk or talk again after a horrific car accident, but gradually, with a great deal of professional help and support from friends like Ali, his body began to repair. His right side is still partially paralysed, he walks with a limp, can no longer run and his speech sounds slightly slurred – a result of the accident, not boxing, it seems – but he remains sharp and articulate, still working as a celebrity speaker.

WBC heavyweight champion Larry Holmes survived some torrid moments in the fifteenth round but fought with a damaged shoulder to beat Ken Norton on a split decision at Caesars Palace in Las Vegas on 9 June 1978. It was Norton's first defence of his title after it had been awarded to him in March.

Larry Holmes – 'The Easton Assassin'

WBC heavyweight title holder 1978–84; IBF title holder 1984–85; generally recognised as world heavyweight champion 1980–85.

'Larry Holmes was a legendary fighter. If he was at his best I wouldn't have stood a chance.'
Mike Tyson, 1988.

Height: 6'3
Peak weight: 209–213 lb.
69 wins (44 stoppages),
7 losses
Born: Cuthbert, Georgia,
3 November 1949

Bad luck, bad timing, bad decisions and an acerbic tongue all counted against Larry Holmes achieving the status his talent demanded, but in the end he came through. He held one or another version of the world title for seven years and defended it 20 times, but when his chance finally came to unify, the fight was cancelled. He was one fight from equalling Rocky Marciano's record for consecutive wins when he lost his title on a debatable decision and then, in the return, was robbed outright. He was never quite forgiven for beating up Ali, and could never quite get George Foreman to share a ring with him. But finally, a couple of decades late, Holmes is gaining the recognition he deserves: as one of the finest heavyweights of all time. The great trainer Emanuel Steward rates him close to the best: 'Holmes would have been a much more difficult fight for Lennox Lewis than Ali because of his strength and that very fast jab.' Frank Maloney, Lewis's former manager, goes further, 'Holmes in his prime would have beaten them all – every heavyweight who ever existed.'

The fight that started to turn it around for Larry was his 11 June 1982 Las Vegas showdown with Gerry Cooney. Holmes had been WBC champion for nearly three years and after 11 defences, including his victory over Ali, was widely recognised as world champion, but he came into the fight as the underdog in every sense. His big, 25-year-old Irish-American opponent was fêted like no other challenger before. Even Ronald Reagan phoned him on the eve of the fight, wishing him luck. Holmes received no such call. Cooney looked and talked the part and he could really fight, with paralysing power in his left hook. Norton, Lyle and Young had all fallen to it and many thought the smaller, older Holmes would follow and that Cooney would become the first white heavyweight champion in 23 years. There was more than a hint of racism in the build-up with some nasty comments from extremists on both sides of the racial divide. It was taken seriously enough for police snipers to be positioned on the roofs of the hotels surrounding Caesars Palace.

The event was broadcast to 150 countries – the highest grossing fight in boxing history at that point. Cooney had been out of the ring for 13 months while awaiting this chance but he had youth, size and, most of all, power on his side. At 6'6 and 225 lb. he was three inches taller, 13 lb. heavier and seven years younger. His strategy was to work past the jarring Holmes jab to land his left hook, but Cooney lacked anything approaching Holmes's seasoning. All those years sparring with Joe Frazier and Muhammad Ali, working his way through the ranks and all those title defences had sculpted the complete boxer – a jab to rival Ali's and Liston's, a hard right cross, left hook and uppercut plus perfect balance and footwork, and a multi-layered defence.

Larry Holmes relaxes at home after winning the WBC title from Ken Norton in Las Vegas, Nevada. The 28-year-old entered the bout with a torn left triceps muscle. This affected his ability to use his best weapon – his jab. In the end it came down to the fifteenth round when the 209 lb. Holmes got the better of the 220 lb. Norton, deservedly winning a split decision after one of the greatest heavyweight battles.

Holmes dropped Cooney with a right in the second round, but the New Yorker rose and fought back furiously so that for the next four rounds the action was intense. The more experienced, more active champion held a slight edge and knew how to pace himself. In round nine he dropped Cooney for a second time and was now in total control. Repeated low blows cost Cooney three points but Holmes kept his composure and increased the pressure. In round 13 Larry sensed he was ready to go and stepped it up another notch. Gerry's legs went from the impact of a heavy right cross and with his back to the ropes and his head in a daze his trainer Victor Valle threw in the towel.

As one of 11 children of a single mother on welfare and charity handouts, Larry grew up living hand-to-mouth in Easton, Pennsylvania. He supplemented the household income by working at a shoeshine stand and later, after quitting school, at a car wash. He began boxing in his late teens but his progress was halted by the experienced Duane Bobick in the heavyweight final of the US Olympic trials – an embarrassing experience since it was televised and Larry made a dire impression. No heart, no punch, they said. He ended his amateur career with a record of 19 wins and three losses and began boxing professionally in March 1973, earning $150 for outpointing Rodell Dupree in Scranton, Pennsylvania. His first real exposure was at Madison Square Garden in his fifth fight when he won a unanimous decision over the Canadian prospect Bob Bozic. Two fights later he was dropped for the first time by fellow novice Kevin Isaac but got up to win in the third round. He was invited to serve as Joe Frazier's sparring partner, as 'Smokin Joe' built up towards his second fight with Ali. Joe was ruthless on the hired help but Larry impressed with his ability to fight back, but eventually had to leave with a broken rib.

Holmes sparred a few times with Ali when he turned professional, walking away as the proud owner of a closed eye, courtesy of 'The Greatest'. Then, after nine fights, he was employed on a longer-term basis. Ali was notoriously lazy in sparring and invariably held back, laying on the ropes and practising defensive moves. An encouraged Larry unwisely told a reporter he was better than his employer. When Ali heard this he opened up on Larry while telling him how wonderful he was. Holmes often fought on Ali undercards but by 1975 Larry felt he was no longer learning from his mentor. In October 1975 Holmes entered the world rankings and there was talk of a fight with Foreman until the former champion lost to to Jimmy Young in Puerto Rico and retired.

His moment arrived when he won a world title eliminator against Ernie Shavers. Holmes won all 12 rounds putting on a brilliant performance, but he was still the underdog when challenging Ken Norton for the WBC title in Las Vegas. Holmes tried to keep it quiet when he tore his left triceps muscle six days before the fight, but the news leaked out. The injury meant he could not use his jab properly, but he still won the early rounds comfortably – too quick and skilled for the older man. Norton broke through in the second half, landing heavily to the head and body but most ringside observers had Holmes several rounds ahead going into the 15th. It turned out he needed those three minutes to win. He threw everything he had at Norton – and got plenty in return – but in the end Larry had more left, hurting Ken towards the end of the round to take the fight, and the WBC belt.

Once Ali retired, Holmes became recognised as the world number one. Stoppage wins over Spain's European champion Alfredo Evangelista and the unbeaten Puerto

Rican Ossie Ocasio were followed by a routine defence against contender Mike Weaver on 22 June 1979. Holmes went ahead with the fight despite a viral infection, dropped Weaver in the 12th then battered him to defeat. Nine months later Weaver won the rival WBA title. In Holmes's next defence on 28 September 1979 against Shavers, he proved his resilience. A huge right to the jaw that dropped Holmes heavily cured his seventh-round complacency and he fought back to stop Shavers in the 11th, winning high praise for his powers of recovery. But it was only after beating Ali that Holmes's claim to be world champion was established beyond serious dispute and he continued to consolidate with wins over Trevor Berbick, Leon Spinks and Renaldo Snipes (who also knocked him down).

After his win over Cooney there were signs of slippage. Holmes beat Randall Cobb and France's Lucien Rodriguez but he seemed to have lost his spark. On 20 May 1983 he defended his title against 'Terrible' Tim Witherspoon, who had won all 15 of his fights. The 6'3, 219½ lb. Witherspoon showed his defensive prowess by catching Holmes's jabs and for most of the bout gave Larry a torrid time. The referee hovered anxiously in the ninth round as Witherspoon battered Holmes but somehow the veteran dug deep, fought back, and in the twelfth forced Witherspoon into retreat and emerged with a split decision win. Despite subsequent problems with drugs, alcohol and promoters, Witherspoon went on to win both the WBC and the WBA titles.

While waiting to take on new WBA champion Gerrie Coetzee – a match that failed to happen – the WBC stripped Holmes of his title for failing to defend against their number one, Greg Page. Holmes was recognised by a new control body, the International Boxing Federation, and retained general recognition as world champion. His next challenger was the 6'4, 227 lb. James 'Bonecrusher' Smith, who had recently

Larry Holmes pumps his jab into the 38-year-old face of Muhammad Ali. Ali's corner refused to allow him out for the eleventh round. The 211½ lb. Holmes won every completed round on all three judges' cards, giving the 217½ lb. Ali his only stoppage defeat. After this victory Holmes was generally recognised as the legitimate world champion.

Larry Holmes raises his arms after stopping his former employer, Muhammad Ali, after ten totally one-sided rounds. This victory gave him widespread recognition as the linear world heavyweight champion although the WBA withheld recognition, preferring to give their belt to lesser heavyweights – several of them former Holmes victims.

broken the unbeaten record of Britain's Frank Bruno by knocking him out. The 35-year-old Holmes stopped him in the 12th round. Smith went on to win the WBA title. Four months later Holmes stopped the unbeaten David Bey in ten rounds and then defended against another unbeaten contender, 25-year-old Carl 'The Truth' Williams. This seemed an extremely close fight with the busier challenger outjabbing the master jabber. At the end of fifteen rounds it looked like it could go either way and it was a surprise when Holmes won by a wide, unanimous margin.

His 21st challenger was the quick, unpredictable and hard-hitting world light heavyweight champion Michael Spinks on 21 September 1985. Spinks hot-footed it around the perimeter of the ring, coming in with quick flurries before moving away again. Holmes lacked the speed to cut off the ring but pursued doggedly, using his jab effectively and with occasional combinations, without ever cornering his elusive and tiring prey. When asked before the fight about the possibility of breaking Rocky Marciano's record for 49 consecutive wins, Holmes replied, 'I'm 35 fighting young men and he was 25 fighting old men-to-be. Marciano couldn't carry my jockstrap.' To Larry, this was simply common sense: how could a crude little bleeder, 30 lb. lighter, five inches shy in height and 14 inches shorter in reach be considered his equal? But his remark had exacerbated the anti-Larry mood in American boxing circles and it hardly endeared him to people such as boxing judges. Larry's days of getting the benefit of the doubt were over and Spinks was awarded a unanimous decision. Afterwards, an unrepentant Larry repeated his previous insult: 'If you want to get technical about it,' he said. 'Rocky couldn't carry my jockstrap.'

The 36-year-old trained harder for the Spinks return in Las Vegas on 19 April 1986, and this time there seemed to be no doubt about the outcome. Larry broke his thumb in the third round and failed to pull the trigger when he had Spinks going in rounds five, nine and fourteen. Holmes thought he had done enough as did one judge, Joe Cortez, who gave it to Larry by 144-141 but was over ruled by Jerry Roth (144-142) and Frank Brunette (144-141). It was a shameful decision, prompting Holmes to retire in disgust.

Larry's love of money prompted his decision to accept promoter Don King's $3-million short-notice offer to face Mike Tyson, in Atlantic City on 22 January 1988. At the age of 38, after 21 months out, four weeks was not nearly enough time to train. 'I knew I wasn't ready,' he admitted. Holmes, at a career-heaviest of 225 lb. – ten more than Tyson – held his own while boxing in retreat for three rounds but in the fourth his right got caught in the ropes and Tyson exploded with a rapid-fire combination. Holmes went down, made it up in time, and Tyson put him down again with a sickening right and the fight was over five seconds from the end of the round. Holmes later described this as his worst-ever performance.

He returned to retirement for over three years, enviously watching Foreman's success. Then in 1991, aged 41, he returned, although at first there was not much to write about except his success in a street fight against former opponent Trevor Berbick. He strung together five wins and then took on the unbeaten 1988 Olympic heavyweight champion Ray Mercer, who had scored several notable victories including a brutal knockout of Tommy Morrison for the World Boxing Organisation title. The WBO, in a rare fit of misspent conscience, was so concerned about this mismatch with Holmes that they stripped Mercer of their worthless title when he insisted on going ahead. Holmes, at 233 lb. and 42 years old, dished out a comprehensive boxing lesson – moving to his right, slamming his long, accurate jab into the 30-year-old's face and tying him up when he came close. At one point Larry took time out – while holding the ex-Marine sergeant off – to sneer at ringside spectators, before romping home with a unanimous decision. Four months later he managed to take four rounds off Evander Holyfield, while cutting and frustrating him, and then put together seven wins before holding a drugs-ravaged Oliver McCall to a hairline decision for the WBC title – at the age of 45.

He took out his frustrations with verbal attacks on Lennox Lewis and George Foreman, particularly after the Lewis camp turned down his training offer. Meanwhile, he fought on, outboxing the unbeaten Dane Brian Nielson for another meaningless title in Brondby, Denmark, in 1997 only to be robbed with a split-decision verdict. However, in his next fight he was adjudged a split decision winner over Maurice Harris – a fight he clearly lost. He hung around to fight Foreman but when the event was cancelled he unleashed another tirade against George. After this he had three more fights, easily stopping former victims Bonecrusher Smith and Weaver before using that jab to outpoint the 33-year-old, 334 lb. novelty heavyweight, 'Butterbean', when he was nearly 53.

Larry, who still lives in Easton, has five children and a growing batch of grandchildren and has made good money – around $700,000 a year, he says – investing in real estate, endorsing health products, making personal appearances and running his own restaurant. He still trains and still talks a good fight. 'I'm the most underrated heavyweight champion who ever lived,' he says with that combative smile .

Michael Spinks – 'The Jinx'

World heavyweight title (generally recognised) 1985–88;
(IBF title holder to 1987); world light heavyweight champion 1983–85
(WBA title holder from 1981).

'If you don't take chances, you can't do anything in life.'
Michael Spinks

Height: 6'2½
Peak weight: 170–209 lb.
31 wins (21 stoppages),
1 loss
Born: St Louis, Missouri,
13 July 1956

The name Michael Spinks is most commonly associated with three fighters: Mike Tyson who unified the world heavyweight title by blowing him away in 91 seconds; Larry Holmes, who was robbed of the decision in their second fight; and older brother Leon Spinks. This is a pity because Michael was one of the finest fighters, pound for pound, of the late 20th century. He went from winning the Olympic middleweight gold to unifying the world light heavyweight title and being the first world light heavyweight champion to lift the world heavyweight title, defending it three times. Spinks did not have the most attractive style but it was extremely effective. He was quick, hard to hit, unpredictable and courageous, with an impressive array of punches. His speciality was his right cross, known as 'The Spinks Jinx'.

His greatest achievement was his win over Larry Holmes in Las Vegas on 21 September 1985. Spinks broke the jinx on light heavyweight champions becoming the cream of the heavyweights because he had at his disposal the advances in training and nutrition his predecessors lacked. Long runs gave way to wind sprints, weights and resistance machines were brought in and he was put on a high protein, supplement-rich diet. Ten weeks of intense work brought his weight up to 199¾ lb. Spinks attacked from the start, edging the early rounds with smash-and-grab raids and keeping out of Holmes's range. The heavyweight champion pursued doggedly and the focus required by the smaller man was so immense he would collapse in his corner at the end of each round, panting heavily. Holmes began timing Spinks's attacks, forcing him to keep his distance, and he also started to land his right more frequently. But Spinks survived to get a unanimous points decision. Spinks bulked up to 205 lb. for the rematch but this time Holmes was sharper and more aggressive. He landed more frequently with his right, despite breaking the thumb, hurting Spinks in the fifth round. Using his mobility Michael shaded the middle rounds but Holmes shook him again in round nine and particularly 14 when Spinks was out on his feet. The younger man managed an impressive late flurry to take a split decision, although this verdict was widely condemned.

Michael was three years younger than Leon but came across as the older brother – more careful, mature and brighter. The 20-year-old middleweight was the first to reach the Olympic finals but both brothers emerged with gold. Michael went on to an amateur record of 93 wins (35 stoppages) out of 100. With his sophisticated style and one-punch knockout power he was thought to be more likely to succeed, although at first he played a dutiful supporting role. When Leon fought Ali for the world

Michael Spinks cries out, 'Thank you God', following his win over Larry Holmes in a 15-round unanimous decision on 21 September 1985. Going into the final round two judges had the fight even while the third had Spinks two points up. Spinks took a hard right after which he kept his distance. All three judges gave him the round, prompting a unanimous decision. Holmes remarked that the judges 'must drink before coming to the fights' although he later admitted that Michael's punches 'came from places I never saw before'.

heavyweight title, Michael was on the undercard. Over the next two years he put his own ambitions on hold – managing just two fights – while he tried to keep Leon in line. Eventually, he decided it was time to kick start his own stalling career and fought his way near to the top of the world rankings before challenging the outstanding WBA champion Eddie Mustafa Muhammad. Falling behind after five rounds Spinks changed tactics and before long the champion was bleeding over both eyes. Spinks dropped Muhammad with a right and went on to win. He made five title defences, winning all of them inside the distance before agreeing to meet the rival WBC champion, Dwight Muhammad Qawi, in a unification bout in Atlantic City on 18 March 1983. Qawi, his skills honed in prison, was short, powerful and highly skilled, having wreaked havoc in the light heavyweight division since his release. On the eve of the bout both men had catastrophes. Qawi developed pneumonia but rejected medical advice to withdraw, while Michael's girlfriend was killed in a car crash, making him the single father of their three-year-old daughter. An hour before the event she asked him when her mother would arrive to watch the fight, and he struggled to hold back the tears. However, when the first bell rang he was completely focussed, boxing in retreat to secure a unanimous verdict.

After four defences Michael moved up a division to beat Holmes – the first time that brothers had won the world heavyweight title. He handled his crown with more care than Leon, treating it as a long-term investment. He featured in beer commercials and made cameo appearances in films before opting for an easy defence in Las Vegas on 6 September 1986 against European champion Steffen Tangstad. Spinks dropped the Norwegian three times before stopping him 58 seconds into the fourth round. The IBF insisted he take on Tony Tucker – an option worth $1.5 million – but instead he accepted a $5 million offer to fight Gerry Cooney. The decision meant he was stripped of his IBF belt, although he retained recognition as linear world champion.

Cooney had taken two years out after losing to Holmes – encountering depression, drink and drugs – before returning to action with a couple of wins in 1984; then another break, and another win in 1986. Although he had managed only three fights in five years and had started drinking heavily again, he was the favourite against Spinks. Michael had built himself up to 208 lb. but was still dwarfed by the 238 lb. Cooney, but once again he gave a masterful performance, using lateral movement to prevent his giant opponent from using his lethal handy hook. The first four rounds were close but in the fifth Spinks started opening up, landing hard and fast on Gerry's vulnerable chin. The years of inactivity and drinking sapped the big man's resistance, he wilted then fell and, with nine seconds to go, referee Frank Cappuccino stopped the fight.

Michael was out of the ring for over a year, waiting for the pension plan offer he needed before risking his life against Mike Tyson for the undisputed world title – set for Atlantic City on 27 June 1987 and billed by the co-promoter, Donald Trump, as 'Once And For All'. Spinks bulked up even further, to 212 lb. – six less than Tyson – but was not helped by a right knee injury sustained in training nor by conflicting advice. His trainer Eddie Futch instructed him to move laterally but his manager, Butch Lewis, wanted a blitz attack. Spinks also feared his ferocious opponent. Before the fight Tyson was cranking up the fear factor by saying, 'I'll break him, I break 'em all. When I fight

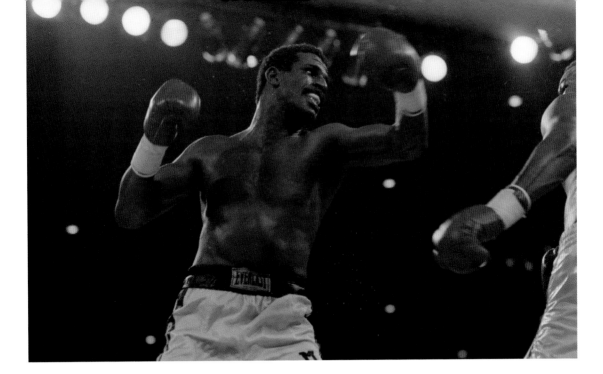

someone I want to break his will.' Having seen the trail of destruction wrought by Iron Mike, Spinks took this to heart. 'Fear was knocking at my door big time,' he admitted. When he walked to the ring there was a look of sheer terror on his face – a fact that did not escape Tyson's notice. 'I could see the fear in his face and I knew it was gonna be a first-round knockout,' he said. 'I hurt him with the first punch I threw. He wobbled a little, but I knew he would try to fight back. There were only two things he could do: try to get lucky or try to run around all night.' Michael tried the first option but Tyson simply did not walk into punches. Using his speed Tyson cut off the ring and exploded his hooks on Spinks' chin. Michael went down, rose, but was counted out by Cappuccino after just 1 minute 31 seconds of the first round.

Soon after, having just turned 32, Michael Spinks announced his retirement. He had earned $25 million from his five heavyweight bouts and had invested it well, resisting the periodic temptation to return to the ring. He was not quite the angel of his most generous portrayals, however. In November 2000 he was arrested after a fight with his girlfriend and charged with third-degree assault. He eventually pleaded guilty to the lower level domestic violence charge of 'offensive touching' and was sentenced to a year's probation, a fine and a course of counselling. Unlike many of his contemporaries, he admitted he was wrong and said he would never do it again. He has since returned to the celebrity guest appearance circuit while working with Butch Lewis in boxing management and in assisting his nephew, Cory Spinks, in his rise to become the undisputed world welterweight champion.

Michael Spinks survived a torrid fourteenth round in his return fight with Larry Holmes but fought back to retain his IBF title with a 15-round split decision on 19 April 1988 in Las Vegas, Nevada. Holmes battered him around the ring but could not put him away. Still, there was virtual unanimity at ringside that the 36-year-old Holmes had done more than enough to regain his world title.

Mike Tyson – 'Iron Mike'

World heavyweight champion 1988–90, WBC title holder 1986–90; WBA, IBF title holder, 1987–90; WBC, WBA title holder 1996.

'There's the future heavyweight champion of the world. This is the one I've been waiting for all my life – my third champion, the best one of all.'
Boxing trainer Cus D'Amato on seeing the 13-year-old Mike Tyson in action.

Height: 5'11
Peak weight: 215–221 lb.
50 wins (40 stoppages),
6 losses, 2 no contests
Born: Brooklyn, New York,
30 June 1966

No one in boxing history has shocked, shaken and enthralled quite like Mike Tyson during his reign of terror through the 1980s. He was the most destructive heavyweight of all time, in every sense. It is said that while Ali became the best-known sporting figure on earth for all the right reasons, Tyson got there because of his dark side – through the public's fascination with his depravity, cruelty and capacity for self-destruction but that is hardly the full truth. Tyson drew people in because they loved the way he fought.

His ability to destroy was confirmed against Trevor Berbick in Las Vegas on 22 November 1986. In 20 months Tyson had packed in 27 wins – 25 on knockouts and 15 in the first round – to become America's top boxing story. Part of it was the way he looked – a block of bone and muscle topped by a huge head resting on a 19½' neck. His life story also helped – from bullied slum boy to jailed mugger then rescue and re-invention as ring assassin. The crippling blows he unleashed on stricken men were facilitated by his speed, accuracy, timing, reflexes and technique. He crouched behind a high guard, shifted his head and moved laterally, making him an elusive target. Many opponents were too overcome by fear and the assault of heavy leather that confronted them to think too hard about responding in kind.

The boxing world wanted to see what would happen when he met a man who knew how to fight. After two points victories over fringe contenders, James Tillis and Mitch Green, he challenged Canada's Trevor Berbick whose record boasted 32 wins out of 37, 23 of them stoppages. He was unbeaten in over three years. Tyson, dressed, as always, in black, got to work with frightening ferocity. In the second round he pounded Berbick to the canvas, then dropped him again with a monster hook to the temple. Berbick crashed down, rose and collapsed, gasping in shock, after which referee Mills Lane stopped the fight. Tyson was the WBC champion at 20 – the youngest-ever heavyweight title claimant.

Michael Gerald Tyson was born in Brooklyn, the son of a drug addict mother and a heavy-drinking father who left the family when Mike was one. Violence was rife in his childhood and Mike witnessed numerous domestic fights. He lived in a gang-run district where you were either predator or victim. Bullied Mike took many beatings but snapped when a boy killed one of his beloved pigeons. He beat the bully senseless, kicking and punching until the boy was a bloody mess. 'After that I got off on the violence. I saw its power,' he said.

With a gang called the Jolly Stompers he began bag snatching, mugging and robbing other kids, old people, stores and houses, using fists, knives and guns. At the age of 12,

A ferocious Mike Tyson batters a reeling Razor Ruddock in 1991. Their first fight was prematurely stopped so they fought a return three months later. When they met at a pre-fight contest Mike told Razor: 'I can't wait to kiss those great big lips of yours. I'm gonna make you my girlfriend. Don't you know that you're really a transvestite?' He then looked at the audience and added, 'It doesn't count if he is dead.' And back to Razor: 'You're dead, you pretty thing, you.' But the 238 lb. Ruddock put up a tremendous fight taking the 216 lb. Tyson to the final bell. Mike won a unanimous decision.

he was arrested once too often – for purse snatching – and sent to Tryon School for Boys, a detention centre in upstate New York. Here he met former boxer Bobby Steward, who steered the boy to the prison gym and began to teach him on condition he behaved. He was so impressed by the strength and power he witnessed that he called Cus D'Amato, the former trainer of Floyd Patterson, and asked him to take a look.

Cus, who was after a last shot at vicarious glory, took one look and rushed home announcing he had seen his next world champion. The teenager was driven to a 15-room mansion overlooking the Hudson River in the Catskill Mountains, which became his new home. Cus devoted his time to teaching the boy. Every meal time was a seminar – on fishing, astronomy, history and destiny, but mostly on boxing. A grateful Mike said, 'He broke me down and built me back up. I became his slave.'

Mike was expelled from school after transgressions with girls but developed rapidly in the ring to a point where Cus launched his amateur career in 1981. After early setbacks he won the US under-19 super-heavyweight title in 1983 and the national Golden Gloves heavyweight title in 1984, but fell short in the Olympic trials.

Tyson was still 18 when he launched his professional career with a first round stoppage of Hector Mercedes on 6 March 1985 and it was soon clear that his style was more suited to the rules of prizefighting. D'Amato, who had become Tyson's legal guardian after Mike's mother died of cancer, decided on a two fights a month and was delighted with the progress of his pupil, but he never got to see the fruits of his labour. On 4 November 1985, three days after Mike's 11th fight, he died of pneumonia.

HBO organised a 'tournament' to create an undisputed champion – a much-needed development at a time when the upper ranks of the various boxing organisations were populated with men who were fat, drug-dependent or mediocre. After destroying Berbick, Tyson fought WBA champion James 'Bonecrusher' Smith in Las Vegas. Bonecrusher had been in with all the big names but was thoroughly spooked and clung on for 11 rounds. In the 12th he rocked Tyson with a hard right, but it was too late.

Tyson followed this by knocking out the former WBC champion Pinklon Thomas in six rounds and outpointing IBF champion Tony Tucker who had won all 35 of his fights. Next came the unbeaten Olympic super-heavyweight champion Tyrell Biggs. Tyson hated Biggs for the way he had 'disrespected' him during the Olympics and was out for revenge. Tyson punished him with brutal severity before knocking him out in round seven. He claimed Biggs 'screamed like a woman every time I hit him to the body'. Three months later he stopped Larry Holmes in four rounds and followed this in Tokyo with a two-round stoppage of another former WBA champion, Tony Tubbs. He then fought the linear world champion Michael Spinks, in Atlantic City on 28 June 1988, delivering an emphatic performance to become the first undisputed world heavyweight champion in a decade. He dropped the frightened Spinks with a combination and then knocked him flat on his back with a right uppercut – all within 91 seconds. Explaining his mindset he said, 'When I fight someone, I want to break his will. I want to take his manhood. I want to rip out his heart and show it to him.'

All was well in the ring but outside was chaos. It was becoming clear he was unable to cope with life as a celebrity. 'I love to hit people,' he said. 'Most celebrities are afraid someone's going to attack them. I want someone to attack me. No weapons. Just me and

him. I like to beat men and beat them bad.' Women were even more of a problem. He married the TV actor Robin Givens but she said he regularly beat her – backhanding her across the room before their marriage, bashing her in the face with a phone, 'choking me, kicking me and things like that'. She claimed that when the beating was over, 'he'd cry like a baby and I used to hold him and console him.' She said that throughout their time together he was constantly propositioning other women. Givens left with a large chunk of Tyson's money while promoter Don King, through his step son, Carl, took over Mike's management. After this, there were signs of decline in the ring, while the problems outside continued. He broke his hand beating up former opponent Mitch Green in a street fight. He drove a BMW into a tree in an apparent suicide attempt and there were further allegations of assault and sexual harassment.

Having previously fought every two months he waited eight months before his next fight, against Frank Bruno in Las Vegas on 25 February 1989. Bruno wobbled him in the first round, but even a faded version of Tyson was too quick and resilient for the Briton who was pounded to defeat five seconds from the end of the fifth. Five months later Tyson stopped Carl Williams in one round in Atlantic City.

He pulled out of a fight with the dangerous Donovan 'Razor' Ruddock, claiming pneumonia, and by the time of his next defence, against James 'Buster' Douglas in Tokyo on 11 February 1990, he had spent only one-and-a-half minutes in the ring in the previous year. It later emerged he was having problems while taking drugs for venereal disease and depression.

His preparations were chaotic, while his corner for the Douglas fight seemed to have no clue of what to do in a crisis. Douglas was a 42-1 underdog but he boxed with the

Mike Tyson in action against Evander Holyfield for the WBA heavyweight title on 11 September 1996. Don King considered the apparently declining Holyfield an ideal opponent but 'The Real Deal' withstood his punches, dropped him in the sixth round and stopped him in the eleventh.

assurance of a confident world champion, using a hard jab to block Tyson's advance and excellent footwork to keep away. Tyson dropped him with an uppercut in round eight but Douglas beat the slow count and went on to knock out Tyson in the tenth. Don King tried to get the result reversed because of the long count and the WBC's compliant president, Jose Sulaiman, played along for a while. In the end popular sentiment forced them to back down and – at the age of 23 – Tyson's reign had ended.

His third comeback opponent was the Canadian he had previously avoided, 'Razor' Ruddock, but the fight was controversially stopped in Tyson's favour in the seventh. At their 28 June 1991 return Ruddock matched Tyson punch for punch but Tyson got the decision although it was clear that the speed and combination punching of his younger days were a thing of the past.

Three days later Tyson went to the Miss Black America pageant in Indianapolis where he fondled the buttocks of the 23 contestants and made graphically obscene suggestions. He settled on an 18-year-old college student, Desiree Washington, later claiming she agreed to see him after he explained what he had in mind. The former convent girl had a different story and alleged rape. Tyson was charged but turned down the option of pleading guilty in exchange for a six-month sentence, saying he would rather go to jail for 100 years than admit to a rape he did not commit. He was sentenced to six years in jail and four on parole – a verdict upheld on appeal. While in prison he was cleaned of his substance abuse problems and given an incentive to learn – even becoming an avid reader. In his first comeback fight, on 19 August 1995, he was paid $22 million to bowl over the inept Pete McNeely in one round. He followed this by flattening Buster Mathis Jr in three, setting himself up for a shot at the WBC heavyweight title, held by Frank Bruno. Bruno looked terrified, crossing himself over and over. Mike had no trouble getting inside, battering him for two rounds and then finishing it 50 seconds into the third.

Don King refused to allow Tyson to defend against his mandatory challenger, Lennox Lewis, instead paying Lewis $4 million to step aside. When the Londoner's camp persisted, Tyson relinquished the WBC title in preference to fighting Lennox. Evander Holyfield looked like damaged goods, which made him the ideal opponent for Tyson's next fight in Las Vegas on 11 November 1996. Mike had slackened off in training. Why work hard for another quick outing against a faded veteran, smaller and older than Bruno? Evander trained with a religious devotion for 15 weeks and went into the ring feeling sure of victory. Tyson tired first, a victim of his truncated training, before Evander unleashed a volley of hard punches to get the fight stopped in the tenth round.

The much-awaited return, set for Las Vegas on 28 June 1997, was even rougher than the first fight. Holyfield got away with butting continuously without drawing a warning. One of these butts drew blood from Tyson's eye and a rare complaint from his mouth. Going into the third round the fight was evenly poised. Tyson came out without his gumshield and was sent back for it. He waited until they clinched and then bit a piece out of Holyfield's ear, spitting it onto the canvas. Two points were deducted and, after a delay of nearly four minutes, Tyson bit Evander's other ear. Astonishingly, the fight was allowed to continue until the end of the round when referee Mills Lane finally decided it was time to disqualify Tyson. Mike was fined $3 million and banned for a year.

Tyson was short of cash and blamed Don King, demanding money from him. When this was refused he was alleged to have kicked his promoter in the face. He then dumped King, suing him for $100 million. The case was eventually settled out of court when King paid Tyson $14 million to drop it. By then Tyson had four children with various women and spent time with them. His new wife, paediatrician Dr Monica Turner, described him as far more intelligent than portrayed in the media – a view anyone who has interviewed him would affirm. But his behaviour did not usually reflect this intelligence. During his year out he fell asleep riding his unlicensed motorbike and crashed it, breaking a rib and piercing a lung. 'I know I'm going to blow one day,' he said while recovering. 'My life is doomed the way it is. I have no future. I feel bad about my outlook, how I feel about people and society, and that I'll never be part of society the way I should.'

He returned to the ring in Las Vegas on 16 January 1999 against a former IBF title claimant, Frans Botha, and once again the public interest was enormous. As he put it, 'I could sell out Madison Square Garden masturbating.' Tyson resorted to trying to break Botha's arm in a clinch while being handily outboxed, but late in round five a single right cross put the South African out for the count.

Tyson had been involved in a road rage incident before the fight, kicking one man in the groin and punching another in the face, and this delayed his progress. Pleading 'no contest', he was sentenced to a year's imprisonment, a fine and two years of probation. He ended up spending time in solitary confinement after a 'disturbance' and was released after five months. On 23 October 1999 he fought former contender Orlin Norris in Las Vegas but after one round the bout was declared a 'no contest' because Tyson felled him after the bell. He then fought twice in Britain, showing his best behaviour in knocking out the British and Commonwealth champion Julius Francis in two rounds and the worst in knocking out the American Lou Savarese in 38 seconds – bowling over the referee and continuing to throw punches after the fight was stopped. He told the Glasgow crowd, 'I am the most ruthless, brutal champion ever. I am Sonny Liston and Jack Dempsey. There is no one who can match me.' With that off his chest he directed his rage at Lennox Lewis: 'I want to eat your heart out. I want to eat your children [*sic*].'

His volatility was attributed to his inconsistent use of an anti-depressant drug, of which he said, 'It has really messed me up and I don't want to be taking it, but they are concerned about the fact that I am a violent person, almost an animal, and they only want me to be an animal in the ring.' In his next fight, however, he behaved sensibly enough, dropping Andrej Golota in the second round, prompting the big Pole to retire to his corner, claiming a broken jaw, although the result was changed to 'no contest' when Tyson tested positive for cannabis.

He was out for a year but returned in Copenhagen, Denmark on 13 October 2001, weighing a career-heaviest of 239 lb., to stop the 259 lb. Dane Brian Nielsen in seven. Soon after, he signed to fight Lewis for the world title but the bout was almost scuppered by his behaviour at a New York press conference. Tyson marched towards Lewis, knocked over one of his bodyguards and brought his hands up to the punching position. Lewis then dropped him with a right at which point Mike sunk his teeth into Lennox's thigh.

Mike Tyson sits on the canvas after being knocked out by Danny Williams on 31 July 2004. He was fully conscious but looking dispirited and exhausted, and suffering from a twisted knee, he took the full count. A year later he lost to the inept Kevin McBride and retired.

The real fight was rescheduled for Memphis, Tennessee on 8 June 2002 and Tyson went off to the Hawaiian Island of Maui to train, while reflecting on his standing in the world. 'Mike Tyson is a bad nigger but he's very popular,' he said. 'I'm just a dark shadowy figure from the bowels of iniquity. I wish I could be Mike who gets an endorsement deal but you can't make a lie and truth go together. I would love to be Tiger Woods. I would love to be Michael Jordan.'

It sounded like reflective logic but with Tyson self-pity inevitably followed. 'I love my babies, don't crucify me for what I am. You guys have written so much bad stuff about me. I can't remember the last time I fucked a decent woman. I have to go with strippers and whores and bitches because you put that image on me.' He told a female journalist that he did not do interviews with women unless he was having sex with them; then told the male journalists that he wished he could stomp on the testicles of their children, 'so you could feel my pain'.

Despite all this nonsense he worked hard, sparring 160 rounds and building up his strength with the idea of overpowering Lewis quickly. He said his objective was 'to be professional and kill him – to take his soul and smear his pompous brains all over the ring'. Instead the 234 lb. Tyson took the most severe beating of his career. He attacked furiously in the opening round and landed several hard punches, but from then on it was one-sided. The 249 lb. Lewis was so much bigger and stronger and Tyson struggled to get inside his heavy jab. When he did, he was met by hurtful uppercuts or simply pushed away. Lewis cut him up, dropped him heavily in round four – officially ruled a push – and beat him up badly. In round eight Tyson took a count after going down on his haunches from a left uppercut and right cross and was knocked out by a massive right hook to the jaw, taking the full count, with blood dripping from every

KINGS OF THE RING

orifice, at the 2 minutes 25 second mark. It took half a minute before he could stand again, after which he approached his conqueror, gently stroking his face while saying, 'He knows I love him. He knows I have respect.'

The beating was so one-sided it was essential to rebuild his reputation before the contracted return. First up was former contender Clifford Etienne in Memphis on 22 February 2003. But Tyson, who three weeks earlier was divorced from Monica (with whom he had two children), disappeared, re-emerging with a Polynesian facial tattoo while claiming to be ill. He was coaxed back to work. 'They offered me more money and that makes you better real quick,' he said. 'If I didn't get it, I'd have been sick again.' He knocked out Etienne in 49 seconds and was then set to fight on the undercard of a Lewis bill but withdrew. 'I got some serious demons I'm fighting,' he explained. 'I hate my life now. Maybe in the next life I'll have a better life.'

Instead of earning $20 million from fighting Lewis he earned a community service sentence after beating up two aggressive autograph seekers in a hotel lobby. Tyson, who had earned $300 million during his career, was declared bankrupt and began selling his mansions to pay his $40 million debts. 'I've got nowhere to live. I've been crashing with friends, literally sleeping in shelters,' he claimed. 'Unsavoury characters are giving me money and I'm taking it. I need it.'

He went 17 months without fighting, saying 'it's probably too difficult to get into shape now' but resumed his career because he had no other way of earning money. His opponent in Louisville, Kentucky, on 30 July 2004 was the 265 lb. Englishman Danny Williams. Tyson shook him up him in the first round but then twisted his own knee. After that he was not able to punch properly and was knocked out at the end of the fourth round – fully conscious but unwilling to rise.

He tried again on 11 June 2005, against the 271 lb. Kevin McBride. When he was unable to put away the slow, clumsy Irishman he resorted to butting, tried to break McBride's arm in a clinch and bit his nipple. He was ahead on points by the end of the sixth round but, exhausted, he decided to retire in his corner. The fighter who, in his prime, said: 'How dare they challenge me with their primitive skills?' admitted his own skills had deteriorated to the point where he had nothing left. 'If I can't beat McBride I can't even beat Jill or Joe,' he said. 'I just don't have this in my gut anymore. I'm not going to disrespect the sport by losing to this calibre of fighter. I most likely won't fight anymore.'

Mike Tyson's career lasted more than 20 years although his peak as a fighting man was brief – an orgy of destruction from 1986 until 1988. During those two wonderful years he was one of the finest heavyweights ever to lace on a pair of gloves. His power and aggression drew the punters, but it was complimented by extraordinary speed, excellent balance, footwork and head movement, brilliant combination punching, sharp defensive technique and a fine left jab. Outside of the ring, there was no control. He spoke for the ghetto, but not in any considered way. Rather, he symbolised its unpredictable dangers, its violence, its sense of desperation. He was the rapist, the thug, the metaphorical killer, until, slowly, the venom burned out and near the end he became a figure of pathos – a poke-him-and-see-if-he-snarls parody of his terrifying past. Still, he was boxing's last iconic champion – a man whose reputation outgrew his sport, albeit for reasons that were invariably negative, frequently vile and, in the end, simply sad.

James 'Buster' Douglas

World heavyweight champion 1990.

'Buster Douglas gave me the blueprint on how to beat Tyson. You look at that fight and you say, OK, this is when Tyson was supposed to be his most ferocious and this guy's mother's dying, he's out in Japan by himself and everybody's against him, yet he came out on top.'
Lennox Lewis, 2004

Height: 6'3¾
Peak weight: 226–232 lb.
38 wins (25 stoppages),
6 losses, 1 draw, 1 no contest
Born: Columbus, Ohio,
7 April 1960

If fighters were rated solely on their finest moments then James 'Buster' Douglas would fit right in with the elite. His shock victory over Mike Tyson in Tokyo on 11 February 1990 was not merely the result of Tyson's forgetfulness in the training department. Buster boxed out of his skin – showing the speed, power, strength and mindset of a superior champion.

The reigning champion's troubles were legion: drugs, depression, alcohol, a cavalier disregard for his opponent and an incompetent pair of trainers. But Douglas also faced obstacles. He had recently separated from his wife and then his mother, Lula, died of leukaemia shortly before he departed for Tokyo.

From the first bell the 42-1 underdog Douglas boxed with intelligent aggression using fast, heavy jabs but in round eight he relaxed and Tyson caught him with a massive right uppercut. He waited for the referee to count eight and then rose. It later emerged the count lasted 12 seconds. Douglas bounced back and in the tenth kept on landing big right hands and Tyson became disoriented. A blistering combination, ending with a big right, finally put him down on his back and out for the count. Don King claimed the 'slow count' voided the victory and although the WBC initially complied, public pressure forced them to change their minds and recognise Douglas's victory.

Buster grew up in Columbus, Ohio, and after a decent amateur career turned professional with a run of 22 wins in 25 fights leading to his first title fight against the talented and unbeaten Tony Tucker for the vacant IBF title. Douglas boxed well for nine rounds but in the tenth Tucker trapped him on the ropes, landed a few hard punches and Buster turned away and gave up. He was branded a quitter. But once he realised what he'd thrown away, he emerged a more resolute fighter.

However, after beating Tyson he regressed. His first challenge was against the extremely self-confident Evander Holyfield. Buster's manager and trainer did their best but after seven months of partying they struggled to get him into presentable shape and he waddled in at 246 lb. Holyfield, in contrast, was a ripped 208 lb. Douglas was slow and sloppy. A minute into the third round Holyfield hit him with a stiff, well-timed right cross counter and Douglas went down for the count – looking like he was conscious enough to drag himself up but couldn't be bothered. After this he couldn't be bothered to do anything but eat. His weight passed the 350 lb. mark and on 8 July 1994 he was rushed to hospital, slipping in and out of a diabetic coma. He realised that he would soon die unless he lost weight and the only way he knew to do this was through boxing. He went back to the gym, got his weight down to 233 lb. and made a brief comeback career, winning eight out of nine fights, before retiring to a successful career in property.

James 'Buster' Douglas knocking out Mike Tyson on 1 February 1990, Tokyo. After going down for the first time in his career Tyson groped for his gumshield, stuck it halfway into his mouth and was counted out. 'There I was preparing for one of the biggest nights of my life and all the things in my life were going bad, but I stayed focused and was able to lean on boxing to bring me through that storm.' Douglas said.

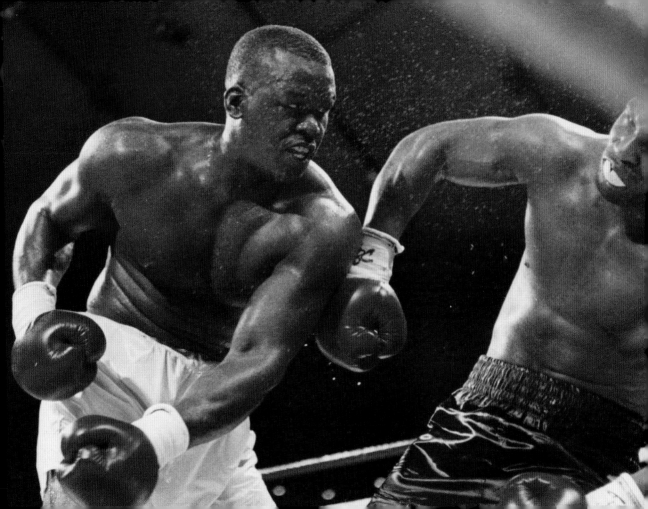

Evander Holyfield – 'The Real Deal'

World heavyweight champion 1990–92, 1993–94; WBA heavyweight title holder 1996–99; 2000–01; WBA/IBF heavyweight title holder 1997–99; world cruiserweight champion 1988; WBA cruiserweight title holder 1986–88; WBA/IBF cruiserweight title holder 1987–88.

'One thing you've got to realise with Evander: there are better boxers and bigger punchers, sure, but no fighter, ever, has invested so much in winning; no fighter has his drive and willpower; no fighter is as competitive. No fighter has his heart.'
Lou Duva, Holyfield's first professional trainer.

Height: 6'2
Peak weight: 187–218 lb
38 wins (25 stoppages),
8 losses, 2 draws
Born: Atmore, Alabama,
9 October 1962

No world heavyweight champion has had more lives than Evander Holyfield. Every time he was written off, he reinvented or at least reinvigorated himself. He was not a consistent performer at heavyweight, often fought dirty, made elaborate excuses when beaten, and as he got older the gaps between the failures shrank. But whatever the outcome, that extraordinary warrior spirit – a combination of faith in his God, faith in himself and that inability to own up to weakness – was truly a wonder to behold.

And never more so than during first his victory over Mike Tyson, in Las Vegas on 9 November 1996, when he started out as a 22-1 underdog. He was only picked by Don King because he looked terrible in his previous two outings. When Mike's co-manager Rory Holloway speculated that Mike might just kill Evander, the sense of outrage was made that much more shrill by the perception that this might just happen.

Evander believed Tyson was the man God picked for him to conquer. Right from the start the 215 lb. Holyfield showed he was not intimidated, which meant the 222 lb. Tyson was deprived of his usual psychological dominance. Mike went out with his big guns but Evander held firm, clinched and fought back. The champion realised he was in with a man who could match him for strength and surpass him in boxing ability, and he soon ran short of ideas. The battle developed into an intense, often scrappy one. The 34-year-old challenger grabbed, butted, and threw quick, hard punches and then grabbed again – in this way sapping Tyson's strength, knowing he could be confident in his own superb conditioning. He landed a well-timed left hook in the sixth round and Tyson went down on his backside, sliding across the canvas. He recovered but with each round Holyfield's lock on the fight became harder to break. At the end of the tenth he hammered Tyson with heavy, unanswered punches on the ropes. Tyson wobbled back to his corner, dazed and depleted. Holyfield pounced on him at the start of round 11, driving him into the ropes where he pounded Tyson into a state of complete defencelessness until the referee, Mitch Halpern, stopped the fight.

Evander was the youngest of five sons and four daughters of single mother Annie Laura Holyfield. They moved to Atlanta, Georgia when he was a child and he said he had a 'respectable working-class childhood'. His ambitions focussed on achieving greatness on the football field but he was intrigued at what went on in the restricted zone of the Warren Memorial Boys Club. Eventually he laced on the gloves and gave it a try

With a $100 million in assets many questioned Holyfield's need to fight Mike Tyson, the most feared unarmed man on the planet. Emanuel Steward, who trained him for two fights, offered this insight, 'Everyone who doesn't know Evander thinks of him as this humble nice guy but I've never met anyone with an ego like his. That's why he's doing it. He had an obsession about being the best: best fighter, richest man, best in bed, best body, best in the eyes of God.'

and excelled through a combination of natural talent and extreme dedication. After leaving school he worked pumping airplane fuel and as a lifeguard at a local pool, but by then his true ambition was to win the world heavyweight title. In 1984 he won a place at light heavyweight on the US Olympic team and was rated as the most mature and 'professional' of the boxers on the squad, but he was disqualified in the semi-finals for felling his New Zealand opponent on the break – going home disappointed with the bronze medal. His amateur record stood at 160 wins (75 stoppages) and 14 losses.

Two months later, at the age of 22, he turned professional at light heavyweight, trained by Lou Duva and the former middleweight contender George Benton. They moved him to cruiserweight and after 18 months as a professional and 11 bouts, he was ready to challenge the formidable Dwight Muhammad Qawi for the WBA title in Atlanta on 12 July 1986. Qawi battled him at close quarters, with both men taking heavy punishment, but Holyfield closed stronger to take a split decision. They fought a return in New Jersey 17 months later, but this time Evander dominated, winning on a fourth round knockout. He then fought IBF champion Ricky Parkey, who was stopped in three rounds. He finally unified the cruiserweight title by stopping the WBC champion Carlos de Leon in eight rounds in Las Vegas on 9 April 1988.

Evander then picked up six heavyweight wins to earn his shot at the heavyweight title. The toughest of these came against the rejuvenated former WBA heavyweight title holder Michael Dokes in Las Vegas on 11 March 1989. Dokes hit the 208 lb. Holyfield low several times so when Evander returned to his corner Lou Duva told him, 'You go out there, get your right hand and put it right into his cup. You got that? Hit him low.' Holyfield said, 'OK,' and, as Duva recalled, 'He goes right out there and boom! Dokes is falling over and calling foul and he had to have a rest, so I hollered out to him: "You damn dog, next time I'm gonna rip your balls off if you keep hitting my boy low." And he did it no more. If I told him to walk through a wall, he'd just say "okay" and he'd do it.' After an intense battle he stopped Dokes in the tenth round.

His third round world title victory over Buster Douglas in Las Vegas on 25 October 1990 was anticlimatic in comparison. Buster was in such poor condition and folded so easily that Evander wasn't given much credit. He then outboxed the 42-year-old George Foreman in Atlantic City on 9 April 1991 and wobbled him a few times, but was criticised for failing to put him away. Tyson was supposed to come next but he suffered a rib injury in training. The unbeaten Italian Francesco Damiani came in as a late replacement but he broke his ankle in training. At the last minute the former cruiserweight contender Bert Cooper stepped in. Holyfield dropped him in the first round but then in the third round was smashed into the ropes. The 215 lb. Cooper was about to finish the badly wounded champion with his big right when the referee stepped in and administered the first count of Holyfield's career. He recovered and was fortunate that the ill-prepared Cooper was in no state to capitalise. Holyfield stopped his spirited challenger in the seventh round, but the general view was that he was lucky he wasn't fighting Tyson. His third defence, in Las Vegas on 19 June 1992, was against 42-year-old Larry Holmes who frustrated and cut him, winning four of the 12 rounds.

For his next fight, against the unbeaten Riddick Bowe in Las Vegas on 13 November 1992 , he came in at 205 lb. – his lightest in over four years. They fought with fervour

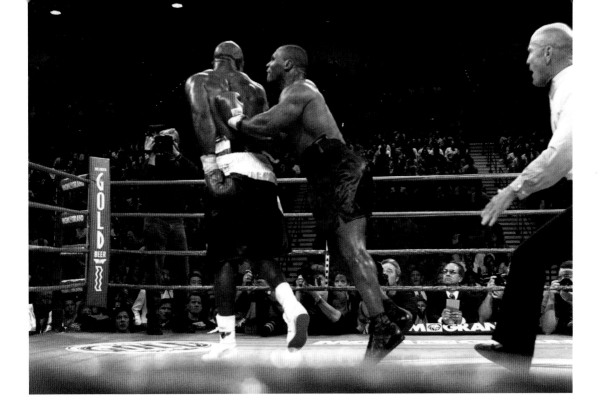

and skill, with Bowe's 30 lb. weight advantage giving him a slight edge, confirmed at the end of the ninth when he hurt Evander with a right. Bowe shook Holyfield with a wicked uppercut in the tenth and proceeded to pour it on, dishing out a sustained battering. Then, just when it looked like Holyfield was finished, he started firing back with his own hooks, driving Riddick across the ring. Early in round 11 Holyfield moved into a clinch and Bowe slipped under his arms and landed a right hook behind the head, dropping him. Once again Evander fought back but the knockdown sealed the result and Bowe won on a unanimous decision.

Holyfield went quiet for a while but returned seven months on to outpoint a former opponent, Alex Stewart. Then in Las Vegas on 6 November 1993 he fought his return with Bowe. Right from the start it was clear Holyfield was hitting considerably harder than before, driving Bowe back, moving in and out with telling combinations, while avoiding the young champion's big right cross. By the halfway mark Riddick looked exhausted while Evander was still fresh, hammering the champion on the ropes. It was starting to look like a stoppage might be possible when, two minutes into the seventh round, a parachutist flew through the hole in the Caesars Palace roof and landed with one leg over the ring ropes, at which point Bowe's goons pounded him into unconsciousness. This strange incident gave Bowe 21 minutes to recover and he regained control and completely dominated the final round. But Holyfield's early work deservedly secured him a majority decision. He was world champion again.

Instead of trying to reunify the title by fighting the WBC belt holder Lennox Lewis, Holyfield opted for a defence against Michael Moorer in Las Vegas on 22 April 1994.

Evander Holyfield recoils in agony after being bitten by Mike Tyson on 28 June 1997. In the second round Holyfield used his head to open a cut above Tyson's eye, but the first two rounds were scored evenly by the judges. In round three Tyson bit off a piece of Holyfield's ear, but amazingly the referee, Mills Lane, allowed the bout to continue. Tyson bit again, and finally at the end of the round Lane disqualified him.

Evander Holyfield goes down during a bout against Riddick Bowe at Caesars Palace, Las Vegas, on 4 November 1995, in which Bowe won the fight with a technical knockout in the eighth round. It was his first of two stoppage defeats and he was dropped six times. At the end of his career Holyfield refuted suggestions that he was starting to slur his speech as a result of brain damage and declared, 'I am not fearful and I ask you not to be, but instead have faith as I do.'

His efforts seemed strangely lethargic. He dropped Moorer in the second round, but failed to make much impression after that and lost a fair majority decision.

Holyfield was out for over a year, coming back with an impressive performance in outpointing Ray Mercer over ten rounds. This set him up for a third bout with Bowe in Las Vegas on 5 November 1995. Both men showed signs of deterioration but they nevertheless fought another intense battle. The big man shaded the early rounds but in the sixth the 213 lb. Holyfield poleaxed the 240 lb. Bowe with a cracking left hook to the chin. It looked like it was all over but he made it up and survived the round. After this Holyfield had very little left. He had one last try in round eight but left himself open. Bowe caught him with a right cross and he went down. He clambered up but Bowe dropped him again and referee Joe Cortez stopped the fight. Holyfield blamed a pre-fight illness and returned six months later to stop the former light heavyweight and cruiserweight champion Bobby Czyz in five rounds but looked curiously weak – spindly legs, 30-inch waist and an absence of those mighty biceps – but the surprise victory over Iron Mike erased all the doubts and established Evander's reputation as the great comeback king.

For the return, in Las Vegas on 28 June 1997, the 6-4 odds favoured Tyson and it was hard to tell from the three completed rounds what would have happened if Mike hadn't lost his head by biting Evander's ears. Some ringsiders felt the 218 lb. Holyfield had shown his dominance and that Tyson started chomping as a way out because he knew he was going to lose; others that the 218 lb. Tyson was gaining an edge and that he had merely responded in a state of rage to Evander's headbutting and the failure of the referee to do anything about it. In any event, after two bites in the third round, with one little piece of Evander's ear lying on the canvas, the fight was stopped and awarded to Holyfield on a technical knockout.

Evander's next fight, again in Las Vegas on 8 November 1997, saw him gaining revenge over Moorer to unify the WBA and IBF titles, dropping him five times before the ringside doctor advised the referee to stop the fight at the end of the eighth round.

His rival for the right to call himself world champion was Lennox Lewis, who held the WBC title, and after two years of negotiations, Evander's promoter Don King agreed to a two-fight deal – the first leg taking place at Madison Square Garden on 13 March 1999. Evander trained with his usual intense focus but found himself unsettled when Lewis called him a hypocrite – pointing to the contradiction between his frequent professions of his gospel quoting fundamentalist Christian faith, and his continued practice of fathering children outside of his three marriages. These accusations got to Evander, who claimed to have seen a vision of victory – knocking out Lewis in the third round.

The 246 lb. Lewis outboxed the 215 lb. Holyfield for two rounds but in round three Evander threw himself into a violent attack. Lewis responded by boxing in retreat before taking over again. Holyfield admitted, 'I knew I'd done wrong picking the round. It gave him an advantage, no question, when I failed to knock him out.' Evander tried everything he knew – hooks, head butts, low blows – but he failed to unsettle Lewis. He ended the fight with his face swollen and lumpy and it seemed clear he was beaten by a wide margin. He'd thrown 348 punches to Lewis's 613 and had been outlanded 2½-1. But the official result was a draw, prompting an outpouring of rage and condemnation.

No proof of corruption was established and Don King was permitted to promote the return in Las Vegas on 13 November 1999. Evander trained even harder while Lennox found it hard to motivate himself for what he assumed was an easy assignment. The result was an intense battle of attrition, fought mainly at close range. Holyfield delivered his finest performance since the first Tyson fight, while Lewis delivered one of his worst, neglecting his jab. Evander landed plenty of low blows and head butts but his fists were also working efficiently. He absorbed huge uppercuts, crosses and body punches and kept on coming. But Lewis closed the last two rounds stronger to take a unanimous decision.

Lewis was forced to give up the WBA portion of his unified title (the result of a prior contractual agreement with Don King), and so, on 3 March 2000, Holyfield won a disputed points decision over John Ruiz to claim the belt, but it was clear he had deteriorated markedly. His last good fight was on 1 June 2002 when he met former world champion Hassim Rahman in Atlantic City. Holyfield boxed well although it was his head that caused a grotesque swelling around Rahman's eye. The bout was stopped in the eighth round and went to the scorecards, with Evander winning by a split decision. After losing a wide points decision to Chris Byrd he fought the 35-year-old IBF cruiserweight champion James Toney and looked strong for two rounds, after which he ran out of ideas and was beaten up. In round nine he was dropped for the sixth time in his career and his trainer, Don Turner, threw in the towel. He fired Turner and returned at the age of 42, as an undercard fighter, still declaring it his goal to regain the world title, but instead was outboxed by the unrated Larry Donald, losing 11 out of 12 rounds. After this the New York State Athletics Commission took away his licence.

Since then Holyfield, who owns his own dance studio, has taken part in a nationally televised ballroom dancing competition, but, ominously, he occasionally talks about fighting on. 'I still want to leave boxing as the undisputed heavyweight champion of the world.'

Michael Moorer – 'Double M'

World heavyweight champion 1994; IBF heavyweight title holder 1996–97.

'Michael Moorer was definitely one of the greatest light heavyweights in the history of boxing.'
His first trainer, **Emanuel Steward**, 2003.

Height: 6'2
Peak weight 175–222 lb.
47 wins (37 stoppages),
4 losses, 1 draw
Born New York,
12 November 1967

The fight epitomising the best and worst of Double M was the one that delivered the world title – in Las Vegas on 22 April 1994. The 26-year-old Moorer had won 34 straight with 30 knockouts but his signs of a dodgy chin, lethargic attitude and habit of getting disorderly when drunk, made him an unpredictable commodity. Late in round two Moorer walked into a right cross and a left hook and went down. Holyfield failed to capitalise and Moorer came back, hurting the older man with solid southpaw left crosses. But in the eighth Moorer eased off, allowing Holyfield back. With Teddy Atlas, Moorer's agressive trainer, imploring him to act, Moorer did a bit more in the last two rounds – enough to pick up a deserved majority decision.

Michael grew up in Monessen, Pennsylvania, a hyperactive child who began boxing after a psychologist suggested it would be good for him. He was not a consistent trainer but clearly had talent and power. In 1986 he joined Emanuel Steward's famed Kronk Gym in Detroit, and began his professional career with a one round stoppage win and within eight months he had won the low-rent WBO light heavyweight title. Soon after his final light heavyweight bout he was arrested for brawling – one of several drink related run-ins with the law.

He moved to heavyweight, dropped Steward, changed his style from banger to boxer and won the world title. He chose the nearly 46-year-old Foreman for his first defence and it went as expected for nine rounds, with Moorer dominating. But 20 seconds into round 10 Foreman connected with Moorer's fragile chin, sending him down for the count. It was a devestating experience he could never escape. 'That's all people want to talk about,' he later moaned.

He regrouped to outpoint Axel Schulz for the vacant IBF title and successfully, if unspectacularly, defended it against Frans Botha and Vaughn Bean, and prepared for a unification bout with Evander Holyfield. Moorer initially had the edge, landing hard and accurately, but in the fifth Holyfield got that glass chin. He went down five times before the fight was stopped. For three years he stayed away from boxing, getting into more drink-related trouble before quiting drink and beginning training for a comeback. After four wins and a technical draw he accepted a bout with the big-hitting heavyweight David Tua. With one left hook it was over – 30 seconds including the count: the 11th knockdown and the third stoppage defeat of his career.

His final bout was on 9 December 2004 against Vassily Jirov, who outboxed Moorer for eight rounds before being flattened with a single left cross. Moorer decided this was a good note to end on– apparently satisfied with his achievements and no longer the sullen insecure brooding presence of the past.

Winning the IBF title fight against Axel Schulz was not one of Moorer's better displays. At one point, when he returned to his corner, he found his emotional trainer, Teddy Atlas, sitting on his stool, sarcastically offering to take over. Still, he seemed to win clearly, although the official result was a split decision victory. This was the second time he held a version of the heavyweight title. He also held the WBO light heavyweight title for over two years.

Riddick Bowe – 'Big Daddy'

World heavyweight champion 1992–93.

'I've got no one to blame but myself.'
Riddick Bowe, 2003

Height: 6'5
Peak weight: 225–243 lb.
42 wins (33 stoppages), 1 loss, 1 no contest
Born: Fort Washington, Maryland
10 August 1967

The sight of Riddick Bowe, waddling around at 280 lb., getting shaken to his boots by a small journeyman is not pretty, but still more hopeful than the wife-beater, kidnapper, jailbird, or even the Marine drop-out. He might sound ridiculous talking about his desire to face the retired Lennox Lewis while fighting the occasional no-hoper, but by the standards of his previous decade, this is an improvement. It is hard to talk about 'Big Daddy' without a sense of pathos. What might have been is never far away. Bowe was a boxer of superior talent: serious power, impressive punch variety and an ability to fight inside or at a distance. A flawed fighter, perhaps, and a dirty one certainly, but he could've been a contender for greatness. What he lacked was the mind of a champion.

Only once in 44 fights did Bowe reveal his immense potential: in his first encounter with Evander Holyfield in Las Vegas on 13 November 1992 when he won the title. Riddick was emerging as the darling of HBO and the New York media: a big, talented heavyweight, with a great triumph-over-adversity story to tell and a sense of fun. He was the anti-Tyson – proof that even the worst ghettos have their Cinderellas. And yet he also came with niggling doubts about whether he had the discipline and strength of character to prevail. There were also doubts about Bowe's abrasive, thin-skinned manager Rock Newman although everyone loved his wizened old trainer, Eddie Futch.

Futch honed Bowe's conditioning to a hard 235 lb. – 30 lb. more than the underweight Holyfield. 'I'm going to knock out that little man you call the heavyweight champion of the world,' he said. What followed was 47 minutes of the best action the division had ever seen – a back and forth thriller, packed with power, skill and courage. Bowe used his heavy jab to make openings for his cross and when they fought up close he used short hooks and uppercuts, showing his mastery of infighting. Holyfield responded with rapid-fire combinations, boxing with skill and aggression. They took turns to turn it on. By the end of the ninth Bowe's size and power gave him a three point edge in the eyes of two judges (the third had Holyfield up one point). In the tenth Bowe detonated an uppercut under Holyfield's chin and battered him around the ring with huge, accurate, unanswered hooks, uppercuts and crosses. Evander was taking a terrible beating and the referee, Joe Cortez, looked like he might step in. But then Bowe began to tire and Holyfield regrouped, driving the bigger man across the ring with his own hard hooks. 'He was laying a lot of leather on me,' Holyfield explained. 'He hurt me and he had me going from pillar to post, yet I felt, "This is the round I have the chance to knock him out." Even though he had me hurt he was expending a lot of energy. I knew he was going to miss one and I was going to have a chance to catch him. I did catch him but he proved he was a champion by staying in there.' Still, it was Bowe's round and by dropping Holyfield with a right behind the head in round eleven and closing strongly

Riddick Bowe in November 1993 shortly before losing his heavyweight title in a return with Evander Holyfield. He had a disappointing title reign that saw him facing two inept no-hopers rather than the man who had beaten him in the Seoul Olympics, Lennox Lewis.

in the twelfth he won a clear decision. The bout strengthened Holyfield's reputation for bravery and reinvented Bowe as a big man with the commitment, courage and energy to go with his size and talent.

Child number 12 out of 13 of headstrong Dorothy Bowe, Riddick grew up in the same Brownsville district as Tyson. Uzi-wielding crack dealers controlled their tenement block at 250 Lott Avenue. People were regularly shot and every night they could hear screams. But Riddick sidestepped the drug merchants and seemed such a sunny character. Despite an official IQ of 79 he was clearly no fool, with a particular talent for spot-on mimicry (Ronald Reagan, Bill Cosby, Muhammad Ali and Stevie Wonder were his favourites). But this was not the whole truth. Bowe might have avoided the gangs but his environment left its scars. Rock Newman later conceded his protégé came from 'a pretty dysfunctional family', adding that he was 'not a guy with a lot of self-motivation' and that 'he could be very mean-spirited'. It left its scars in more direct ways too. His sister, Brenda, was stabbed to death by crack dealers in 1988. Then Riddick learned that one of his brothers was dying of Aids. Shortly after the Olympics the *Daily News* quoted Dorothy on her son's achievements amid such scum. One of her daughters sent a bouquet to congratulate her on speaking out. It arrived on her doorstep in a garbage can that also contained the murdered delivery man, prompting Riddick's decision to move them to Maryland. But in the build-up to the Olympics they were still in Brownsville – Dorothy, Riddick, his wife Judy, their two children, a brother and a sister – seven in a two-bedroom apartment, waiting for deliverance.

The 21-year-old Riddick was the best amateur super heavy in America but not in the world. He was dropped twice in losing to Cuba's Jorge Luis Gonzalez, but when Cuba boycotted the Seoul Olympics the Americans were convinced their man was a sure thing for the gold, despite the fact that Canada's Lennox Lewis had done rather better against Gonzalez – losing a dubious split decision and then winning a wide decision in the return. Predicting he would 'take this Canadian to school' he bloodied Lewis's nose in a scrappy first round but was deducted a point for dangerous use of his head and by the end of the round was being driven back. Early in the second he was caught with two hard jabs and a blistering right-left-right combination. Bowe wobbled and fell on the ropes, breathing heavily from the shock of being hit so hard. The German referee stepped in to issue a standing eight count. Lewis bashed him with another right that rocked his head back and then a left hook. The referee issued another standing count. Bowe turned around with a dazed look in his eyes, and the fight was waved off. When the Canadian anthem was played the devastated Bowe asked Lewis if he could join him on the top step. Lewis refused and Bowe responded, 'See you in the pros.'

He was auditioned by Lou Duva and George Benton, who were unimpressed. 'Piece of shit,' Duva concluded. 'No heart, no balls. I had him here three times until finally Tyrell Biggs knocked him out in sparring by hitting him in the belly and then we threw him out for good. When the going gets tough he's not going to be there.' Riddick was about to join the Marines when he was approached by a chubby, chip-on-the-shoulder radio talk show host who sold his BMW to finance Riddick's career. Rock Newman fought tenaciously for him, sometimes physically (like the time when an opponent fouled Riddick and Rock leapt onto the ring apron and throttled the fellow). They tried various

trainers, until finally the 77-year-old Eddie Futch gave the lad a try. Futch, who had trained 17 world champions, told Bowe to run alone in the hills of Las Vegas at 5 am. Bowe agreed. Futch – or Papa Smurf as he was known – drove to the hills at 4.45 and waited. Fifteen minutes later he spotted Riddick labouring up the hills. He had passed his trial. 'This boy has been misunderstood,' he declared and he started teaching him the tricks learned from his 60 years in the game.

Bowe launched his career by stopping future contender Lionel Butler in two rounds in March 1989 and picked up 14 wins by the end of his first year and eight more by the end of his second. In 1992 the boxing promoter Dan Duva (Lou's son) negotiated a four-way 'box-off': Riddick would fight Holyfield if he got past Pierre Coetzer, while Lewis would meet Razor Ruddock, with the winner meeting the Holyfield–Bowe victor. An overweight Bowe laboured his way through the Coetzer fight landing several low blows along the way. Late in round seven, he buried his fist deep into Coetzer's groin and the South African bent over in agony. Riddick belted him a few more times and the referee, Mills Lane, pulled him off – awarding Bowe the fight on a technical knockout with one second to go. Asked why he kept pounding the 6'3 Coetzer in the groin, the 6'5 Bowe explained: 'I hit him low because I never fought anyone so tall.'

After winning the world title Bowe and Newman took a cynical approach, picking two of the worst challengers since Joe Frazier's reign 20 years earlier. First came the fat, 34-year-old, drug-addicted Michael Dokes – stopped in one round. Then the tough

Riddick Bowe and Jorge Luis Gonzalez during their bout at the MGM Grand in Las Vegas, Nevada on 17 June 1995. Gonzalez had knocked him down twice as an amateur and the pair had an intense hatred of each other. Riddick trained harder than in any fight since winning the world title in 1992 and won in six rounds.

Ray Mercer was proposed but the former Olympic champion lost a decision to journeyman Jesse Ferguson, and so Bowe fought Ferguson, knocking him out 17 seconds into round two. In the meantime Newman took him to South Africa to meet Nelson Mandela, to the Vatican to meet the Pope and got him to endorse the disgraced Washington DC Mayor Marion Barry, who had been caught smoking crack. It was hardly ideal preparation for the 11 November 1993 return with a fitter, stronger, heavier and markedly more muscular Holyfield, especially since Bowe was pigging out on fast food, his weight rising to over 270 lb. Bowe may have been saved by 'Fan Man' James Miller who descended in his parachute in the seventh round at a time when Holyfield was dishing out a beating, but justice was done and Bowe lost on points. His 11 months and 21 days as world champion ended and much of the boxing world breathed a collective sigh of relief.

Newman then decided they needed Lewis, who accepted their challenge for March 1995. But it never happened because Lewis lost his WBC title to Oliver McCall. Riddick was fortunate to get a 'no contest' rather than a disqualification for pounding the unprepossessing Buster Mathis Jr. on the canvas after dropping him. He followed this by punching Larry Donald in the face at a press conference before outpointing him and stopping Britain's weak-chinned Herbie Hide in six rounds. Bowe then fought a more serious opponent, the 6'7 Cuban Jorge Luis Gonzalez who had beaten him as an amateur and was now unbeaten in 23 fights. There was such bad feeling between them that they had to be separated into perspex booths before the fight. Futch worked Bowe into excellent shape while Gonzalez barely trained, and the result was an impressive sixth round knockout for Riddick: his last outstanding performance.

He suffered a heavy knockdown before putting away Holyfield in their 'rubber' match in Las Vegas on 4 November that year – a fight supposed to be prelude to a 'showdown' with Lewis. But the promoters Main Events persuaded Newman that their interests lay in first taking on the unbeaten Pole, Andrej Golota, so once again the Lewis fight fell through. Bowe, who was dumped by Futch for his indiscipline, came in at his career-heaviest of 252 lb. for their fight at Madison Square Garden on 11 July 1996. The 242 lb. Golota marched through his punches and bashed him from one side of the ring to the other. Riddick tried his share of rough stuff – rabbit punches and punching after the bell – but for once he was outdone. Despite his success Golota could not resist the temptation to go for the groin. Late in round seven Bowe sunk to the canvas after being whacked to the testicles and was declared the winner on a disqualification. African-American outrage at Golota's foul tactics and Polish-American outrage at the manner of Bowe's victory prompted a riot, leading to 16 arrests and numerous injuries. One of Bowe's cornermen bashed Golota on the head with a mobile phone, opening a gash, which was more than Riddick managed. They fought again in Atlantic City five months later. This time Bowe arrived at his title-winning weight of 235 lb, but his beating was even more severe. Golota was so much more powerful and delivered a mainly one-sided pounding. Bowe managed to drop Golota once but he was up quickly and knocked Bowe down twice. Yet he could not resist going low. Going into the ninth round he was comfortably ahead and looked set for a stoppage victory but once again he spoiled it by teeing off with three huge blows to the groin, earning another disqualification loss. What was most alarming, however, was the way Bowe spoke after the fight, fluffing his consonants and muffling his vowels – a clear sign of trauma to the brain.

The 29-year-old decided to fulfil his teenage ambition to join the Marines but gave up after a week. Although he hardly needed the money he took a job at $10.49 per hour as a high school security guard and gave that up too. Reports emerged of incidents of domestic violence – against his sister and then against his wife Judy. As he later put it: 'Once I retired everything fell apart. My personal life, everything, just went crazy.' He beat Judy up several times and then in April 1997 knocked her unconscious. 'I remember my youngest boy telling the other kids that daddy killed mommy,' she recalled. 'They had stopped noticing and stopped crying. They had gotten used to too much.' She fled the family estate in Maryland with their five children and headed for the hills of North Carolina. In February 1998 Riddick armed himself with a long knife, duct tape, handcuffs and pepper spray and with his brother as driver pulled into Judy's new home at 6 am, ordered her into the car along with the children. He sat in the back with his knife out, threatening to kill her, and just so she was sure he meant it, he gave her a little cut on one of her breasts. She said she needed the toilet and called the police on her cellphone. The car was pulled over a few miles later and Riddick was arrested for kidnapping. 'How can you kidnap your own family?' he asked. Later he added, 'I wouldn't say I regret it. I regret being there.'

His lawyer Johnny Cochrane made a successful plea for a non-custodial sentence, arguing that Bowe had diminished responsibility because of his boxing-induced brain damage, but the prosecutors appealed and in 2003 Bowe began an 18-month prison sentence in Maryland for 'interstate domestic violence'. By then he had lost all contact with his children and had another wife, Terri, who laid charges after he allegedly hit her, two children and a family friend, but he was acquitted when the witnesses failed to arrive in court. He blamed his troubles on Newman, who never came to visit him, accusing his former manager of stealing his money, later expressing regret when this was disproved. He also claimed his brain damage plea was merely a ruse to get him out of jail, although he continued to slur his words slightly. He started trying to get fit again in prison, and began to talk about a comeback with the idea of fighting Lennox Lewis, to which Lewis's trainer, Emanuel Steward responded, 'There's one guy he should never think about fighting and that's Lewis because Lennox has a really hard attitude towards him and Riddick would run the risk of being seriously hurt because Lennox would show him no mercy.' Lewis, then in his second year of retirement, watched Bowe's first comeback bout – a two round win over multiple loser Marcus Rhode and shook his head, 'I always wanted to fight Bowe but after seeing his last fiasco, I realised he has put on a lot of weight and turned into a big turkey.' Riddick looked even worse in his second bout, getting rocked several times before scraping a disputed split decision over 32-year-old Billy Zumbrun, whom he outweighed by 52 lb. And still Big Daddy pressed on. 'I'm in the process of trying to get back all that I once had,' he explained.

Lennox Lewis – 'The Lion'

World heavyweight champion 1999–2001; 2001–04; WBC heavyweight title holder 1992–94, 1997–2001; WBC/linear world champion 1998–2001.

'Lewis was beyond doubt the greatest heavyweight of all time. He was good enough to compete with anyone.'

George Foreman, on Lewis's retirement in 2004.

Height: 6'5
Peak weight: 227–249 lb.
41 wins (32 stoppages),
2 losses, 1 draw
Born, London, England
2 September 1965

Lennox Claudius Lewis is one of the enigmas of heavyweight history; so hard to pin down as a man and as a boxer. He was a slow burner – an athlete destined for greatness whose career developed in fits and starts until, finally, he outlasted all the opposition. He beat Bowe, Holyfield, Tyson, Klitschko and Don King and retired at the top. He was dogged by personal rumour, derided for his chess player's approach and his reluctance to play the media game, but in the end he was vindicated.

The fight that made him an A-list superstar was, fittingly, one that fell short of closure: the night at Madison Square Garden on 13 March 1999 when he first tangled with Evander Holyfield. Lewis used his 84-inch reach to keep his jab in the smaller man's face until Holyfield exploded in the third round. Lennox covered up, then brought his uppercut into play. He came close to ending it in the fifth. Holyfield wobbled from four massive punches, but Lewis showed too much respect. As he explained, 'When he was covering up on the ropes I asked myself, "Is this his version of rope-a-dope, trying to get me to punch myself out so he can come on in the later rounds?" You have to make sure his strategy doesn't beat yours, but maybe I should've taken more chances.' Lewis battered Evander again in round seven but eased off in rounds nine and ten. Evander tried everything he knew – flurries of punches and regular head butts – but in round 11 Lewis returned to the jab and in the 12th his dominance was absolute, until the swollen veteran had to grab to stay upright. The general view was that Lewis won by at least five points. He outlanded Holyfield by 348 punches to 130 and there was no doubt he hit harder. But the official result was a draw, with the Don King-friendly American judge, Eugenia Williams, scoring for King's fighter, Holyfield.

'IT STINKS', said the *New York Post*. 'IT'S ROBBERY', yelled the *Daily News*. Mayor Rudi Giuliani demanded justice, the New York Senate set up a commission of inquiry and the FBI got involved. But this ludicrous decision made Lennox Lewis. To the Brits, he finally became a wronged hero. To the Americans, he finally became 'The Man' – an attitude shared by Lewis, who did not train as hard as for the return in Las Vegas eight months later. The 217 lb. Holyfield used his head even more than in the first fight and threw several low blows, and his fists were also busier. The 242 lb. Lewis won the early rounds but in the fifth Holyfield opened a cut by the side of Lewis's right eye with a butt. Lewis's rhythm was broken and from then on he wanted to duke it out. He fired hard, single punches up close but Holyfield's flurries were more eye-catching. In round seven Lewis took a hard hook to his jaw and played possum to encourage Evander to go for broke. It worked, Holyfield's punches lost steam while Lewis was still

Lennox Lewis outboxes Hasim Rahman during the second round of their WBC/IBF world heavyweight championship fight at the Mandalay Bay Hotel and Casino in Las Vegas, on 17 November 2001. Dominating behind his jab the 36-year-old Lewis wobbled Rahman in the third round and then knocked him out cold with a right hook in round four, to regain the world title.

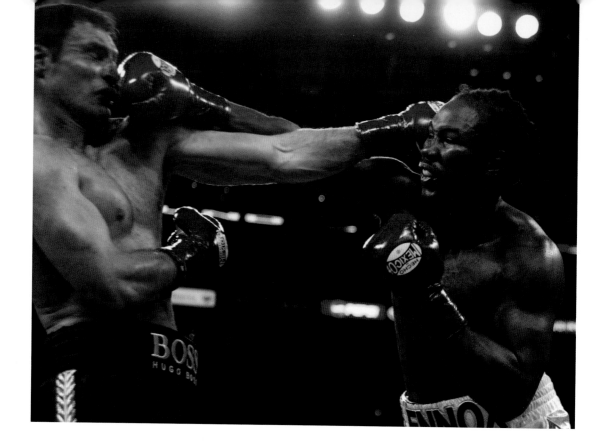

Lennox Lewis lands a punch to the eye of Vitali Klitschko during their WBC world heavyweight championship fight at Staples Center in Los Angeles, 21 June 2003, in his last fight before retiring. Lewis had been out of action for a year and spent the final two weeks publicising the fight he was promoting. He was behind on points when the ringside physician ruled that the hideously cut Klitschko could not continue after six rounds.

landing hard and clean with his uppercut and hooks to the body. Then he began using the jab again and everything flowed. He controlled the final rounds with jabs, hooks, body blows and uppercuts. The three judges gave him a unanimous decision by margins of six, four and two rounds, but it seemed closer than their first fight, a view confirmed by the Compubox statistics which had Lewis landing 195 punches to Holyfield's 137.

Lennox's Jamaican-born mother, Violet, raised him and his half-brother in East London. She then moved to Chicago for a year, leaving her boys behind and returned to find Lennox had acquired a violent temper, which got him expelled from school – for thumping another boy and smashing a window. She tried Kitchener, Ontario but after six months sent Lennox home. Five lonely, vulnerable years later the 12-year-old finally joined his mother in Canada. He found his way to the boxing gym after some toughs they had encountered failed to show for a fight. Junior, as he was called, decided to have a go, and after a bloody nose, began to excel under the benign influence of a kindly father-figure and trainer, Arnie Boehm. When he was 17 Boehm took him to the Dominican Republic where he won the heavyweight gold medal in the World Junior Championships. He then fought in the Los Angeles Olympics, losing in the second round to gold medallist Tyrell Biggs. He turned down huge offers to turn professional, before making it to the 1988 Seoul Olympic finals to face the US favourite, Riddick Bowe. Lewis took over in the second round, wobbling Bowe with a combination for a standing count, and then doing it again, ending the fight.

KINGS OF THE RING

He returned to London to start his professional career, managed by a publican, Frank Maloney, promoted by wing-and-prayer entrepreneur, Roger Levitt, with ex-Marine John Davenport as trainer. After 16 months he won the European title by stopping France's Jean Chanet in six rounds. His next fight – his 15th – came at a time when the empire of his fraud-accused promoter collapsed. A new backer was found in professional liquidator Panos Eliadis and the fight went ahead. The powerful British champion Gary Mason had 35 fights, 35 wins, 32 stoppages and was rated number five by the WBC. Lewis absorbed some heavy blows, used his jab to close Mason's eyes before stopping him in the seventh. He moved to the top of the ratings but Bowe got first shot at Holyfield's title, with Lewis promised first shot at the winner provided he beat Razor Ruddock in London on 31 October 1992. Now trained by Pepe Correa, the 227 lb. Lewis knocked down the 232½ lb. Canadian with an overhand right in the first round, and then twice more in the second to end the fight. George Foreman was asked if he'd consider fighting Lewis. 'Are you crazy?' he said. 'That man's dangerous.'

Bowe won the world title 13 days later and Lewis received a torrent of abuse and then a refusal to honour an agreement about his first defence. He admitted he came close to laying into Bowe without the gloves on but felt sure he'd eventually get his chance in the ring. 'I always wanted that chance because I believe Bowe deserved to be treated for what he did. I had marked in my mind: "Yeah, you called me a faggot. All right. You'll see, redemption will come." But with Bowe, it never arrived. Instead, his first defence came against former IBF champion Tony Tucker, who'd won 14 in a row since being outpointed by Tyson. Fighting with a damaged hand Lewis dropped Tucker twice but was shaken by a heavy right flush in round nine before jabbing his way to a wide points win. Next came British rival Frank Bruno on a rainy autumn night in Cardiff. The 238 lb. Bruno used his jab effectively and in the third round shook the 229 lb. Lewis with a right on the temple. But Lennox took over in the fifth, winning the jabbing battle. With his back to the ropes, Lewis landed a devastating left hook to the jaw in the seventh round. After several more huge punches, ending with a brutal right to the jaw, Frank collapsed, the ropes breaking his fall. Lewis followed this with an eighth round stoppage of Phil Jackson before taking on Oliver McCall, who had the most reliable chin in heavyweight history. He had knocked Tyson down in sparring but neither Iron Mike nor anyone else managed to drop him. Lewis's preparations were disrupted by a back injury and compromised by tensions within his camp resulting in him skimping on training. The 6'2 McCall, at a ripped 231¼ lb., came out aggressively but the 238 lb. Lewis won the first round and Correa's final words after the break were, 'Keep on him.' He lunged and McCall closed his eyes and blasted his right – its impact doubled by Lewis's momentum. Lennox was up at 'six', nodding and raising his gloves when referee Lupe Garcia asked if he was OK. But Garcia waved his arms when Lennox's legs shuddered. Even McCall's trainer, Emanuel Steward, agreed with Lewis that the stoppage was premature.

Lewis fired Correa, employed Steward and picked up four wins, including a one-sided sixth round stoppage over Tommy Morrison and a hard-fought war with Ray Mercer. But the WBC replaced Lewis with Tyson as their top contender, prompting a period of legal action that forced their hand. Don King refused to allow Tyson to defend against

Lennox – first paying him $4 million and then, when Lewis pressed his case, relinquishing the WBC title. The organisation then nominated the deposed Oliver McCall as Lennox's opponent for their vacant title, finally set for Las Vegas on 7 February 1997. McCall's substance-abuse problem prompted incidents of crazy behaviour, and he only kept out of jail on condition he went into rehabilitation. The test was whether his mind would hold. Lewis at a huge 251 lb. put him under pressure from the first bell. Oliver landed several hard punches but they just bounced off and in the third round Lennox took over completely. A hook and right to the chin caused McCall's legs to buckle for the first time in his career and his confidence disintegrated. He refused to sit at the bell and in round four grabbed, blocked and wept without punching. Lewis landed 15 unanswered punches early in round five and referee Mills Lane stopped it 'because Oliver refuses to defend himself'.

The disappointment was not helped when, in his first defence, the unbeaten, 6'7 British-born Nigerian Henry Akinwande clung for dear life, refusing to let go until Lane disqualified him. His second defence was against the big Pole Andrej Golota, whose only losses in 30 fights came via disqualification against Bowe. Lewis dropped him twice and stopped him halfway through the first round. Next came 'linear' champion Shannon Briggs, who earned this status by outpointing George Foreman. Briggs gave Lewis a scare with a hard hook to the temple in the first round, but by the fifth round, after four knockdowns, Briggs was so unsteady that he fell flat on his face. Lewis' fourth defence was against the unbeaten Zeljko Mavrovic, who lost a wide points decision. But it took his two fights with Holyfield before he won universal acceptance as champion.

His next fight was against the 6'7, 250 lb., 27-year-old Michael Grant, who had won 31 straight, 22 on knockouts. Lewis knocked him down twice in the first round and finished him off in the second. Two months later Lewis returned to London to face Frans Botha, who had once held the IBF belt (stripped for steroids abuse). In the second Lewis landed a right cross that lifted Botha off his feet to end the fight. Next came the 5'9½ 245 lb. David Tua – the hardest puncher in the division with one of the best chins. Lewis boxed masterfully behind his jab, cruising to a wide unanimous decision. After this he called himself a 'pugilist specialist' and began to think of himself as invincible.

Responding to an invitation from Nelson Mandela, Lewis chose Brakpan in South Africa for his next defence, against Hasim Rahman on 22 April 2001. He fell out with his promoter Panos Eliadis and they both sued each other (Lennox winning $6 million for civil fraud and $1.175 million from their lawyer Milt Chwasky). He arrived in high altitude Johannesburg (6,000 feet) eleven days before the fight and came in at a soft 253½ lb. Rahman trained for seven weeks in the Catskills and four in Johannesburg and weighed a muscular 238 lb. Lewis was soon panting heavily, his movement sluggish. He neglected his jab but still won three of the first four rounds. In the fifth, with Rahman pawing at his cut and swollen eyes, Lewis bounced off the ropes with his hands down and Hasim launched a right cross that landed flush on his jaw – 'one of the greatest right crosses I've ever seen', said Steward.

Rahman had signed an agreement to fight Lewis within 150 days if he won, but afterwards Hassim signed with King who had other ideas. Lewis took them to court and, once again, beat King. The return was set for Las Vegas on 17 November 2001.

Meanwhile Lennox parted ways with Frank Maloney, and was now completely self-managed and promoted. He trained far harder this time and when it was time to fight the 246½ lb. Lewis settled into a state of steely calm. He took control from the start by using his jab effectively, cutting Rahman and shaking him up. Midway through the fourth Rahman tried to block a decoy hook, leaving the left side of his chin open, and Lewis followed through with a right hook that landed with impeccable timing. The Rock was out cold before he crashed down and when he woke up he asked the doctor what happened. 'I didn't see the punch,' he said, when she explained, and then, after looking at the replay on the screen above his prone head, he added: 'Wow! He's the real champion.'

A fight against Mike Tyson was almost scrapped by Iron Mike's pre-fight leg-biting antics, before being shifted to Memphis on 8 June 2002. The 234 lb. Tyson came out fast, trying to overwhelm the 249½ lb. Lewis but Lennox controlled the action with stiff jabs, hard rights and draining body blows, shoving Mike away when he tried to clinch. He dropped Tyson with a right in round four but referee Eddie Cotton ruled it a push. Lewis landed a left uppercut and a right cross in the eighth to buckle Tyson's knees and Cotton ruled it a knockdown. A minute later Tyson put all his weight into a right uppercut. Lewis absorbed it, stepped back and jabbed, opening the way for a momentous right hook to the chin. Tyson's legs gave way and he collapsed, landing on his back, with blood dripping from his nose, mouth and both eyes. He was counted out and it was 30 seconds before his legs had the strength to hold him.

While waiting for Tyson to decide on a return, Lewis arranged a fight in Los Angeles on 21 June 2003, but his opponent pulled out so he agreed to fight his mandatory challenger, the 6'7½, 248 lb. Vitali Klitschko. Lennox had been out for a year, was lax in training, spent the last two weeks promoting his fight and came in at his heaviest ever, 256½ lb. His last moments in the ring were brutal for a man known for caution – he found his chin and will tested over and over, but he dug deep, rocking the white giant with uppercuts while hideously ripping his face open, until the ringside physician said 'enough!' Klitschko's wounds took 63 stitches to close. At the age of 38 Lewis found his thirst for blood was quenched and he retired as reigning champion in 2004, 'All I was doing was feeding other people's wishes,' he said. 'It's you guys who want me to carry on, but you don't take the punches and I do.' This first-time father, who later married his girlfriend Violet Chang, added with obvious contentment: 'I tried to show people that boxing has to do with more than brutality and blood and now I want to show that as much as I love this sport, there really is more to me than just being a boxer. Now I have to think about my whole life.'

Lennox Lewis wears all of his heavyweight title belts after defeating Evander Holyfield on 13 November 1999 in Las Vegas, Nevada. Lewis won a fairly wide unanimous decision but most ringsiders felt the fight was a lot closer than their first one, which Lewis dominated despite the official drawn decision.

Hasim Rahman – 'The Rock'

World heavyweight champion 2001.

'The second time is going to be a sweeter and a longer run for me. And I can't wait. I feel that I'm destined to be two-time heavyweight champion of the world and I'm not going to let anyone stand in my way. Anybody who gets in my way has got to fall!'
Hasim Rahman, 2005

Height 6'2½
Peak weight 230–245lb.
41 wins (33 stoppages),
5 losses, 1 draw
Born Baltimore,
7 November 1972.

It's hard to know where to place Hasim Rahman on the spectrum between good luck and bad, dedication and neglect. He twice suffered injustice at the hands of boxing officials in key fights with David Tua but was fortunate to secure a title fight with Lennox Lewis – and to find the champion in poor form. He showed grit in driving himself to beat Lewis and several other top men, but blew big chances through his inclination to lose focus and overeat, and he made foolish promotional decisions that saw him squander a potential fortune. Off-form he struggled with journeymen but he could also be an excellent boxer with a ramrod jab and a killer right.

Being with the right people at the right time secured Hasim his wild card title shot in Brakpan, near Johannesburg on 22 April 2001. Lewis needed a patsy for his South African gig and Rahman got the offer because he was promoted by Cedric Kushner, who had close connections with the South African promoters. Lennox figured this 15-1 underdog was easy meat and trained accordingly. Rahman grabbed the $1.5 million purse, spent seven weeks training in the Catskills, then worked for nearly four weeks in an old-style Johannesburg gym known as the 'House of Pain'. He was sure if it came to a drawn-out fight he would outlast the ill-prepared champion.

Hasim absorbed several hard jabs but pressed forward, using his 81-inch reach to good effect. He landed a hard right and a solid combination in the second round but Lewis came back with a left uppercut-overhand right combination, followed by a right to the ear and another to the eye, although this effort had him panting heavily – a product of lax training and late arrival in Johannesburg. In round three the sluggish champion abandoned the jab, throwing hurtful hooks and uppercuts. By round five Hasim's left eye was bleeding and he was taking heavy punishment. He got in a powerful right to the jaw but Lewis came back with hard uppercuts and crosses. The no-hoper began touching his cut and turning away with a look of distress in his eyes while his corner yelled: 'Get off the ropes! Throw some punches!' According to Lewis's trainer, Manny Steward, Rahman admitted he was ready to quit, but Hasim said. 'I kept pawing at my eye because there was blood dripping into it. I really couldn't see Lennox's punches and he was trying to finish me, but I knew the general area he was in.' When Lewis bounced off the ropes Hasim fired a right cross that landed with immense power on the side of the jaw. Lewis called it a 'lucky punch' but later admitted, 'It was a great punch. I never put my left hand in position to block it and I may have taken him a bit lightly but I didn't realise he was able to throw a punch like that.' Lewis and Steward

Hasim Rahman celebrates after beating world heavyweight boxing champion Lennox Lewis in their world title bout in Brakpan, South Africa, on 22 April 2001. Rahman, 28, took the title off the 35-year-old champion with a fifth round knockout, but lost it in four rounds in the return six months later.

Hasim Rahman connects with a left to the head of world heavyweight champion Lennox Lewis during their first world title fight. He lost three of the first four rounds but later in the fifth landed one of the hardest rights in heavyweight history to stop the tiring Lewis.

insisted he made it to his feet in time and the count was short, but Hasim replied, 'The referee could have counted to twenty and Lennox wouldn't have been able to go on.'

Hasim grew up in a working-class Muslim family in Baltimore. He managed to avoid drugs and alcohol but couldn't resist the lure of a life as a street enforcer. At the age of 18 he was shot five times and survived. Soon after, he was involved in a car crash in which his best friend died. This left him with severe scarring around his right eye and cheek and a broken arm. 'They literally had to put my face back on,' he said. He decided he survived for a reason and started boxing. He beat a steadily improving batch of opponents, including a few on the fringes of the ratings. By the end of 1998 his record stood at 29 straight wins, 24 knockouts. With his strength, power and great jab he was even compared to Sonny Liston and was earning rave reviews. On 19 December 1998 he fought the immensely powerful David Tua in Miami in a crossroads fight. Hasim absorbed some heavy digs but kept in front by making good use of his jab. All three judges had him losing just one of the first nine rounds but a second after the bell Tua landed a monstrous hook to the jaw. This should have prompted disqualification or a long recovery period but instead the referee ordered the groggy 'Rock' out for round ten. Tua climbed in and the fight was stopped with 35 seconds to go in round ten.

A bad loss to Russia's Oleg Maskaev (who knocked him through the ropes) was followed by a gutsy win over the quick, hard-hitting South African southpaw Corrie Sanders. Hasim went down twice but kept fighting hard, winning in round seven. He was now back in the world ratings and after another win was picked to fight Lewis.

KINGS OF THE RING

For such an obviously smart man, his behaviour after the Lewis fight was bizarre. He skipped a meeting with Nelson Mandela, went home to Baltimore and got into a car accident from which his three children escaped uninjured but which left him with cuts, bruises and scrapes and his wife with a neck brace. He then went to Mecca and on his return talked of winning $100 million. 'Money! M-O-N-E-Y. It's about the money. We're not fools. This business is a money business. It's the chance for a guy like me to make sure my family is set for life and that's a great motivator. If you have that carrot in front of you, you'd don't get complacent.' In quick succession, he broke with his promoter Cedric Kushner and walked out on a $14.15 million HBO deal for a Lewis return. It soon emerged that Don King had arrived at Hasim's hotel room with a bag containing 5,000 one-hundred dollar bills as a sweetener for a promotional contract culminating, he hoped, in a defence against the estranged Tyson. Rahman signed and King smiled. 'I've been a busy beaver,' he said before offering back-to-back clichés. 'The proof of the pudding is in the eating, the family that prays together stays together.' When King lost a court case against Lewis, Rahman accepted King's $5 million offer for a Lewis fight, in preference to a more lucrative long-term offer from the cable network HBO.

Once again The Rock trained hard although he later said his relationship with his trainer, Adrian Davis, became strained by the end of their time together. He was also winning the verbal war with Lewis. 'I'm in his head big,' he boasted. 'I can punch hard and Lennox knows that now. Even though he's aware of it this time there's nothing he can do to stop it. I humiliated this man and the same thing is coming this time, only faster.' But while Lewis was calm in his dressing room, Rahman was agitated. He felt he was in for a quick knockout, but instead was cut, outjabbed and outpunched in the first two rounds, wobbled with a left hook and right cross in the third and knocked cold with a right hook in round four. 'It was a planned punch, not a lucky one,' Lewis stressed, and Rahman too was full of admiration. 'I just didn't see it coming,' he said, with his arm around his ten-year-old son. 'He blinded me with the left hook and that's how he got in with the right hook. He has an enormous amount of weight and put it all behind that punch. He had a good game plan, he took and fought a very smart, intelligent fight. It wasn't only his jab. It was his distance and footwork and he stopped me landing my own jab.'

Rahman promised he'd be back but the defeat shattered his confidence and motivation. He returned to face 39-year-old Evander Holyfield in a WBA eliminator but came in underweight (at 224 lb.) and underpowered. Holyfield gave one of his best late career performances, but it was his head not his fists that did the real damage, causing a grotesque swelling above Rahman's left eye. The fight was stopped in round eight with The Rock the loser on a technical decision. Ten months later he fought an IBF eliminator against David Tua and this time came in seriously overweight at 259 lb. Yet he succeeded in outjabbing and outlanding Tua for much of the fight and also became the first man to drop him. Unfortunately for Hasim, that right cross landed a fraction of a second after the final bell so it didn't affect the scoring. Although most ringsiders felt he deserved the decision, the judges made it a draw. He then dropped a decision to John Ruiz before regrouping with six wins to earn another world title shot.

Vitali Klitschko – 'Dr Ironfist'

WBC heavyweight title holder and *The Ring* magazine's world heavyweight champion, 2004–5.

'Vitali impressed me. He's an awkward guy to fight with an unusual European style and it took me a while to figure it out. With all that weight coming from behind a punch he's obviously got power and he threw good punches – punches I wasn't used to seeing, especially coming from that height.'
Lennox Lewis, 2003.

Height 6'7½
Peak weight 245–250 lb.
35 wins (34 stoppages),
2 losses
Born: Belovodsk, Kyrgyzstan,
19 July 1971

Vitali Klitschko won widespread recognition as world heavyweight king, partly by achievement and partly by default. Achievement because, after losing on cuts when ahead against Lewis, he stopped the top contender Corrie Sanders for the WBC crown and the prestigious world title belt issued by *The Ring* magazine. Default because the rival champions were so palpably inferior, clinging to their alphabet honours through dubious decisions against nonentities. 'Dr Ironfist' is a flawed boxer – not good on the back foot, prone to injury, lacking fluidity and in-fighting skills and despite his magnificent conditioning he tends to tire in the later rounds. But as everyone who's tangled with him has found, he's immensely strong, with quick, accurate hands, a highly effective, awkward defence, making him difficult to tag cleanly, and unlike his brother, Wladimir, he also has a solid chin – the only heavyweight champion never to have been knocked down (so far, anyway). He's also the tallest champion of all time.

Until 21 June 2003 Klitschko was derided for being robotic and cowardly. The former charge is still levied; the latter, no more. He was winding down his training for a fight against the unbeaten American Cedric Boswell when the call came to fight Lewis, whose own opponent, Kirk Johnson, had pulled out injured. Vitali had watched his brother, Wladimir, play sparring with Lennox on the set of the movie *Ocean's Eleven* in 2001 and felt there were weaknesses to exploit. 'It wasn't a real fight but the movements were real and I was always watching from the corner,' he said. 'I saw some mistakes – ways to keep him off, openings to take advantage of. Lennox has had less than two weeks, preparation for me, which is not enough, but I've been waiting for this fight for three years and I really am prepared.' Wladimir was Lewis's height and although the brothers never did full sparring together, he proved to be a useful foil in preparing for the world championship. His cause was aided by the fact that Lewis, nearing 38, hadn't fought for a year and had been preparing for a smaller, inferior opponent. 'I could have been in better shape,' Lennox later admitted. 'If I'd been in Tyson shape or Rahman rematch shape it would have been better.' He was too heavy at 256½ lb. while Klitschko came in at his peak weight – 248 lean, hard pounds. To make matters worse, Lennox took on a huge load in terms of publicising the bout he was promoting, which meant his final training suffered. But still, it seemed a long shot for the LA-based Ukrainian.

Lewis went out to test his heart and found it sturdier than expected. He bulled forward, missed with a jab and hook and then wrestled Klitschko in a clinch. But this

Vitali Klitschko lands a right to the face of South African Corrie Sanders during their WBC heavyweight title fight at Staples Center in Los Angeles, 24 April 2004. Klitschko won the fight on an eighth round technical knockout. *The Ring* magazine awarded Vitali its prestigious world title belt and HBO also declared him the legitimate world champion.

was one man who could match his strength. The next surprise was when Vitali stepped in from the jab and landed a hard cross. He did this three times to win the round. In the second, Vitali absorbed a hard jab and right and came back with his own chopping right, followed with a hard jab and then a perfectly timed cross that landed fast and flush on the chin. 'I had the feeling when I landed that punch I could have ended the fight,' he said. But the surprise for Klitschko was that unlike his previous victims Lewis remained upright, soaking up several more extremely hard hooks and crosses without wobbling. Lewis came out aggressively for round three, landing power jabs, including one that visibly rattled Klitschko, who then pulled back from a right that caught the side of his left eyebrow, zipping it wide open, and the blood began to pour.

Lewis was tired, his reflexes slower than normal, his timing off, but now he had a target and he began to land hard with both hands. At one point, when they went down together in a tangle, Lewis took the opportunity to rub the inside of his glove on the cut. Klitschko's cutman, Joe Souza, struggled to stem the flow. The fifth was brutal. Lewis worked up close to conserve energy, ripping in massive uppercuts, one of them lacerating the inside of Klitschko's lip. Vitali was shaken by this punch but when he held Lewis whacked him to the body 12 times in succession. Vitali then came back, landing several jabs and heavy rights. Lennox responded with a clubbing right that caused swelling around the left eye, two jabs that opened cuts on the left cheekbone and another that opened a more serious cut on the left eyelid. Klitschko's trainer, Fritz Sdunek, told him he needed a knockout soon. Vitali came out to fire hard, accurate jabs and rights but as he stepped in Lewis caught him with a massive uppercut that slammed his head back. It deepened the cuts in his mouth, jellied his legs and drained him of strength. Klitschko clung on, panting heavily, and then tried again, but this time Lewis was able to walk through his jabs and land some of his own, followed by another jarring uppercut and a short right to the jaw. Klitschko was hurt again and grabbed and Lewis pushed him off but when he grabbed again, Lennox allowed the challenger to walk him to the ropes while he caught his breath.

Both men sagged to their stools after the bell, utterly exhausted. Lennox's chest was heaving and Vitali, who had lost the sixth badly, looked to have little left. The ringside physician, Dr Paul Wallace, a plastic surgeon, visited the challenger's corner to inspect the damage. The hole on his left brow was horrific and he was also leaking from his nose, mouth and the cuts below his eye. But the damage that worried the doctor most was the cut on the eyelid, which now had horizontal and vertical flaps, placing the optic nerve at severe risk. 'I asked him to look at me,' said Dr Wallace. 'When he did, his upper lid covered his field of vision. He had to raise his head to see me. There was no way he could defend himself or see a punch coming. I had no option but to stop the fight.' Sixty-three stitches were later required to close his wounds, but Vitali remained defiantly determined to fight on. 'No! No! No!' he shouted. 'I see everything.'

Lewis also felt disappointed by the stoppage, which denied him the chance to win spectacularly: 'I was getting my second wind,' he said. 'I brought Vitali into deep water and if the doctor hadn't stopped it he would have drowned. I would have knocked him out sometime in the next two rounds.' Steward emphatically agreed. 'When Lennox hit him with those two tremendous uppercuts in round six I knew the fight was over. He was badly hurt. It wasn't going to be a great polished victory but Lennox would have knocked him out without any doubt. The important thing is what direction was the fight going when it was stopped? Definitely in Lennox's direction. He'd have put Klitschko to bed – probably in the seventh.' But Klitschko felt he was unjustly denied the chance of victory and called himself the 'People's Champion', noting that he was ahead by two points on each of the judges' scorecards. 'I have some feeling Lennox Lewis lose energy and lose his condition and you've seen my record. I can punch hard for all 12 rounds and I think I have very big chance later in the fight. Lennox is a great fighter but I don't give him the chance to use his great weapon, the right hand. I controlled the fight but it was not easy to fight Lewis – he's good. He makes great fight, but I know I would have won. I don't feel like the loser. Many people doubt that's world champion. I beat him on points.'

Vitali and his younger brother Wladimir grew up in a military family, the sons of a Soviet air force colonel who moved from one base to another in the old Eastern bloc. He took up boxing at the age of 14 when they were based in Czechoslovakia and Wladimir soon joined him. But while the younger brother stuck to the conventional boxing, the older brother developed an obsession for a variety of martial arts. He won the European professional heavyweight title in kickboxing and the world military gold medal in amateur boxing. Both were picked to represent the Ukraine at the 1996 Atlanta Olympics, Vitali at super heavyweight and Wladimir at heavyweight, but the older brother, who claimed an amateur record of 195 wins (80 stoppages) and 15 losses, was struck off the squad after testing positive for steroids. He claimed he'd received them from a doctor for a calf injury sustained in kickboxing. Wladimir replaced him at super heavyweight and came home with the Olympic gold medal.

The lads did everything together, with Vitali, the taller, harder one, leading the way. They were both Magic Circle members, both spoke four languages, both excelled in chess, both completed PhDs at Kiev University, and they both turned professional together. Their mother, Nadia, received offers from several promoters, including Don King, and plied them with vodka to see how they would react. She was most impressed with the German Klaus-Peter Kohl, and so they started fighting for pay in Hamburg on 16 November 1986 with Kohl's Hamburg-based Universum group as their promoter. Vitali won in the second round and Wladimir in the first. They continued to train together, without any sign of competition. 'It's the closest a brother relationship can be,' said Vitali. 'Our ambition is to win every heavyweight championship belt and to hold it in the family. We promised our mother that we will never fight against each other. It would hurt her. It would break her heart.' At the start it was the broader-shouldered, better-looking, smoother-boxing Olympic champion who drew most of the plaudits but in December 1998 Wladimir suffered a shock knockout defeat against the journeyman Ross Purrity (whom Vitali later stopped). A few months later Vitali – by then European champion – widened the gap by knocking out Britain's Herbie Hide in two rounds to win the lightly regarded WBO title.

Then they changed places again. In his third WBO defence, in Berlin on 1 April 2000, Vitali took on the small elusive Chris Byrd. The 244 lb. Ukrainian had no trouble outboxing the 210 lb. American, picking him off with long, well-timed punches, to win seven of the first eight rounds. But when throwing a punch Vitali severely tore his rotator cuff muscle and ligaments in his shoulder. With only two rounds to go and an unassailable lead he quit in his corner. HBO's ringside analyst Larry Merchant decided this was clear proof of congenital cowardice. 'The Klitschkos have no balls,' he declared and the charge stuck despite Vitali's protests. 'The injury to my shoulder was very, very bad,' he said. 'I did not want to stop fighting but I knew if I continued the injury could have become so much worse and I may not have been able to fight again for the rest of my life. The shoulder could have been irreparably damaged. The doctor who performed the surgery said the pain I went through was enough to make me go blind – to see black and nothing else. It was terrible.'

Wladimir outclassed Byrd six months later, dropping him twice on his way to a shut-out decision, and he consolidated his position as crown prince of the heavyweight division with a series of impressive wins over genuine contenders. Vitali was out for eight months and then worked his way back via the European title. The conventional wisdom was that the younger sibling was the star but not everyone shared that verdict. 'Vitali's the better of the Klitschko brothers,' Joe Byrd, Chris's father, declared. 'He's so strong and I think he's the better scientific boxer. He keeps that left hand taped to the side of his face. He was really beating Chris until he came undone with that shoulder problem and he's been underrated ever since.' The pecking order was reversed again after Wladimir defended his WBO belt against the Lennox Lewis-promoted South African, Corrie Sanders, in Hanover on 8 March 2003. Twice in the first round and twice in the second the crown prince found himself on his back until the fight was stopped, prompting the distraught, protective Vitali to have a go at Sanders in the ring. After this the idea of the Klitschko brothers as a seamless package began to fade. Wladimir's style was more fluid and pleasing but the taller, leaner, stronger, harder-chinned Vitali was far more resilient and ultimately more effective. He would pick off opponents with long, accurate, quick punches, using his hands, arms and reflexes to catch whatever came back. With his upright, legs-wide-apart stance and his chin tucked behind his shoulder, he would hook off his jab and then drop in hard, chopping right crosses. It was seldom aesthetically pleasing but it seemed to work and after five more wins he was back at the top of the WBC rankings.

The Lewis fight transformed his reputation. Having moved to Los Angeles he was adopted as a local hero, praised for his courage in wanting to fight on despite his horrific eye injuries, and, absurdly, even viewed as a victim of a premature stoppage. His sin of bailing out against Byrd was forgotten and he was paraded around the circuit of Jay Leno, Jimmy Kimmel and morning television. He returned as soon as his cuts healed, stopping Kirk Johnson in two impressive rounds. Lewis talked of a return in which he would 'bust up the other side of his face', but instead, after months of prevarication, he announced his retirement when the WBC put him on the spot. Vitali, who by then was self-promoted (the brothers broke with Kohl after an expensive contractual wrangle) faced Sanders for the vacant WBC title in Los Angeles on 24 April 2004. Sanders got in quickly with a powerful left cross but Vitali slowly ground the South African down, finally battering him to defeat in the eighth round. He was then recognised as world champion by HBO and, more importantly, *The Ring*.

It helped his cause that the rival champions were so ill-qualified. The slowing IBF champion Chris Byrd was the beneficiary of an outright robbery against the Puerto Rican Fres Oquendo in his first defence and was lucky to get a draw against Andrej Golota. Even worse was the boring WBA champion John Ruiz who lost his title to light heavyweight champion Roy Jones, then, after regaining the vacated belt, clung on to it with a dubious decision against Golota, only to lose it to the fat, 37-year-old former middleweight, super middleweight and cruiserweight champion James Toney. But Toney tested positive for steroids, so the result was changed to a 'no contest'. Ruiz renounced his retirement and, to the groans of boxing fans, returned as WBA belt holder. The idea of either of these men testing Klitschko began to look absurd.

Vitali hoped to fight Mike Tyson, but when Tyson was stopped by Britain's Danny Williams in four rounds, he accepted Williams instead for his first defence in Las Vegas on 11 December 2004, dropping him four times on the way to a horribly one-sided eighth-round stoppage, which suggested the gap with the rest of the division had widened. His bid to consolidate his crown was delayed in 2005 by a bone spur on his spine that required surgery to repair – an operation that followed shortly after the birth of his third child, Max, named after his friend and hero Max Schmeling.

A battle-scarred Klitschko following his WBC and IBO title fight with heavyweight champion Lennox Lewis. The bout was stopped on acount of the Ukrainian's cuts which required 63 stitches. Klitschko, who was ahead on points, won praise for his courage in wanting to fight on despite his injuries. Two fights later he won the WBC title.

The Future

John L Sullivan and James J Corbett – the last bare knuckle champion and the first to win his title with gloves – called themselves Irish but were born in American cities, where they learnt to fight. Vitali Klitschko lives in Los Angeles but he is a Ukrainian who learnt to fight in the Soviet Union and Germany. For over a century the best heavyweight in America was synonymous with the best in the world. Irish-Americans were edged out by African-Americans, but whatever the direction of the hyphenation it ended with the word 'American'. Today's boxing's centre of gravity is shifting and the heavyweight division, the last bastion of US hegemony, is under siege. In the America of Sullivan, Dempsey, Louis and Marciano every boy with even the vaguest interest in sport followed boxing. By the 1960s Muhammad Ali's overwhelming presence kept the game in the headlines. After that, however, it slipped off the back pages. The promoters found they could earn more money for themselves and their charges through cable networks, and at the top of the game through pay-per-view, which meant boxing lost its foothold on terrestrial television, and in the process lost much of its mainstream American audience (while at the same time gaining ground in Hispanic America).

It hardly helped that the American side of the game was devoid of federal control, which meant it was run by a handful of venal promoters who in turn controlled a growing proliferation of corrupt or nepotistic businesses which attached words like 'world' to their names even though they were nothing of the sort. These alphabet bodies trade in 'world' titles – which is all very well for their investors but means the public no longer knows what's what. This in turn meant the sporting press lost interest unless one of the tiny band of celebrity fighters like Tyson, Holyfield or Lewis was involved. Boxing became a niche sport at the fringes of public consciousness, competing for space with the make-believe world of all-in wrestling and the all-too-real world of cage fighting.

Without the oxygen of publicity the participating end of the American game struggles to hold its own. Big, athletic, working-class boys these days are unlikely to venture into boxing. Even if they happen to have an amateur boxing gym in their area, they tend to conclude that the odds of making a decent stash are stronger in basketball, football or baseball, to take the more honest end of the range. Which is one of the reasons why the supply line that produced Louis, Ali, Holmes and Tyson seems to be blocked. There is little doubt that boxing in America, or at least non-Hispanic America, if not quite dead, certainly smells a little funny, as Frank Zappa might have put it.

That might sound like a pretty gloomy and rather dumb point to make at the end of a book on boxing, but the other side of this truth is that America is not the world. The professional end of the game is flourishing in Britain, Brazil and Germany; taking off in Russia and the rest of the former Soviet bloc; while Nigeria, Ghana, South Africa, Japan, Thailand, the Philippines, Mexico and the rest of Latin America remain as devoted as ever. And some day Cuba, which produces the world's best amateurs, will join the fun, providing another huge injection of excitement. So, the reports of boxing's death have been greatly exaggerated. It has a wider base of international talent than ever, and this applies as much to the heavyweight division as any other.

Still, it is hard to dispel the prejudice that standards are slipping – that the current crop is simply not up to those of the past. Boxers and their writers have been saying the same thing for over a century. Bob Fitzsimmons, who learnt at the feet of the bare knuckle masters, muttered that the champions of his youth were 'gone, never to return' and those of the future would be 'as children' compared with his heroes. Gene Tunney pontificated on how men of his time, like Dempsey, and before his time, like Corbett, would have handled Joe Louis with ease. Louis ranted about how he would have beaten the stuffing out of Ali, a view shared by that old curmudgeon Nat Fleischer, who wrote a whole chapter in one of his boxing books on the evils of masturbation, and, as he grew older, increasingly preferred fighters of his father's generation at the expense of the moderns. Larry Holmes continued this tradition with his regular disparaging comments along the lines of: 'Lewis was an OK fighter but I don't think you can call him one of the greats. I'd have beat his butt.'

So, have ancient arts really been lost in the dim mists? Were the old masters really so much harder, wilier, more skilful? Today, with the evidence of the long-lost films of past greats to reinforce the logic of the time, there is no point disputing that boxers like Corbett and Fitzsimmons simply did not have anything close to the arsenal of offensive or defensive possibilities later generations enjoyed. It took another 30 years before combination punching became integral to the game, which in turn made the old upright, head-high style more risky than in the days when boxers had to avoid one punch at a time. And the stylistic innovations didn't stop in the 1930s. Advances in diet, conditioning and resistance training (quite aside from the use of banned performance enhancing drugs, particularly among heavyweights) mean that, on average, modern fighters are stronger and fitter than their predecessors. With heavyweights there is the added factor of natural size. If the unusually powerful Evander Holyfield, who averaged 215 lb., found men like Riddick Bowe and Lennox Lewis a bit too big for comfort, how could the 185 lb. Marciano or the 165 lb. Fitzsimmons cope?

We also have to consider that the conditions of the past made boxing a different game. To go back a century, men fought for 25 rounds and more under the hot sun – meaning they were forced to preserve their energy – with horsehair gloves weighing 6 oz. or less, no gumshields, no protective cups, no standing eight count and no neutral corner rule. Today heavyweights fight with far springier 10 oz. gloves, for a maximum of 12 rounds; when they are dropped their opponents are kept away for at least eight seconds and fights are stopped quicker than before – and still men get knocked cold, and suffer brain damage and, occasionally, die in the ring.

With all these differences and advances, the game of comparing heavyweights of different eras is inherently silly. It's enough to rate them against their contemporaries and appreciate them for what they were in their own time, and to do the same with the current crop – secure in the knowledge that in 50 years' time they'll be saying, 'Aah, Tyson, Holyfield, Lewis, Klitschko – they don't make them like that any more.'

Index

KINGS OF THE RING

Several people helped me with this book. In particular I would like to thank my agent Euan Thorneycroft, who made the connections, and my editor Matthew Lowing, who worked to the wee hours to get it ready in time. I would also like to thank Don McRae, who helped make it possible and George Zeleny, who supplied me with films of the heavyweight greats going back to the 19th century. And also my family – Pat, Tessa and Caitlin – who put up with a good deal of inattention while I reverted to trainspotting mode.

First published in Great Britain in 2005 by
Weidenfeld & Nicolson

This paperback edition first published in 2007 by
Weidenfeld & Nicolson
10 9 8 7 6 5 4 3 2 1

ISBN 978 0 297 85345 9

Printed and bound in Italy by Printer Trento srl

Weidenfeld & Nicolson
The Orion Publishing Group Ltd
Orion House
5 Upper Saint Martin's Lane
London WC2H 9EA
www.orionbooks.co.uk

With the exception of the following all photographs are
courtesy of Corbis:

Neil Leifer/*Sports Illustrated*/Offside: pages 145, 152, 177, 187;
Getty Images: pages 13, 25, 67, 198;
Popperfoto: pages 16, 93, 96, 100, 104, 113, 137;
Action Images: 3, 28–9, 185, 201, 223;
The Bridgeman Art Library: page 36;
Pugilistica.com boxing memorabilia: page 55;
Topfoto: page 77, 86;
Weidenfeld & Nicolson: page 80;
Sports Illustrated Pictures/Offside: pages 139, 141;
James Drake/*Sports Illustrated*/Offside: pages 159, 170;
Brad Mangin/*Sports Illustrated*/Offside: page 165;

Designed by Nigel Soper
Edited by Matt Lowing
Design Direction by David Rowley
Design assistance by Justin Hunt
Picture Research by Katie Anderson, Brónagh Woods
& Tomas Graves
Editorial by Graham Lowing, Jennie Condell, Slav Todorov
& David Atkinson
Index by Chris Bell
Additional research by Keily Oakes

Right: Jack Sharkey lying on the
canvas after having been knocked
down at the end of his career.